BUSTING
THE
BARRICADES

What I Saw at the Populist Revolt

LAURA INGRAHAM

ALL
POINTS
BOOKS

324. 27327
ING

For Chris Edwards

and

my faithful listeners and viewers

BUSTING THE BARRICADES. Copyright © 2017 by Laura Ingraham.
Preface copyright © 2018 by Laura Ingraham. All rights reserved.
Printed in the United States of America. For information, address
St. Martin's Press, 175 Fifth Avenue, New York, NY 10010.

www.allpointsbooks.com

The Library of Congress has cataloged the hardcover edition as follows:

Names: Ingraham, Laura, author.
Title: Billionaire at the barricades : the populist revolution from Reagan to
    Trump / Laura Ingraham.
Description: First edition. | New York : All Points Books, 2017. | Includes
    bibliographical references and index.
Identifiers: LCCN 2017036170 | ISBN 9781250150646 (hardcover) |
    ISBN 9781250150653 (ebook)
Subjects: LCSH: Trump, Donald, 1946– —Influence. | United States—Politics
    and government—1989– | Right and left (Political science)—United States. |
    Presidents—United States—Election—2016. | Populism—United States—History.
Classification: LCC E912 .I54 2017 | DDC 324.973—dc23
LC record available at https://lccn.loc.gov/2017036170

ISBN 978-1-250-15163-6 (trade paperback)

Our books may be purchased in bulk for promotional, educational, or business
use. Please contact your local bookseller or the Macmillan Corporate and
Premium Sales Department at 1-800-221-7945, extension 5442, or by email at
MacmillanSpecialMarkets@macmillan.com.

Previously published as *Billionaire at the Barricades*

First All Points Books Paperback Edition: October 2018

10 9 8 7 6 5 4 3 2 1

CONTENTS

PREFACE TO THE
PAPERBACK EDITION

Y ou would have thought that the "political experts" who failed to understand, let alone predict, the rise of Donald Trump in 2016 might have learned something by now. They haven't. While they obsess over silly side issues that do not concern most Americans, President Trump has been methodically making stunning progress in his pledge to undo the policies of his predecessor and pursue others that are improving the lives of working men and women.

Despite the hundreds of hours of media reports about the number of times Trump played golf, staff turnover at the White House, his television-viewing habits, and of course the investigation by Special Counsel Robert Mueller, we see that the American public is generally feeling better about the direction of the country and their own lives. It turns out that Donald Trump's style—at times brash, unconventional, and even unpredictable—is largely irrelevant to voters who just want more control over their own lives, more money in their pockets—a shot at a better life.

By Day 500 of his presidency, Trump was the most popular Republican president among members of his own party since World War II, with the exception of George W. Bush after 9/11. The 87 percent of Republicans approving of his job performance were focusing not on cable chatter, but on some of his achievements. Trump's record at that point:

- Quarterbacked tax reform that saved more than 80 percent of Americans money and spurred massive job growth and investment in the United States.
- Appointed dozens of phenomenal judges to the federal courts, including Supreme Court Justice Neil Gorsuch.
- Cut the federal payroll by 24,000 jobs.
- Eliminated 16 regulations for every one added.
- Boosted our energy sector by removing barriers to the building of the Keystone XL Pipeline.
- Historically low unemployment rates for African Americans.
- Withdrew from the Paris climate accord.
- Repealed the Obamacare individual mandate.
- Defunded Planned Parenthood funding via Title X.
- Reinstated an expanded Mexico City policy blocking foreign aid from being used for abortions.
- Overhauled the Department of Veterans Affairs.
- Enacted new protections for religious liberty.
- Cracked down on MS-13, "sanctuary cities," and deported thousands of criminal aliens.
- Successfully renegotiated our trade deal with South Korea and began process with Mexico and Canada (the North American Free Trade Agreement).
- Reset our trade relationship with China after years of bad-faith actions by the communist regime.
- Held historic talks with North Korea with the goal of averting a nuclear showdown in the Korean Peninsula.
- Moved America's embassy in Israel to Jerusalem, which prior presidents promised but never delivered.

As impressive as the above list is, it's far from comprehensive, and Trump's team insists they are just getting started. Contrary to what the Bushes, Obamas, and Clintons contended, Trump's "America First"

approach to governance hasn't and doesn't result in isolationism, nativism, and/or protectionism. If properly executed, it results in more
prosperity for more Americans, less dangerous and wasteful military interventionism—more happiness, and less hopelessness here at
home. Plus, let's fact facts—with $20 trillion in debt and budgets still
wildly out of balance, pragmatism had to replace idealism. Globalism
had to give way to a conservative populism. Policies that don't work had
to be abandoned in favor of ones that return power to the people, where
it rightly resides.

Of course plenty has not gone smoothly. That shouldn't surprise
anyone when a disrupter like Donald Trump rolls into Washington.
From my personal interactions with him, I know that he's a man impatient for change. I happen to think that's a good, not bad, quality.
For decades he observed our government from afar, enriching other
countries with mega trade deals as our own people struggled. He saw
Europe fail to live up to its financial obligations for NATO's military
budget. He saw our borders overrun. *Smart people should be able to
fix this,* he thought, *and it shouldn't be that difficult or take that long.*
Well, anyone who has worked in government knows—nothing transformative happens easily or quickly.

Trump, a newbie to the workings of Washington, stumbled unnecessarily out of the gate. The executive branch is a labyrinthine
behemoth that will swallow you up if not staffed and managed correctly.
He needed to hire more personnel in key positions who knew how
to work with Congress, prioritize policy goals, understand the rule-
making process, and manage the nastiest characters of all—the press.
In other words, staff who know the system. There's simply no time for
"on-the-job training" when you're president. Crises happen. Domestic
and world events take over. If everyone isn't rowing in the same direction, you'll find yourself going in circles. At the Trump White House,
they found themselves defending a hastily worded travel ban instead
of pushing a robust tax reform or an infrastructure bill that included
a border wall.

For more than a year, Trump's Presidential Personnel Office was
understaffed and slow to move on new hires. People with zero history
of supporting the Trump agenda were advanced into positions that

would have been better served by others. Former Exxon CEO Rex
Tillerson was never suited for the job of secretary of state. Replacing
him with CIA Director Mike Pompeo was an astute move. Tom Price
was similarly a swing and a miss. Just because he had served ably in
Congress and practiced medicine didn't mean he was suited to run a
department as massive and unwieldy as Health and Human Services.
To his credit, Trump saw Price's weakness and slotted in the guy who
many of us thought should have gotten the job in the first place—Alex
Azar, former deputy HHS secretary under George W. Bush. (Disclo-
sure: he is a close personal friend going back to our Supreme Court
clerkship days.)

Of course, the high rate of senior staff turnover and occasional
controversies among certain cabinet members became a favorite narrative of the media always desperate to paint an administration in a
constant state of chaos. "Trump Cabinet Turnover Sets Record Going
Back 100 Years," NPR reported.

More white noise to Americans who by the summer of 2018 were
really feeling the strong Trump economy kick in for themselves and
their families.

But he tweets too much! He publicly criticizes his own cabinet! He's
erratic! (Kim Jong-un's "rocket man" one day and a summit partner
the next.) He's too thin-skinned! His older sons are still doing international business deals! His wife looks unhappy! And what the heck
are Jared and Ivanka doing in there?

The more popular and successful the president becomes, the more
unhinged the anti-Trump "resistance" becomes. Ultimately, their
hatred for the president blinds them to what's happening all around
America—more people are working and taking home more pay. The
hard-core left and the bitter Never Trump right seem to be cheering
against America when they fail to recognize that the policies of this
administration are delivering real results and insist that Trump be
removed from office.

The media complex will continue to be a barrier to Trump, but
he manages to bust through daily. By communicating directly to the
people through Twitter, using talk radio, Fox News, OAN, social media,
and various websites, the Trump administration is able to reach more

Americans than ever before, without the usual filter of bias. Trump has made a decision that appearing on networks like CNN or MSNBC is generally not worth the aggravation. That may or may not be the right decision, but it seems to be working for him.

The Mueller investigation also remains a constant distraction. Rod Rosenstein never should have been appointed deputy attorney general and, in turn, he should never have appointed a special counsel in the first place. The more we learn, the worse the story gets. An FBI director—Jim Comey—who lectured others against leaks but who leaked memos to the press to spur the appointment. FBI agents who expressed their political animus against the presidential campaign they were investigating in text messages and their talk of an "insurance policy" as the campaign was drawing to a close. Dozens of "unmasking requests" made by Obama UN Ambassador Samantha Power and still others by his National Security Adviser Susan Rice. Applications for Foreign Intelligence Surveillance Act warrants that failed to disclose Hillary Clinton's funding of the Christopher Steele "dossier" that contained dirt on Trump. News that a "confidential informant" was placed by the FBI in the Trump campaign to investigate its possible ties to the Russian government. Questions swirling about what President Obama and his top staff knew about the investigation into Trump's campaign and when they knew it.

Meanwhile, Hillary Clinton was cleared by Jim Comey and the Obama Department of Justice for conduct that would have gotten any low-level government staffer or U.S. soldier prosecuted. That's Washington "justice" for you. One set of rules for the Clintons. Another for everyone else.

What is most heartening is that Republicans (and I bet a lot of independents) are able to separate the distractions from the reality of President Trump.

Elites always maintained that refashioning our global trade agreements was too complicated, that if we revisited these old decisions the nation would be imperiled. That was total poppycock. Trump's instincts were right and theirs were wrong.

They were also wrong on China becoming a member of the World Trade Organization. They were wrong about allowing open borders.

They were wrong about admitting so many unskilled, poorly educated workers. They were wrong about the formation of the European Union. They were wrong to support German Chancellor Angela Merkel's wave-in of millions of mostly Muslim, male refugees from Syria.

While they keep hoping for a world that will never be, Trump operates in the world as it is. This doesn't mean he won't make missteps. But what it does mean is that before every decision he makes, he will ask the question—how does this affect the life of that working-class family of four in Kentucky? Is America's interest advanced?

Populists don't care how policies make elites feel while at their international forums. They care if they work. Policymaking is supposed to exist for the betterment of your own people first. We tried ceding our authority, our sovereignty, to international organizations and courts, and it was an abject failure. When liberals say other countries don't respect us any longer with Trump as president, they get it exactly backward. Trump demonstrated that America will not be bullied by other governments into losing ground. We have power and we should use it for ourselves—he instinctively understands this. Imagine trying to be Hungary or the Czech Republic or Poland and at odds with entire EU over the key issue of immigration. In America we decide our *own* destinies.

This is the whole point of America—freedom. We were supposed to govern for ourselves. We created the richest, most powerful country in history of the world because our system worked better than others.

Their policies were good for rich elites but not for most people who prefer that we have a middle class.

In 2020, Democrats are going to have to answer this question: how are you possibly going to get better unemployment numbers, better growth, and a better policy toward China? That's a tough climb.

When Democrats aren't railing on about how "embarrassing" Trump is, they're embracing the same high-tax, big government, open borders policies that the voters rejected in the 2016 election. As they spin their wheels, Trump will work to do what George W. Bush could not—expand his base of support.

Why should African-American and Hispanic voters buy into the stale old game of identity politics and feel compelled to stick with the

Democrats? Because Nancy Pelosi and Chuck Schumer support removing Confederate statues and celebrate kneeling for the national anthem? How will that create more jobs? Democrats, once the party of slavery, talk a good game about civil rights as they relentlessly push policies that obliterate religious liberty. Their leaders march for "social justice," but preside over cities where violent crime is the norm and two-parent households the exception.

Today, thanks to a president who is determined to forge a new path, and leave behind the failed ideas of the past, America is back on the right track. Twenty-five years from now, I hope my children will look back on the 2016 election the way I look back on 1980—the time when a man who so many of the "smart people" dismissed, ridiculed, and maligned restored faith in the American experiment.

AN EARLY WARNING SIGN

If I had to pinpoint a single moment that foreshadowed the rise, and ultimate victory, of Donald Trump, I would choose June 10, 2014. That was the day a little-known economics professor defeated the Republican House majority leader Eric Cantor in a primary challenge. It had never happened before in American history. Not a single member of the media or political Establishment saw it coming. Yet Dave Brat's victory didn't come out of nowhere. It was actually a logical outcome after years of a Republican leadership that had grown smug, insulated, and totally out of touch with the concerns of its own grass roots.

In early 2014, when filmmaker and Virginia native Ron Maxwell initially brought Dave Brat to my attention, I was skeptical for the obvious reasons. I'd never heard of him and didn't know anyone who had. But Maxwell, a conservative populist, had done his homework and tilled the ground for several months before I ever entered the picture. Brat appeared on my show several times over the last four and a half months of the campaign. Although we had yet to meet in person, I found him to be humble, courageous, and smart.

Meanwhile, Brat was doing precisely what I had urged interested Americans to do 10 years earlier in my book *Power to the People*— get involved, run for office, and pursue policies that give power back to the people. In 2009, the Tea Party—the first authentically populist movement on the right in decades—emerged in response to Obama's reckless bailouts and gained strength after the passage of Obamacare. Although the Tea Party helped elect a number of people to Congress, it was still a minority within the GOP. Undaunted by the very imposing barricade of Establishment money and power that lay before him, Brat took his case directly to the people. Most aspiring politicians would have been scared off by Eric Cantor's staff of 23, or the $5.4 million he had to spend on advertising. But not Brat. He had a team of two and had raised only $200,000. It was Dave versus Goliath. "They don't take me seriously," he told me a few months before primary day. "And right now, that's just the way I like it."

His drive and determination were inspiring. Disorganized and small in representation, the Tea Party movement had wandered since the 2010 midterm elections, and Brat's brainy fearlessness was exactly what it needed. Besides, I reasoned, how will we ever save America from a corrupt, unresponsive, ineffective federal government if we don't support those with real talent who are willing to stick their necks out and challenge the status quo? Even if Brat could come within striking distance of Cantor, that could spur other independent, strong conservatives to challenge lame incumbents across the country. Such were my thoughts as I weighed whether to throw in with the underdog.

On June 3, 2014, a Tuesday night, my producer, Julia Hahn, another business associate, and I made the two-and-a-half-hour drive from Washington to the leafy Virginia town of Glen Allen to support Dave Brat. The Republican primary vote for Virginia's 7th Congressional District was just a week away, but as we rolled up to the Dominion Club, none of us knew what to expect. Incredibly, not a single national Tea Party group had given Brat any financial support, although the local Richmond Tea Party had endorsed him. The polls showed Cantor ahead by 25–30 points, and he was getting big money air cover in the form of ads from powerhouse lobbying groups like the American Chemistry Council, the Chamber of Commerce, and the National Association of Realtors.

"Let's hope people actually show up tonight besides some snarky reporters," I told Julia, who personally took it upon herself to make my appearance happen. I wondered to myself whether the whole thing was a bridge too far—a total waste of time. We were doing the round-trip in one day, after my three-hour radio show and an appearance on *Fox & Friends. I should be home eating dinner with the kids,* I thought.

But then as we approached the club's driveway, we saw the cars—hundreds of them—lined up, spilling out of the parking lots. The moment we walked into the lobby, I was overjoyed that we had made the effort.

The "Brat Pack" was out in full force.

"Thank you for coming, Laura!" chirped a 40-something woman standing in the hallway with her teenage daughter. "Dave Brat is the MAN!" someone else blurted out. "Our boy's gonna win!" exclaimed a man who introduced himself as "just a plain old farmer." He had come at the last minute after learning about the rally from his neighbor. A few were wearing "Can't stand Cantor" buttons; most were just neatly dressed, everyday middle-class Americans.

"We got him right where we want him," Brat insisted, in reference to the incumbent Cantor, at what was our first face-to-face meeting. I laughed, and wondered if I would be that optimistic were I in his shoes. Tan, with his sandy brown hair combed back, in wire-rimmed glasses, Brat had the look of an all-American prepster. His smile was real and reassuring.

More than the average politician, Brat understood the urgent need to "disrupt" the old GOP hierarchy. Fundamental, conservative change would not be possible in Washington, unless and until the Establishment in both parties was exposed and defeated. For decades, on key issues, they had been in an alliance of convenience, working against the interests of everyday Americans. On no issue was this collusion more apparent than "immigration reform" (aka amnesty).

Over the years, I've developed a pretty accurate rule of thumb for judging the conservatism of Republican politicians. If they refuse multiple requests to appear on my radio show, they're usually up to no good. Case in point: Eric Cantor. Majority Leader Cantor had turned down several invitations from my bookers to join us on air to discuss his 2013 legislation misleadingly known as The Kids Act. It was essentially his version of President Obama's DREAM Act and would have given a path to legalization to illegal immigrants brought here as children. Cantor thought he could dodge the tough questions by simply avoiding them. That told me a lot. Apparently it was that same aloof, "I-don't-need-to-answer-to-anyone" attitude that rubbed the voters of the 7th Congressional District the wrong way, as well.

In the final week before the June 10 primary, we covered the race every day on radio. I begged Glenn Beck to get involved and to his credit he did, by interviewing Brat on his popular radio show. Radio host Mark Levin had been in the pro-Brat camp for some time and was also extremely influential. Likewise, the populist website Breitbart played a critical role in this historic primary by covering the race and the issues motivating Brat's challenge. As for the rest of the media—many of the same people and institutions that look down on talk radio and conservative websites—they barely touched on the race at all.

On June 10, after my radio show wrapped up at noon, I said a silent prayer for a surprise Brat victory. If he could pull off this sneak attack against Cantor and the big corporatist forces that backed him, anything was possible. None of my staff would take bets on the outcome. We were all too nervous.

Later that night, I was celebrating my son Dmitri's sixth birthday at the home of a close family friend. Through dinner and cake, I didn't have my cell phone handy. I was so focused on *his* big day, I had put Brat's big night out of my mind. Their home telephone rang. It was one of my friends—a Brat supporter. "Where have you been? We've been trying to reach you! He won! He won! Dave won!"

"Yes!!" I screamed, with a mouth full of frosting, still sitting at the dining room table. Those gathered must have thought I'd hit the lottery. I ran for my phone where the texts and emails were pouring in. Not long thereafter, I was on Fox News' special coverage of Cantor's loss.

"He really just didn't have very much money, but what he did have was a lot of heart," I said of Brat, in a telephone interview with Megyn Kelly. "I think there will be a lot of people out there saying this could be the beginning of something really big for the Republican Party."

Fox News political analyst Brit Hume disagreed, and he was not alone among conservative commentators in expressing dismay over Brat's massive upset of the GOP Old Guard.

> The margin is amazing. . . . The conventional wisdom on this . . . that this is bad news long term for the Republicans and great news for Democrats. It is argued by some that immigration reform now will never pass with Republicans who were very much chastened by what happened to Eric Cantor. So that's dead for now. That means that Republicans will go forward into the 2016 election without their name associated with immigration reform, which will make it very difficult for any Republican to become president.

Or so he thought.

Every news outlet in America reported on Brat's unprecedented victory. "[O]ne of the most stunning primary election upsets in congressional history," wrote *The New York Times*.[1] "The loss wasn't just big, it was historic," said NBC News.[2] *The Washington Post* called it "a historic electoral surprise that left the GOP in chaos."[3]

As for Cantor himself, he had little to say on election night except that he "came up short."[4] (According to *The Washington Post*, he was so confident on Election Day that he was hanging out with lobbyists at the Starbucks on Capitol Hill.)[5] When approached leaving a DC Italian restaurant the night his heir apparent crashed and burned, Speaker John Boehner had no comment.

Other GOP bigwigs seemed intent on spinning the Brat victory as a one-off. The party's 2012 presidential nominee Mitt Romney dismissed the notion that the Cantor defeat was a harbinger of change to come in the GOP. "I know it's our inclination to look at races and suggest that somehow a national movement is causing what occurs," he told NBC's David Gregory.[6] When asked specifically whether a rising conservative populism was in the air, Romney batted away the suggestion, noting that the Republican senator Lindsey Graham, disliked intensely by the Tea Party, easily won his primary challenge in South Carolina. To his credit, he did cite the frustration of voters on the immigration issue as a driving force in the race.

Contrary to what many pundits and *"Wall Street Journal"* Republicans claimed in the aftermath, Cantor's support for immigration amnesty was a major factor in his loss. Brat pounded that theme relentlessly, along with Cantor's cozy relationship with K Street and his overall disregard of the concerns of his constituents. The six-term congressman had become everything that the Tea Party and other grassroots conservatives hated about the GOP.

The Sunday after the primary, I was part of the ABC panel to discuss the Cantor primary loss. Eric Cantor was on the panel before us. Saying little of interest, he still didn't seem to fathom why he lost. Zero insights. When his segment was over, he exited the studio out of a side door to avoid crossing paths with me.

"Objectively thinking, I really believe it was the beginning of everything that followed—and led directly to Donald Trump," Ron Maxwell posited.

Although Tea Party groups launched other primary challenges against Establishment GOP candidates in 2014 and weren't successful, it didn't matter. Brat's win was cataclysmic—and gave encouragement to conservative-populist activists coast to coast. For the first time, they had proof positive that the Establishment doesn't always win.

One year later, Donald Trump crashed the Republican Party when he announced his presidential bid. Even Cantor's defeat hadn't prepared the Establishment for the possibility that their grip on the GOP was weakening. Yet given the voters' building discontent with Republican politics as usual, they should have seen Trump coming.

His populist counter-insurgency campaign was brash and bold, and entirely predictable after years of failed GOP and Democrat efforts to grow our economy and put America on the right track. If the people were mad enough to oust a sitting majority leader, anything was possible.

THE POPULIST MOVEMENT MADE IT POSSIBLE

The force behind Dave Brat's victory was populism—the belief that people should have power instead of ceding it to elites. Americans are used to left-versus-right political disagreements, like judicial activism versus judicial restraint, union versus nonunion. Populists understand that there's a top and a bottom, too. The Establishment—composed of powerful elites on both the left and the right—does not trust individuals to make decisions for themselves. Instead, they believe Washington "experts" and bureaucrats must fill the void. Populists believe individuals should have more control over their own lives.

Presidential candidates invoke the populist style because it connects with working people. Except for Reagan, all modern presidents of both parties campaigned as populists but governed as globalists. Populism isn't new. It arose in the 1890s when the so-called robber barons—businessmen who gained wealth and influence through unethical business practices—amassed power that hurt workers. Populists revolted and formed a short-lived national People's Party. Its platform was essentially left-wing. It was pro-labor and anti-capitalist and was especially hostile to banks and railroads. That party effectively merged with the Democrats in 1896 and ultimately disappeared in 1908. But the populist style—with its emphasis on the common-sense wisdom of the working class—remained a potent force that Democrats and Republicans both co-opted for years to come.

Because populism is not an ideology, it often appears with a descriptor, like "progressive populism" or "conservative populism." On the left side of the political spectrum, progressive populism wraps big government schemes in the guise of populism. Bill Clinton's Arkansas everyman populist style ultimately gave way to disastrous globalist trade deals; Obama's "hope and change" morphed into a historic growth in government power. In 2016, Establishment Media tried to portray Bernie Sanders as a "left-wing populist." In reality, of course, Sanders was little more than a socialist retread. Nevertheless, he ran an impressive campaign—one that managed to draw massive crowds of over 20,000. (It's amazing what promising young kids free college tuition can do!)

On the surface, Sanders seemed to agree with Donald Trump's populist opposition to bad trade deals, foreign interventionism, and Wall Street corruption. But on domestic issues, Sanders's proposals were the same old failed big government power grabs and massive tax gambits that are antithetical to economic freedom. As President Reagan put it, "as government expands, liberty contracts." Instead of returning power to the people, Sanders's plans would have squelched workers' wealth and freedom. Still, the fact that a man of Sanders's age could be a thorn in Hillary Clinton's side was just as much a compliment to him as a sign that Clinton's candidacy was deeply flawed.

By contrast, conservativism and populism overlap in their opposition to "big things"—big government, big international organizations, big media, big business cronyism. These distant, uncaring entities rob people of decision making and ignore their interests. Pat Buchanan and Donald Trump summarized conservative populism best when each vowed to put "America first."

Conservative populists tend to support a policy of economic nationalism—people-centered economic policies that put the nation and its workers first. They oppose a massive national debt because it weakens America and makes its citizens beholden to lenders. They also believe high taxes are bad because they sap workers' wages and economic freedom. Similarly, they are against huge trade deals and international organizations like the World Trade Organization because they take power out of the hands of voters and give it to a faraway and often hostile global elite.

In foreign affairs, conservative populists oppose broad military interventionism and believe military force should only be used when American interests are threatened. Populism's critics like to toss around the term "isolationism" to dismiss populist foreign policy, but that doesn't describe any populist I've ever known. Throughout the Cold War, populists were among the strongest voices opposing Soviet communism. At the same time, they believe squandering the nation's wealth and blood on unwinnable wars and nation-building is unwise. Instead, they support a pragmatic foreign policy based on achieving "peace through strength" by maintaining a strong military and using it prudently.

If all this sounds familiar that's because conservative-populist Ronald Reagan remade American politics with his two landslide presidential victories in 1980 and 1984. The populist movement that propelled Reagan into office came roaring back in 2016 to produce the most stunning political victory in American history.

This is the story of how a man with zero political experience overcame the Establishment in both parties and a hostile press to capture the presidency. It's also a book about how a lot of us who supported Ronald Reagan, and who worked together for decades, came to disagree so strongly over the next steps for this country.

There is also a caution here. Trump's victory was only the beginning. The forces he overcame during the campaign have now created a barricade to block his—and the people's—agenda permanently. Choreographed and well-funded protests, endless investigations, and a slow-walking of his agenda on Capitol Hill have reinforced the barricades to real reform. To overcome this, the president will have to avoid the mistakes of his predecessors and remain close to the principles and people that got him elected. Donald Trump in his gut understands Americans better than most "experts" who have spent their lives in politics.

Despite conventional wisdom (or whatever it's calling itself today), Trump didn't win because of "free air time" or because he hosted *The Apprentice*.

He didn't win because of his tweets.

He didn't win because he is a celebrity.

He didn't win because of FBI director James Comey.

He didn't win because the Democratic National Committee was hacked.

He didn't even win because Hillary was a lousy candidate and a worse campaigner.

Trump won because his message of economic nationalism and a less-interventionist foreign policy reflects the will of the people. He won because he vowed (à la Buchanan) to put America first again. He won because both parties had gotten fat off the status quo, while many in the middle were being squeezed. He won because he was not a politician, but a self-made outsider who fearlessly called out the collusion among politicians, the media, and even big business. He won because Americans had had it—with Washington's failed promises, with political correctness, with open borders, and with career politicians, consultants, pollsters, and pundits.

In the end, voters in Wisconsin, Michigan, Pennsylvania, and Ohio didn't care about his rough language. They cared about saving their country and knew the only way to do it was to elect a renegade—a disruptor—someone who owed the Old Guard nothing. Ironically, that someone was a Manhattan billionaire. Donald Trump won because on the biggest issues of the day, he had the guts to stand with the "silent majority." Just like Dave Brat and Ronald Reagan before him—he was right and his opponents were wrong.

The elites had been blindsided before—by Reagan's 1980 election. Many in the party dismissed him as well. He was just an actor. He was "too divisive." Remember, after he narrowly lost the GOP nomination in 1976, Reagan came back in 1980 and won big. Southern states that had been Democrat strongholds for decades flipped to the GOP. An anti-Establishment conservative who was almost 70 years old was just the breath of fresh air our country and political system needed.

Sound familiar?

The conservative-populist movement that powered Ronald Reagan to historic landslide victories reemerged in 2016. Against all odds, the people rose up and propelled Donald Trump to the presidency. It did not happen in a vacuum. Indeed, as this book reveals, the forces that aligned and made his victory possible had been gathering for decades as Establishment elites in both parties accumulated ever-increasing power for themselves. Time will tell whether Donald

Trump can clear all the barricades in front of him, make good on his promise to drain the swamp, and return power back to the people. Either way, the conservative-populist movement proved it will remain a dynamic and powerful force for years to come.

Power to the people, indeed.

1.

REBEL WITH A CAUSE

Ronald Reagan and the Populist Wave

Don't trust me, trust yourselves.

—Ronald Reagan

I was four years old when I heard over our small kitchen radio that Dr. Martin Luther King Jr. had been killed. All I knew was that he was very important and it was very sad, so I ran next door to broadcast the news to my neighbors. Not long after I remember seeing scenes on television of buildings burning in American cities (the King assassination riots in Washington, D.C., Baltimore, Chicago, and Kansas City).

After that, my political memories jump to a kaleidoscope of jarring images of injured soldiers being carried onto helicopters, angry kids with long hair and bell-bottoms carrying signs, police in riot gear at colleges and universities, and watching my camp counselors crying in August 1974 on the night Richard Nixon resigned.

Then my recollection takes me back to the summer of 1976, sitting on the colorful braided rug in our living room, playing cards with my friend Pam. In our small red rambler-style home, the television blared the coverage of the Republican Convention. Walter Cronkite, the lead anchor of CBS News, was, to put it mildly, not my parents' favorite, but they watched him anyway. (When he signed off his broadcasts with

"That's the way it is," my dad would often say, "No, Walt, that's the way you *say* it is!") Ronald Reagan came up only 117 delegates short, losing the nomination to the incumbent Gerald Ford. My mother said something akin to "the Rockefeller Republicans always win." (Even though Ford had already scotched Nelson Rockefeller from the ticket, it still had a nice ring to it.) Although I didn't understand what she meant, I did know that I liked Reagan's square jaw and speaking style. Ford, even in victory, was bland and boring. But to this 13-year-old tomboy, Reagan, even in defeat, was mesmerizing and resolute.

When people ask me why I gravitated toward conservatism at such a young age, I usually attribute a good deal of it to my parents, James and Anne Ingraham. Growing up in the Hartford, Connecticut, suburb of Glastonbury, I found my own areas of anti-parental rebellion, but politics was not one of them. I caught the political bug by listening to their conversations (often not flattering) about the media, or politicians—especially liberal Republicans. For instance, they thought Lowell Weicker, former governor and three-term senator from our state, was "just as bad as the Democrats." (Weicker campaigned against a state income tax only to support it after his inauguration as governor.)

Reagan was something else altogether—he was speaking for people just like them: middle-class, hardworking, never-take-handouts, flag-flying, World War II–generation patriots. "He's Goldwater, although a hell of a lot better," my dad used to say of Reagan. Gerald Ford was a placeholder, not an incumbent in the truest meaning of the word since he was not elected, but the "Watergate president," as my father said.

Barely a teenager, I innately understood that, if implemented, Reagan's conservatism would mean the lives of average people like us would get better. We had no special connections and were not born into privilege. Allowing families to keep more of their own money, cutting wasteful government spending, law and order—it all seemed solidly grounded in truth and common sense. It resonated with me because for years I had heard my mother repeat her homespun wisdom, depending on the situation that we faced: "Work and you'll learn the value of a buck"; "Don't spend beyond your means"; or "Don't let anyone push you around." (She also said "don't chase the boys," which I confess I didn't follow too well.)

Perhaps my mother was tough and no-nonsense because she needed to be to survive. Growing up very poor in Willimantic, Connecticut, during the Depression, her mother died when she was only 14 years old. In effect, she became like a mother to her little sister Mickey, and did all the family's cooking, cleaning, and ironing. She worked at the American Thread Mill in town before she married my father in 1952. When I was a kid, she cooked and dished out food in my elementary school cafeteria. After we were all in school, she was a waitress at a local steakhouse—a job she held until she was 73 years old, her hands arthritic from carrying heavy trays for so many years. Polish people are hard workers, she would tell me. "People make fun of the Poles," she would say defensively, "Let 'em say what they want, we'll outwork 'em every time." To her, it was simply unacceptable to be an entitled American; it galled her to see "able-bodied Americans just sitting around, waiting for the mailman to deliver a government check."

In 1976, Reagan was warning of the government that spent too much, the welfare system that robbed people of their incentive to work, and the political ambivalence toward the growing threat of the Soviet Union. From my adolescent perspective, I thought Reagan and my mother would have gotten along very well.

I vividly remember the moment Reagan, at the 1976 convention, mentioned a time capsule in the off-the-cuff remarks he made when a victorious Ford brought him out on stage. We had just buried our own "time capsule" in Gideon Wells Junior High to mark the bicentennial year of the American Revolution, so he got my attention. He asked, what would the people of America, on her tricentennial, think of what we did in 1976?

> Whether they will have the freedom that we have known up until now will depend on what we do here. Will they look back with appreciation and say, "Thank God for those people in 1976 who headed off that loss of freedom? Who kept us now a hundred years later free? Who kept our world from nuclear destruction?"

And if we fail they probably won't get to read the letter at all
because it spoke of individual freedom and they won't be allowed
to talk of that or read of it.[1]

Looking back at the archival footage of that night 40 years later on
YouTube, I relived the experience all over again. Chills. Goose bumps.
Almost as good as being front row at my first Billy Joel concert. Watching the reaction shots in the Kemper Arena, it really did seem obvious
that most people knew they had nominated the wrong guy.

Such a dispiriting defeat would have wrecked many a candidate,
but not Reagan. "It was this incredible, crushing defeat, and it didn't
crush him," recalled Reagan policy adviser Martin Anderson. Describing Reagan's mood on the flight back to California after the painful loss, he noted: "He just came back up, shook his head, and said,
'Okay, what's next?' And that began the campaign for the year 1980."[2]

THE BIGGEST TENT

For those who are too young to remember, Ronald Reagan's presidency was the last one that deserved a real exclamation point for conservatives. The broad-based coalition he built included many different
types of voters. One of the reasons I loved Ronald Reagan was that he
understood how important it was to grow the conservative movement.
Social conservatives, defense hawks (the neoconservatives), populists,
libertarians—they were all drawn to his transformative, bold ideas.
Unlike Mitt Romney, who wrote off 47 percent of America as "unwinnable," Reagan believed his conservative message would have wide
appeal if it was passionately and convincingly articulated. Obviously,
he was right. In 1980, Ronald Reagan won 44 states to Jimmy Carter's
six. Erstwhile liberal Republican-turned-Independent John Anderson
was a third-party pest, but the 6.6 percent of the vote he captured
was not consequential. (Reagan beat Carter by 9.7 percent.) "He built
a stunning electoral landslide by taking away Mr. Carter's Southern
base, smashing his expected strength in the East, and taking command of the Middle West," wrote Hedrick Smith in *The New York
Times*.[3] Then, in 1984, Reagan went even bigger.

I remember that evening vividly. I was a student at Dartmouth College and had served as the editor of the conservative student weekly, *The Dartmouth Review*. Our college election night party at the Hanover Inn in 1984 was a total riot. Few of Dartmouth's liberal faculty showed up, but we at the *Review* put on a great celebration. It was packed. I wish we'd had cell phones back then so I could have captured on video all the seething leftists outside, peering through the glass of the Hayward Lounge where balloons and streamers turned the event into a red-white-and-blue extravaganza. Everyone was in a great mood. God, I loved the '80s.

By the end of the evening, Ronald Reagan had captured 525 out of 538 electoral votes—the highest total ever by a presidential candidate—against Democratic challenger Walter Mondale. That meant that Reagan, the ultimate anti-Establishment candidate, won 97.58 percent of all the electoral votes. In fact, the only state Mondale carried was his home state of Minnesota—and that Reagan would have won with a switch of just 1,876 votes in a state with over two million voters. Were it not for the president insisting that his campaign pull back the reins in Minnesota to give Mondale a shot at winning in his own backyard, the Gipper likely would have won all 50 states.[4] A consummate gentleman.

A big part of the story of the last 30 years is that different people followed Reagan for different reasons. Various right-of-center factions each claim him as a shining textbook example of their beliefs borne out on the presidential stage. Reagan was a genius who combined different categories when he communicated. That's why he won 49 states in 1984. For every libertarian quote from Reagan, you can find a populist quote from Reagan. So it's easy to see why each group now amplifies their favorite Reagan themes and mutes the others.

The core of Reaganism was this: returning power to the people by disempowering behemoth bureaucratic institutions yields the greatest freedom for all. He believed in the individual over the state. Drop in at any point along the Reagan time line—even during his days as a Democrat—and you will hear him declaring his belief that power should reside with the citizens, not government. Today we refer to this idea as "Reaganism," but he would have hated that term. This, after all, was the man who had a plaque on his Oval Office desk that read: "There is no limit to what a man can do or where he can go if he doesn't care who gets the credit."[5] But more than that, he knew that lasting political movements must be built around principles, not personalities. Reagan liked to say, "Don't trust me, trust yourselves." That was his consistent view throughout his political life, and it helped pave the path for the populist movement of the present. It's easy to see why historians have called him "a true American populist."[6]

THE ULTIMATE OUTSIDER

Today we remember Ronald Reagan in almost mythic terms, as a towering figure whose ascendancy and landslide presidential victories were inevitable, even predictable. Yet many of those who claim to have been with Reagan all along weren't—not by a long shot. Libertarians, for example, attacked Reagan's economic populism for decades. Until recently I did not appreciate how many writers who call themselves conservatives are actually libertarians. But as we saw during the 2016 election cycle, the libertarian numbers in the GOP are just not that significant, and the same was true under Reagan.

Here is what the leading libertarian think tank, the Cato Institute, wrote about Ronald Reagan's economic policies in a 1988 policy paper: "If President Reagan has a devotion to free trade, it surely must be blind, because he has been off the mark most of the time."[7] Their beef? Reagan had the audacity to protect American jobs and companies by slapping hefty tariffs on some foreign goods, like Japanese electronics (a 100 percent tariff) and motorcycles (45 percent tariff, a move meant to help Harley-Davidson). Libertarians like to say that we can't criticize how China manipulates markets if our government occasionally interferes with a pure market system. Absurd. For one, that's like saying we could not criticize the Soviet Union for human rights abuses because we occasionally backed allies with less than pristine human rights records. And second, whatever level of interference we impose upon markets, it's infinitesimally small and in no way comparable to China for the simple reason that theirs is not a market economy at all.

For added anti-Gipper libertarian gusto, Cato likened Reagan to the man who presided over the Great Depression and dubbed him "the most protectionist president since Herbert Hoover." It's one of the oldest (and lamest) tricks in the book of the anti-populists: impugn anyone who doesn't worship trade agreements and tariff-free commerce as a "protectionist," "isolationist," or "nativist." All throughout the 2016 election, Trump and any of us who supported him were showered with the "-ists." Should Reagan have had America unilaterally disarm economically against countries that subsidized their industries and manipulated their currency? Since when is it bad to "protect" our nation and its workers? Reagan wasn't picking winners and losers willy-nilly in the marketplace. He was giving *American* industries a fighting chance to compete against nations who rig the rules in their favor. Personally, I've never found libertarianism to be an interesting worldview. Politics takes place in the real world with real people, not in the dusty pages of an Ayn Rand novel.

But libertarians weren't the only one's sniping at Reagan. During the first half of his career, the GOP Establishment didn't have much use for him either. That is, until he dragged them kicking and screaming to seismic political victories that reshaped the contours of U.S. policy. In the 1970s, "the other major GOP players—especially Easterners and moderates—thought Reagan was a certified yahoo," recalls Reagan historian Craig Shirley. "To a person, by the time of Reagan's death in 2004, they would profess their love and devotion to Reagan and claim they were there from the beginning in 1974, which was a load of horse manure."[8]

The political "wise men" on both sides of the aisle had spent years dismissing Reagan as a simpleton. Henry Kissinger once told President Richard Nixon that even though Reagan was "a pretty decent guy," his "brains are negligible."[9] Clark Clifford, adviser to four Democratic presidents and Lyndon Johnson's secretary of defense, infamously labeled Reagan "an amiable dunce."[10] History got the last laugh.

FIGHTING FOR THE LITTLE GUY

Ronald Reagan's populist-conservative instincts annoyed elites of both parties because he was everything they were not. He always fought for the little guy because his people were the "little guys." Reagan was a kid from Dixon, Illinois, with an alcoholic shoe salesman for a father and a degree from tiny Eureka College that he paid for with a football scholarship. The elites knew all the right power players. Reagan knew all the right principles. His respect for the working class was rooted in his own hard-scrabble upbringing. Even as a Hollywood actor, a General Electric spokesman, and later the president of the Screen Actors Guild, Reagan was always most at home with everyday people. As Reagan speechwriter Peggy Noonan put it, "more than any president since [Andrew] Jackson, he spent the years before power with the people, the normal people of his country."[11]

For those who know the real story, that isn't hyperbole. I sometimes have to remind myself that anyone born after 1970 has scant recollections of Reagan's presidency. Even I, as a young speechwriter in the Reagan administration in 1987 (more on that later), did not fully comprehend his improbable path to the presidency.

From 1954 to 1962, Ronald Reagan traveled the country as a spokesman for General Electric. In addition to hosting the TV show *General Electric Theatre*, Reagan's duties as the company's "goodwill ambassador" meant he traveled to over 135 GE factories to meet with and speak to over 250,000 workers in 38 states.[12] The experience changed him forever.

"When I went on those tours and shook hands with all of those people, I began to see that they were very different people than the people Hollywood was talking about," Reagan recalled. "I was seeing the same people that I grew up with in Dixon, Illinois. I realized I was living in a tinsel factory. And this exposure brought me back."[13]

Throughout his Hollywood years, Reagan had been a Franklin Delano Roosevelt New Deal Democrat. But in the eighth and final year as General Electric's traveling ambassador, Reagan made a decision that would transform American politics: he switched parties. His motives were not opportunistic, but pragmatic. Given the expansion of Soviet communism, the explosion of federal government, the soaring tax rates that ate away at the people's wealth, and Democrats' embrace of 1960s countercultural values—Reagan had simply had enough. "I didn't leave the Democratic Party," Reagan famously declared. "The party left me." And it would be that courageous decision of conscience that set off a chain reaction that would change history.

1964–1976: IGNITING
A POPULIST PRAIRIE FIRE

Barry Goldwater was a candidate unlike anyone the nation had ever seen—the college dropout and Arizona senator was devoted not so much to party as to principles. Conservative writer Patrick J. Buchanan, then a young editorial writer for the *St. Louis Globe-Democrat,* would later brand Goldwater "the first great modern conservative of the modern era." My parents were volunteers for Goldwater in Connecticut. Like he, they were staunchly anticommunist, socially conservative, opposed to excessive foreign aid, and thought government had gotten too powerful since the New Deal. The Goldwater campaign was a formative experience for them—even though neither worked on a campaign again, they were more convinced after Goldwater that the worst things that had befallen the GOP could be traced back to the "Rockefeller Republicans," whom they regarded as little different than Democrats.

In 1964, Reagan served as the cochairman of Barry Goldwater's ill-fated California campaign. The relationships he forged in that role proved useful in his future political endeavors. But it was Ronald Reagan's delivery of his televised "A Time for Choosing" landmark speech in support of Barry Goldwater for president that put him on the national political map. The address, which is now known affectionately as "The Speech," moved American conservatism out of the rafters and onto the main stage of politics. In it, he planted the seeds for a revolutionary, populist approach to governance.

Reagan began the speech by pointing out his shift in political parties. His principles hadn't changed, the Democrat Party had. "I have spent most of my life as a Democrat. I recently have seen fit to follow another course. I believe that the issues confronting us cross party lines."

He then made it clear that the established order's doctrine of endless war weakened America. "As for the peace that we would preserve, I wonder who among us would like to approach the wife or mother whose husband or son has died in South Vietnam and ask them if they think this is a peace that should be maintained indefinitely."

Next, Reagan dropped the rhetorical hammer on the governing class of political elites and issued a clarion call for national sovereignty:

> And this idea that government is beholden to the people, that it has no other source of power except the sovereign people, is still the newest and the most unique idea in all the long history of man's relation to man.
>
> This is the issue of this election: whether we believe in our capacity for self-government or whether we abandon the American revolution and confess that a little intellectual elite in a far-distant capitol can plan our lives for us better than we can plan them ourselves.

Goldwater lost in a landslide to Lyndon Johnson. Johnson won 44 states to Goldwater's six. The popular vote was equally lopsided, with LBJ beating Goldwater by a whopping 61 percent to 39 percent— a drubbing by any standard. Among the GOP's Old Guard there was a sense that now that the "kids" (conservatives) had had their fun, the "adults" (Republican Establishment) would be back in charge and running things for the foreseeable future.

Despite Goldwater's historic defeat, Ronald Reagan's speech had been a hit. Soon, California Republicans had recruited him to run for governor. In 1966, Reagan defeated California's political "Goliath," incumbent Democrat governor Pat Brown Sr., in a state with more registered Democrats than Republicans. As California's governor, he broke the mold by shrinking government, cracking down on lawlessness, getting people off of welfare and back to work, and slashing taxes. When his state's budget ran a $100 million surplus, then-governor Reagan told his finance director Caspar "Cap" Weinberger—who would later become his secretary of defense—that he wanted to give the surplus back to the people; it was their money in the first place. (Did you hear that, Washington?) Weinberger said that sounded great but it had never been done before. "Well," said Reagan, "we've never had an actor for governor before either."[14]

Allowing Californians to keep more of their hard-earned money was popular, but many of the other choices he made as governor were not. Although vehemently criticized for his decision to slash spending from California's bloated education budget, Reagan persisted. "I didn't come up here to get reelected," he was known to tell the party apparatchiks who warned that he was hurting his chances at reelection.[15]

Voters in both parties had grown accustomed to politicians whose primary goal was maintaining their vice-like grip on political power. Reagan was different. He built up his political capital so he could spend it on conservative policies that returned power to the people of his state. It was an honest approach to governing that voters found refreshing. In many ways, Donald Trump's bluntness evokes a similar level of authenticity; his brawler style is clearly about driving home his populist principles, not pandering to boost his personal popularity. Reagan's approach was more polished than Trump's. But like Reagan, Trump speaks bold truths, regardless of the polls.

Still, Republicans at the time lacked a nationally viable example of a conservative-populist who had cracked the code on how to communicate populism in ways that could win a presidential election. Then in 1968, midway through Ronald Reagan's first term as California governor, Richard Nixon energized the Republican Party with a broad-based populist message that captivated the working class. We don't usually think of Nixon as a populist, but as a staunch anticommunist whose presidency included liberal social policies and a globalist China policy. Yet Nixon's campaign style and oratory often evinced strong populist appeals. As a young man growing up in a hardworking Quaker household of modest means, Nixon gravitated toward populism's concern for the plight of working people and a rejection of elites. As he put it in his White House diary, he opposed the "American leader class" who "whine and whimper" and instead sided with "labor leaders and people from middle America who still have character and guts and a bit of patriotism."[16] His populist 1968 campaign, therefore, spoke to working Americans who played by the rules but had been left behind by Washington elites.

In his acceptance speech at the Republican National Convention in Miami, Nixon vowed he would restore law and order and would fight for "the great majority of Americans, the forgotten Americans— the non-shouters, the non-demonstrators." As Nixon said, "They are good people, they are decent people; they work, and they save, and they pay their taxes, and they care."[17]

After winning the presidency, Nixon declared that government must heed the will of the "silent majority"—the everyday Americans who play by the rules, pay the taxes, love their country, and quietly earn a living. It was an iconic and enduring phrase that had originally been coined by populist legend and Nixon speechwriter Pat Buchanan.[18]

The Nixon administration also took big media to task. Nixon's first vice president, Spiro Agnew, blasted the TV networks for being "a tiny and closed fraternity of privileged men, elected by no one, and enjoying a monopoly sanctioned and licensed by government. . . . the airwaves do not belong to the networks; they belong to the people." He excoriated them as an "effete corps of impudent snobs"—a line also penned by Buchanan. Indeed, every Republican president since Nixon has had to contend with a hostile press, but liberal media have been particularly nasty toward populists.

Then the Watergate scandal engulfed the nation and destroyed the populist promise Nixon had created. As Pat Buchanan lamented, Watergate was "the lost opportunity to move against the political forces frustrating the expressed national will" and squandered the chance to win "a political counterrevolution in the capital."[19] The scandal ended with Nixon's resignation, but not before he had shown the GOP how to craft a people-centered message capable of attracting massive national support. Indeed, his 1972 reelection landslide campaign over Democrat George McGovern swept every state except Massachusetts and received over 60 percent of the popular vote.

In the aftermath of Watergate, Republicans spent years wandering in the wilderness until Ronald Reagan led them out by mobilizing the conservative-populist movement against big government with an anti-Establishment insurgency of his own. After two terms as a Republican governor of the most populous state in the union (and one of the most progressive), Reagan left office shortly after Nixon's resignation. Unlike Nixon, Reagan exited on a wave of popularity. He was so popular, in fact, that conservatives clamored for him to do something crazy: mount a serious primary challenge to the incumbent president, Gerald Ford.

When Ford became president upon Nixon's resignation on August 9, 1974, GOP elders had hoped putting the presidency in the steady hands of a reliable "party man" would stabilize the Watergate fallout for Republicans. But conservatives opposed Ford's selection of liberal Nelson Rockefeller as his vice president (ergo the term "Rockefeller Republican"). Indeed, far from moving the party and nation toward conservatism, members of the movement viewed Ford's policies as a continuation of Nixon's globalist views on international affairs and his strategy of Soviet appeasement.

Enter the Gipper. Reagan's 1976 decision to make a serious run against President Ford was more than a long shot. No sitting president had lost his primary nomination in nearly a century. What's more, Reagan "was opposed by nearly every state organization," recalls Craig Shirley. "He had practically no editorial support"—a harsh reality Donald Trump's anti-Establishment campaign experienced as well.[20]

Party leaders were irked by Reagan's decision to run. President Ford was furious. Before he announced his candidacy, Reagan called the president to alert him of his decision, and to extend his best wishes for a competitive race. Ford was having none of it, and recalled the icy phone call in his autobiography:

> "Hello, Mr. President," Reagan said, and then he came right to the point.
>
> "I am going to make an announcement, and I want to tell you about it ahead of time. I am going to run for President. I trust we can have a good contest, and I hope that it won't be divisive."
>
> "Well, Governor, I'm very disappointed," I replied. "I'm sorry you're getting into this. I believe I've done a good job and that I can

be elected. Regardless of your good intentions, your bid is bound to be divisive. It will take a lot of money, a lot of effort, and it will leave a lot of scars. It won't be helpful, no matter which of us wins the nomination."

"I don't think it will be divisive," Reagan repeated. "I don't think it will harm the party."

"Well, I think it will," I said.[21]

President Gerald Ford entered the Republican primary with a political wound. That's putting it charitably. Ford's pardoning of President Richard Nixon had crippled his candidacy in ways that ultimately cost him the 1976 presidential election. Still, despite Ford's obvious weaknesses, the GOP Establishment trashed Reagan the instant he entered the race. Richard Nixon said "Ronald Reagan is a lightweight and not someone to be considered seriously or feared in terms of a challenge for the nomination."[22] And Republican Illinois senator Chuck Percy viewed a Reagan presidential nomination as the equivalent of political suicide for the Republican Party: "A Reagan nomination, and the crushing defeat likely to follow, could signal the beginning of the end of our party as an effective force in American life."[23]

Percy turned out to be as accurate as NeverTrump leader and *Weekly Standard* editor-at-large Bill Kristol was during the 2016 cycle. Yet the only thing the ad hominem attacks and intellectual snobbery managed to do was lower expectations for Reagan—a mistake the "smart set" later replicated with Donald Trump.

President Ford started the 1976 Republican primary strong, but from the beginning there were signs that Reagan's fierce anti-Establishment message, combined with his muscular foreign policy stance of doing away with détente and strengthening American sovereignty, were going to give the Establishment major heartburn.

On November 20, 1975, Ronald Reagan launched his presidential campaign with a heat-seeking missile of a populist speech. "Government at all levels now absorbs more than 44 percent of our personal income," said Reagan. "It has become more intrusive, more coercive, more meddlesome, and less effective." He then honed in on the core problem. "In my opinion, the root of these problems lies right here—in Washington, D.C.," said Reagan. "Our nation's capital has become the seat of a 'buddy' system that functions for its own benefit—increasingly insensitive to the needs of the American worker who supports it with his taxes."

That last sentence is rhetorical dynamite. Reagan pinpointed how corrosive bipartisan cronyism eats away at the people's power. Notice he didn't say "the citizens" or "voters"—no, Reagan made a specific appeal to the "American worker," whom he believed had been ignored. (Sadly, the problem didn't go away after Reagan and grew worse in subsequent decades.)

He continued: "Today it is difficult to find leaders who are independent of the forces that have brought us our problems—the Congress, the bureaucracy, the lobbyist, big business, and big labor." It's hard today to appreciate how unorthodox a statement that was in 1975. For one thing, criticizing "big business" was considered political heresy. Recall again that these were the days when liberal, blue blood, country club Republicans possessed outsized GOP influence. And more importantly, Reagan redefined strong leadership as something "independent of the forces that have brought us our problems." And what were those forces he believed had usurped the people's power? Large institutions packed with unaccountable elites.

Then Governor Reagan revealed the solution: "If America is to survive and go forward, this must change. It will only change when the American people vote for a leadership that listens to them, relies on them, and seeks to return government to them. We need a government that is confident not of what it can do, but of what the people can do."[24] At every turn in his short speech (just 557 words), Reagan reinforced the idea that "the people"—not bureaucrats—must remain the arbiters of government power. Is it any wonder populists flocked to Reagan's cause?

Still, despite the power of his announcement speech, the GOP Establishment continued to scoff and dismiss Reagan as little more than a nuisance, a former B actor who was trying to resurrect the corpse of conservative populism that had been buried when Goldwater lost in a landslide 12 years earlier. Goldwater's loss was supposed to be the conservative movement's tombstone. Instead, it became a touchstone. Again brushing aside the doubts of the "experts," Reagan and many of the conservative stalwarts who had worked on that campaign refused to give up the dream of overturning the liberal policies that had been borne out of the New Deal. "We're Americans and we have a rendezvous with destiny," Reagan said in a March 31, 1976, campaign address. "We spread across this land, building farms and towns and cities, and we did it without any federal land planning program or urban renewal." But now, Reagan said, "a self-anointed elite" in Washington "practice government by mystery, telling us it's too complex for our understanding. . . . Tell us what needs to be done. Then, get out of the way and let us have at it."[25]

First up, New Hampshire. Reagan suffered one of the closest primary defeats in the state's history at the time. Out of the 108,331 votes cast, Ford beat Reagan by just 1,317 votes. The Ford campaign hoped the painful loss would make Reagan pack up and go home. It did the reverse; it emboldened him. "I truly believe that the closeness of the New Hampshire loss made him more confident that all he needed was his message and the right moment," recalled Reagan strategist and pollster Dick Wirthlin.[26]

The Reagan campaign's moment wouldn't come until they had lost five consecutive primaries and crawled into North Carolina moribund and broke. On the campaign trail, Reagan routinely blasted President Ford and his Secretary of State Henry Kissinger for a weak and feckless foreign policy.

"Henry Kissinger's recent stewardship of U.S. foreign policy has coincided precisely with the loss of U.S. military supremacy," Reagan said. "Under Messrs. Kissinger and Ford this nation has become number two in military power in a world where it is dangerous—if not fatal—to be second best."[27] Far from being a call for military interventionism, Reagan's populist foreign policy was premised on the belief that the surest path toward peace and security was to maintain a level of military strength and dominance that protected U.S. sovereignty while deterring the nation's enemies by assuring their inevitable destruction.

In one particular stump speech Reagan tried out a new angle of attack by hitting President Ford for his administration's intention to hand over ownership of the Panama Canal to the government of Panama. With our humiliating withdrawal from Vietnam still fresh in voters' minds, this seemed like yet another instance of American retreat and another wound to our national psyche. As usual, the GOP Establishment was out of touch and couldn't understand why the people would see it as another sign of waning national sovereignty. But Reagan did understand. Sovereignty is an issue that galvanizes the populist movement. Without it, the people cease to have control over their own country.

"We built it, we paid for it, it's ours, and we're going to keep it!" was Reagan's legendary line about the Canal giveaway. (The line was so good, Senator Ted Cruz repurposed it in a 2016 speech on President Obama's decision to shut down the Guantànamo Bay detention camp).[28] Reagan's campaign decided it was worth spending the money it would cost to broadcast the speech highlighting Ford's Panama Canal debacle. The response was overwhelming. Phone lines at the Ford campaign headquarters lit up with calls from angry voters demanding to know why President Ford was giving away the Panama Canal, a charge his campaign denied.[29] Reagan not only won his first primary state, he beat President Ford by 10 points.

He went on to rack up victories throughout the South, West, and Rocky Mountain states, including two of the biggest delegate jackpots in Texas and California. Ford won victories across the Northeast, Rust Belt, and Florida. By the time Republicans gathered for their national convention that August in Kansas City, Missouri, no one knew what would happen. Back then, presidential conventions actually meant something more than a four-day infomercial for political parties. Ford had won 27 states, Reagan 24. When the 2,257 delegate ballots were finally tallied, Gerald Ford beat Ronald Reagan by just 117 votes.

When President Ford took the stage to declare victory, he did something unexpected. He called Ronald Reagan down from the upper deck seats of the Kemper Arena to speak. Reagan's totally impromptu speech rocked the house—and made more than a few Republicans think they had nominated the wrong man. "We must go forth from here united, determined that what a great general said a few years ago is true: There is no substitute for victory," Reagan said from the rostrum. Reagan had upstaged Ford, even in defeat. As California state senator H. L. Richardson told the *Los Angeles Times* during the convention: "Reagan could get a standing ovation in a graveyard. Ford puts you to sleep by the third paragraph."[30]

On the outside, the Gipper projected his usual happy warrior demeanor. The so-called "experts" believed Reagan's political career was finished. And just as had happened 12 years earlier with the Goldwater defeat, the Establishment hoped that Reagan's loss would wash the nascent populist movement away with it. Instead, it motivated supporters to keep trying even harder.

"The Republican Party, absent the 1976 contest, would most likely have remained a moderate 'Tory' party that never becomes a majority governing party," said political scientist and Reagan alum Dr. Donald Devine. Reagan biographer Craig Shirley agrees. "Without Reagan's 1976 campaign, Americans would not have witnessed the reordering of the two major political parties and the shift in our political universe, with one party becoming predominately conservative and the other predominately liberal."[31]

Before Reagan left the Kemper Arena, he huddled a few hundred members of the California delegation and his closest campaign staff together and delivered a second, far less known off-the-cuff speech. In it, Reagan foreshadowed the future by reciting the words of an old Scottish ballad. "I will lay me down and bleed a while. Though I am wounded, I am not slain. I shall rise and fight again."

A CERTAIN SOUND

It would have been understandable if Ronald Reagan's story had ended here. He was 65 years old when he lost to Gerald Ford. Moreover, he had already lived the American Dream. A kid from nothing hit it big in Hollywood, appeared in over 50 films (watch *Knute Rockne, All-American* and *Kings Row* with your family), found and married his beloved Nancy, enjoyed a successful television career, and won two terms as California governor—not a bad run by anyone's standards.

But Reagan's dreams were much bigger than all that. Not for himself, but for America. There was more wood to chop, more work to be done. "He wasn't in it for ego," wrote Reagan speechwriter Peggy Noonan. "He was actually in it to do good."[32]

In the second speech of his ill-fated 1976 presidential run, Reagan had said this: "There's a passage in the Bible that says, 'If the trumpet gives an uncertain sound, who shall prepare himself to the battle?' [1 Corinthians 14:8] Well, just to make sure no one mistook the sound of the trumpet, I took it to Washington this morning to announce my candidacy for the presidency. I chose Washington because it is such an intimate part of our troubles: inflation, recession, unemployment, bureaucracy, and centralized power."[33]

Reagan's trumpet never made an uncertain sound. His values and vision were unwavering. The populist movement he led was rooted in the firm belief that Americans must always come first. He also knew that nothing changes if patriots are unwilling to do the heavy lifting of history. So he rode to the sound of the guns, which meant marching his populist revolution to Washington—the place where, as he put it, so many of "our troubles" reside.

ARE YOU BETTER OFF THAN YOU WERE FOUR YEARS AGO?

After four years of President Jimmy Carter, the nation was reeling from a rudderless Cold War foreign policy, rising unemployment, soaring inflation, crushing taxes, byzantine regulations, dependency-breeding welfare policies, and a smug Washington elite who harbored utter contempt for the values of everyday working people. It was so bad, even Carter acknowledged the nation's downward trajectory in his infamous July 15, 1979, "Malaise" speech. Carter never uttered the word "malaise" in his address, but what he said was in many ways worse. "It's clear that the true problems of our nation are much deeper—deeper than gasoline lines or energy shortages, deeper even than inflation or recession," President Carter said. "I realize more than ever that as President I need your help." As if that weren't alarming enough, Carter went on to issue an ominous warning: "The erosion of our confidence in the future is threatening to destroy the social and the political fabric of America."[34]

Foreign affairs were even worse. Americans were furious that our countrymen were being held hostage by the Iranians. Hard hats kept a tally of the passing days—444 before Reagan secured their release—on a construction platform in New York City. The Iranian hostage crisis was a humiliating display of weak presidential leadership in the face of foreign aggression. Then the first week of January 1980, President Carter addressed the nation and announced that the Soviet Union had just invaded Afghanistan, a development that threatened to "further Soviet expansion." Carter's solution? Beg for the help of the United Nations and the International Court of Justice. It was precisely the kind of weak, sovereignty-squelching deference to global institutions populists vehemently opposed. And it further paved the way for Ronald Reagan's populist revolution.

To restore America, though, Ronald Reagan first had to win a hotly contested GOP primary that included favorites of the Old Republican Guard, including: former CIA director George H. W. Bush, Kansas senator Bob Dole, Senate minority leader Howard Baker of Tennessee, Illinois congressman Phil Crane, liberal Illinois congressman John Anderson (who later ran as the Independent candidate in 1980), and former Texas governor John Connally. Just like his 1976 primary run, Reagan encountered immediate opposition from within his own party.

"People on our side of the spectrum in 1980, we thought [Reagan] was a nutcase," said David Lucey, son of Anderson's running mate Pat Lucey.[35] Republican national Conservative Caucus chairman Howard Phillips said "some (of us) suspect that Reagan is only a script reader, not a script writer." And many questioned whether Reagan's age (he would turn 70 shortly after Election Day) meant he lacked the stamina to be commander in chief. A *Wall Street Journal* column claimed that Reagan's "lackluster" speeches and "aloofness" had "revived feelings that Mr. Reagan is too old and too indolent for the nation's top job."[36]

The age issue became a constant refrain throughout the race. Reagan's youthful demeanor and good looks helped mute the attacks, but they still got to him. "What am I supposed to do, skip rope through the neighborhood?" Reagan said to reporters.[37]

Despite the barbs, Reagan stuck to the same conservative principles he always had: return power to the people, reduce the size of government, maintain peace through strength. Then on January 21, 1980, the day of the Iowa caucuses, Bush pulled off a surprise victory and beat Reagan by just 2,182 votes. The loss rattled the Reagan campaign. *Time* called it a "jarring defeat" and said it "prompted many of his followers to wonder whether he could ever make a comeback."[38] The February 26 first-in-the-nation New Hampshire primary would test Reagan's mettle.

Three days before Granite State voters went to the polls, Reagan put on a legendary rhetorical performance at the Nashua debate moderated by the *Nashua Telegraph* newspaper's executive editor Jon Breen. The Reagan campaign had agreed to cover the cost of the debate when the Federal Election Commission said the paper could not pick up the tab. At the beginning of the evening, Breen interrupted Reagan.

"Would the sound man please turn Mr. Reagan's mic off for the moment?" said Breen.

The crowd howled in protest. Reagan shot up from his seat and grabbed the microphone.

"Is this on?" Reagan asked. As Reagan tried to speak, the moderator interrupted him again. "I am paying for this microphone, Mr. Green!" thundered Reagan.

The crowd screamed and cheered. Even the four Republicans on stage clapped. Reagan had even mispronounced the moderator's name and called him "Mr. Green" instead of Mr. Breen. But it didn't matter.

As *The Washington Post* later reported, Reagan "stole the show while Bush seemed not to know quite what was going on." Afterward, Bush press secretary Peter Teeley tried to soften the blow to his candidate with dry humor. "The bad news is that the media is playing up the confrontation," Teeley told Bush. "The good news is that they're ignoring the debate, and you lost that, too."[39]

Reagan went on to win 44 primary contests to Bush's seven. But not before Bush called Reagan's economic plan "voodoo economics." Bush trashed Reagan's supply-side economic philosophy that cutting taxes raises, not lowers, total revenues. It should have been an omen to Republicans. When Reagan tapped Bush as his vice presidential running mate, many voters dismissed the line as a sharp elbow thrown in the heat of political battle.

During his general election matchup against President Carter, Reagan's populist message emphasized his fundamental trust in the people versus elites. As he put it in his July 17, 1980, acceptance speech at the Republican National Convention in Detroit:

> Back in 1976, Mr. Carter said, "Trust me." And a lot of people did. Now, many of those people are out of work. Many have seen their savings eaten away by inflation. Many others on fixed incomes, especially the elderly, have watched helplessly as the cruel tax of inflation wasted away their purchasing power. And, today, a great many who trusted Mr. Carter wonder if we can survive the Carter policies of national defense.
>
> "Trust me" government asks that we concentrate our hopes and dreams on one man; that we trust him to do what's best for us. My view of government places trust, not in one person or one party, but in those values that transcend persons and parties. The trust is where it belongs—in the people.[40]

Any conservative leader who wants to know how the GOP Establishment in subsequent years ran Reaganism off the rails and how to get us back on track need only read the above passage from Reagan. For years, Establishment Republicans yelled "Trust us!" and then did everything in their power to thwart the people's will. On trade, immigration, government spending—you name it, the Establishment repeatedly tried to cram unpopular and unwanted Donor Class–directed policies down our throats.

The term "Donor Class" refers to the elite group of the nation's wealthiest and most active political contributors. Some of these individuals are well-known, such as George Soros on the left and the

Koch brothers on the right. But most are unfamiliar to the majority of Americans. Some donors give millions of dollars to political causes out of a deep and sincere patriotic desire to see their favored candidates prevail and the country improved. Others, however, view their donations as a down payment on policies that will enrich their businesses, regardless of the impact they will have on the people. Immigration amnesty, for example, is supported by many wealthy Republican donors who desire cheap labor that fattens their bottom lines.

Aiding them in this effort are often members of the Political Class, a coterie of well-connected and overpaid consultants and "professional" think tank "scholars" beholden to the edicts of the Donor Class. Major ideological nonprofits rely on Donor Class contributions. Not surprisingly, their "research" and "studies" often reflect the issues donors care most about. Likewise, political consultants also make big bucks creating advertisements and issue campaigns for candidates and causes that members of the Donor Class support. All of this contributes to a system that favors elite interests over those of the working class—something Reagan fought against throughout his career.

Reagan's belief in the people represented a stark contrast with the big government failures Jimmy Carter's policies produced. During the first and only presidential debate between Carter and Reagan, the Gipper told Americans to ask themselves a fundamental question: "Are you better off than you were four years ago?" If not, Reagan suggested voters should consider voting for him. Why? Because as governor of California, "we did give back authority and autonomy to the people," he said.

There was also another critical issue that arose during that debate, one that hit home with me even in my youth: the Iranian hostage crisis.

Long after my mother went to bed, during my four years at Glastonbury High School, I would be up doing homework in my bedroom, usually with the TV on in the background. My dad had given me an old small black-and-white set that was propped up on an antique school chair from the late 1800s, next to my bed. When ABC's *Nightline* started in March of 1980, I was ecstatic. I loved Johnny

Carson and *The Tonight Show,* but this program was something different. Anchored by Ted Koppel, unlike traditional newscasts, it focused on the biggest story of the day—at that time, the Iranian hostage crisis, in which 52 diplomats and soldiers were paraded in blindfolds for the world to see. It was heartbreaking humiliation at the hands of the rabid supporters of the Ayatollah Khomeini. I remember hearing "America Held Hostage. Day . . ." every night. *How can this be happening?* I wondered to myself, *We are the United States of America!*

Carter's attempt to rescue the hostages in April 1980, called Operation Eagle Claw, was an abysmal failure. Eight American servicemen died. This embarrassing ordeal hung like an anvil around the neck of the Carter campaign. It translated into one overriding message: weakness. When Reagan won the election in a landslide, I felt hopeful he could do something to help free our hostages.

Then in his very first hours on the job, the news broke on Inauguration Day that the hostages had been released. I was headed to varsity basketball practice when it happened. All of us on the team were high-fiving each other. "The Reagan Effect," I proclaimed confidently.

But this was only the beginning. Reagan did much more than wax eloquent. He fought and won historic brass knuckle policy battles in Washington that reordered the political universe.

MONEY IS POWER, SO GIVE IT BACK!

Economic populism rests on a simple axiom: if "money is power," as the old saying goes, the more money workers are allowed to keep, the more empowered they grow. Ronald Reagan believed that no one knows better how to spend your money than you do. Your wealth is your property; the government doesn't have a boundless right to confiscate it. He also believed that high tax rates squelch investment, work, and total revenues.

It wasn't just Reagan who understood this; President John F. Kennedy believed it as well. "In short, it is a paradoxical truth that tax rates are too high today and tax revenues too low, and the soundest way to raise revenues in the long run is to cut rates now," Kennedy famously said. By 1980, top tax rates in America stood at a staggering

70 percent.[41] On July 29, 1981, Congress approved President Reagan's 25 percent across-the-board tax cut known as the 1981 Economic Recovery Tax Act.[42] When the bill cleared the House 238–195, veteran Chicago Democrat congressman and the chairman of the tax-writing Ways and Means Committee Rep. Dan Rostenkowski picked up the telephone and called President Reagan. "Well, Mr. President, you're tough," said the old Chicago pol. "You beat us. . . . It means you're working at your job."[43]

Reagan wasn't finished. In 1986, he came back and cut taxes even more. He created two tax brackets—15 percent for the middle class, 28 percent for top earners—and closed tax loopholes. The economic results were dramatic and long-lasting. "The American economy grew mostly between 4 and 5 percent annually for over 25 years," said economist Larry Kudlow, who served as the associate director for economics and planning in the Office of Management and Budget (OMB) during President Ronald Reagan's first term.[44] The 1981 success of the 25 percent cut spawned bipartisan support for the 1986 cut. So much so that the measure passed the Senate 97–3.[45] In politics, everyone loves a winner; success begets success.

"I knew my ideas were working when the media stopped calling it Reaganomics," Reagan liked to say.[46]

Reagan's economic agenda put millions of Americans back to work and put real money back in the pockets of working people. Inflation cratered and per capita real disposable income jumped 18 percent from 1982 to 1989, a standard of living increase of nearly 20 percent. Between 1984 and 1989, the poverty rate fell every single year.

Legendary Reagan economist Art Laffer (of Laffer Curve fame), who served as a member of President Reagan's Economic Policy Advisor Board and helped devise Reagan's tax cuts, said this about the Reagan economic boom:

We call this period, 1982–2007, the twenty-five year boom—the greatest period of wealth creation in the history of the planet. In 1980, the net worth—assets minus liabilities—of all U.S. households and business . . . was $25 trillion in today's dollars. By 2007, . . . net worth was just shy of $57 trillion. Adjusting for inflation, more wealth was created in America in the twenty-five year boom than in the previous two hundred years.[47]

It's easy to see why President Reagan tapped Professor Laffer as his economic guru; Laffer is as smart as they come. Of note, when all the "experts" and pollsters were predicting a Donald Trump defeat, Laffer stunned—and outsmarted—everyone by predicting months in advance that Donald Trump would win easily.[48] Laffer has touted Donald Trump's Reaganesque tax policies and says that, if implemented, they will lead to economic "nirvana" in America.[49] Let's hope he's right (again). President Trump's tax plan would shrink the current seven tax brackets into three: 10 percent, 25 percent, and 35 percent. It would also double the standard deduction, repeal the Alternative Minimum Tax, repeal the death tax, and "eliminate most of the tax breaks that mainly benefit high-income individuals," except for "home ownership, charitable giving, and retirement savings."[50]

Working-class Americans today could sure use another economic jolt after eight lugubrious years of the Obama economy. Here's hoping Congress can get its act together and pass significant tax relief consistent with President Trump's proposals.

PEACE THROUGH STRENGTH

Progressives trashed Reagan throughout his presidency as an unstable Cold War "cowboy" with a trigger-happy finger hovering over the nuclear red button. "Ronnie RayGun," they used to call him. As usual, they had Reagan all wrong. He was a lover of peace who believed in good and evil. Above all else, Reagan's goal was to protect Americans. After witnessing decades of escalating Cold War tensions, Ronald Reagan set out not to end but *win* the battle with Soviet communism. When he was asked what his Cold War strategy was, Reagan responded with his hallmark clarity and confidence: "We win; they lose."

Populists supported Reagan's Cold War strategy because they knew Soviet communists sought global domination. Again, the canard that the populist movement is isolationist is just that—a fallacy.

Populists believe military responses are warranted when American interests are threatened. Put simply, you can't empower people if you allow them to be killed or captured by hostile enemies. What was so brilliant about Reagan's populist foreign policy approach was that he found a way to apply maximum winning leverage against the Soviet Union without bloodshed.

In the end, even his harshest critics were forced to concede that he accomplished what he set out to do. "Mr. Gorbachev, tear down this wall," he thundered in front of the Brandenburg Gate. It was a vision he had the very first time he traveled to Berlin in November 1978. Outraged and appalled by what he saw, Reagan turned to Richard Allen (who would later become his national security adviser) and said, "We have got to find a way to knock this thing down."[51] And soon he did, faster and more peacefully than anyone dreamed. As liberal lion Ted Kennedy put it after Reagan's passing, "On foreign policy he will be honored as the president who won the Cold War."[52]

How did he do it? And why? The answers are critical for the conservative-populist movement's commitment to maintaining national security in a dangerous age.

Go back to the beginning. Soviet communists had long articulated their desire for global domination. It wasn't just rhetoric; they had backed it up with a massive amount of blood and carnage. Reagan was alive throughout Joseph Stalin's 30-year rule. Stalin's Great Terror (sometimes called the Great Purge) to consolidate power by exterminating dissidents and rivals through execution and internment in the slave prison camps known as the gulags claimed millions of lives. The tyranny and brutality made such an impression on Reagan that in 1950 he joined a group called the Crusade for Freedom to liberate the slaves of communism and to thwart Soviet expansion. When communists in Hollywood began muscling their way in to seize control of Hollywood trade unions, Reagan fought back at great risk to himself and his family.[53]

Faith in God was at the center of Reagan's determination to defeat communism. Communists were waging a war on religion and he knew it. "Communism begins where atheism begins," said Karl Marx.

Similarly, Vladimir Lenin wrote in 1913 that "There is nothing more abominable than religion."[54] That was a view whose spread Reagan would not allow.

From the start, Reagan believed that the idea of mere containment, or détente—the accepted "realist" approach pursued by Richard Nixon and Henry Kissinger—was a strategy that was fatally flawed. Reagan's strong stance against Soviet appeasement infuriated the Establishment. *Leave well enough alone,* they yelled, *Soviet communism is here to stay and isn't going anywhere.* Reagan wouldn't listen. As even *The New York Times* was forced to concede after his death, "Mr. Reagan's stubborn refusal to accept the permanence of communism helped end the Cold War."[55]

How did he do it? By announcing in March 1983 the beginning of a little thing called "Star Wars," formally known as the Strategic Defense Initiative (SDI). The so-called "experts" in Washington thought it was nuts, but Reagan threw down the gauntlet in an arms race with the Soviet Union by declaring that the United States would pursue the technological development of a "peace shield"—a missile defense system that could knock down incoming intercontinental ballistic missiles (ICBMs). It was part of his dream to render nuclear weapons useless, thereby increasing peace and security. But it was also a deft move to hasten the fall of the USSR by drawing the Soviets into a high rollers arms race that the already-rickety Russian economy could never win.

For added leverage, President Reagan announced two years later that once SDI was built, and once the Soviets had agreed to reductions in offensive weapons, the United States would be willing to give the Soviet Union the technology to create an SDI system of their own. In October 1985, during an interview with the BBC, President Reagan was asked the question directly:

> BBC: But the Russians, presumably, would have to make their own SDI. You wouldn't offer it to them, would you, off the shelf?
> PRESIDENT REAGAN: Why not? . . . I would like to say to the Soviet Union, we know you've been researching this same thing longer than we have. We wish you well. There couldn't be anything

better than if both of us came up with it. But if only one of
us does, then, why don't we, instead of using it as an offensive
means of having a first strike against anyone else in the world,
why don't we use it to ensure that there won't be any nuclear
strikes?

The BBC interviewer could hardly believe his ears. He tried once
more.

BBC: Are you saying then, Mr. President, that the United States,
if it were well down the road towards a proper SDI program,
would be prepared to share its technology with Soviet Russia,
provided, of course, there were arms reductions and so on on
both sides?
PRESIDENT REAGAN: That's right.[56]

The Kremlin was terrified. The reason was clear. The Russians
knew darn well—just as President Reagan did—that they didn't have
the rubles to go toe-to-toe in an arms race to build Star Wars. And
even if America did agree to share the technology, what good would
that do if they lacked the money to build and maintain it? I can "give
you" the plans to build a fortress, but if you don't have the *money* to
build a fortress, what good are the plans? Worse, if your enemy (the
United States) does have a fortress (SDI), and you don't, your enemy is
guarded by a shield of security and you are left naked and vulnerable
to attack.[57]

The Soviets knew they had to kill SDI somehow. They made their
move in 1986 during Mikhail Gorbachev and Ronald Reagan's historic summit in Reykjavík, Iceland, to broker a deal to drastically reduce each country's strategic missiles. Gorbachev promised Reagan
the moon: he would agree to eliminate all ballistic missiles. But there
was a catch. Gorbachev looked at Reagan and said, "This all depends,
of course, on you giving up SDI." That was the moment Reagan became livid. It was also the moment Reagan knew just how deeply the
Russians feared SDI. Reagan turned to George Schultz and said, "The
meeting is over. Let's go."

That was the beginning of the end of the Soviet Union. As former Soviet spokesman Gennady Gerasimov later admitted, "Reagan bolstered the U.S. military might to ruin the Soviet economy, and he achieved his goal. Reagan's SDI was a very successful blackmail. The Soviet Union tried to keep up pace with the U.S. military buildup, but the Soviet economy couldn't endure such competition."[58]

As for the SDI system itself, Reagan wasn't bluffing. We really did spend tens of billions of dollars developing the technology. "Indeed, technologies developed under SDI contributed to ballistic missile capabilities the United States has today," note former Heritage Foundation president Jim DeMint and vice president James Carafano. "Moreover, SDI research produced innumerable benefits beyond missile defense: cheaper and more capable computer chips, optics equipment, and specialized materials that businesses and consumers now take for granted."[59] It was all part of Reagan's strategy to maintain "peace through strength."

Some have argued that Reagan's military buildup cost too much money. Others say it was a small price to pay to win the Cold War, liberate millions from communism's murderous grip, and keep America safe in a nuclear age. One thing is certain: even Reagan's critics concede his Cold War victory defied all the odds. "Against waves of 'expert opinion,' he pursued his belief that the Soviet Union would crack under the pressure of an accelerated arms race, and he lived to see the Soviet empire crumble and a degree of freedom and democracy come to Russia itself," wrote liberal *Washington Post* columnist David Broder.[60]

The underreported part of Reagan's strategy against the "Evil Empire" was his alliance with Pope Saint John Paul II. Reagan and the pope had survived assassination attempts only six weeks apart in 1981 and felt they had been spared for a larger purpose. Each saw a common enemy in the communist menace. Reagan relied on John Paul's spiritual power, and he shared military intelligence with the pope—data critical to the resistance in Poland. The Solidarity movement—a populist uprising led by a humble electrician, Lech Walesa—and the deep faith awakened by John Paul's visit to his homeland in 1979 would weaken the grip of the Soviets in Poland and start the fall of communism.

As she often did, the Iron Lady, Prime Minister Margaret Thatcher put it best: "Ronald Reagan had a higher claim than any other leader to have won the Cold War for liberty and he did it without a shot being fired."[61] For those with eyes to see, this bold approach bears striking similarity to President Trump's engagement with the world's great religions during his first foreign trip in 2017. Only the goal this time is peace in the Middle East.

SPEECHWRITING IN THE REAGAN ADMINISTRATION

During Reagan's second term I was blessed to have a bird's-eye view of history as a young speechwriter in the Reagan administration. Washington was totally new to me. Frankly, I had no idea what I was getting into, but even in the era of Iran-Contra and the Bork hearings, for a young conservative like myself, it was a dream come true.

I started off in 1986 as the speechwriter for Undersecretary of Education Gary Bauer during William Bennett's tenure as secretary. Bauer was a strong Christian conservative with a big heart and a keen understanding of the Reagan Revolution. Years later, he told me he hired me because of my work as a conservative student journalist at the infamous *Dartmouth Review*.

Bill Bennett's young staffers were, like myself, all recent college grads. My new colleagues were exceptionally bright and dedicated. Speechwriters like Gene Scalia, John Cribb, Julie Cave, Bill Armistead, Pete Wehner, and I all hung out together. We were young and single, so after work it was softball on the Mall and maybe a beer (or two). Those were fun days. We were Reaganites, and we believed we were part of something big.

Being in Washington also afforded us the chance to meet fascinating figures outside the administration. My then-boyfriend Dinesh D'Souza and I had breakfast in the summer of 1986 with Edward Teller, the physicist who was known as the "father of the Hydrogen bomb." We met near my office, at Vie de France bakery, which was right near the subway stop for the U.S. Department of Education. A short, stooped-over man with big bushy gray eyebrows, he told us riveting stories in his thick Hungarian accent about his time at Los Alamos Laboratory in New Mexico, working with J. Robert Oppenheimer. With colorful details and the passion of a scientist a half-century younger, he shared some of the personal dynamics that made the World War II Manhattan Project work even more challenging, along with how he successfully lobbied President Harry Truman on the urgent need to develop the H-bomb. Teller was a staunch advocate of America's nuclear weapons program and a supporter of Reagan's Strategic Defense Initiative, which we had covered closely at *The Dartmouth Review*.

At age 78, Teller was unrepentant about his exile from much of the scientific community after his public falling out with Oppenheimer. (Dinesh recalls that he was frustrated that Oppenheimer and others treated him like some kind of "Dr. Strangelove.") Through the hour-and-a-half-long breakfast, he railed against the no-nukes movement that sought to, as he described, "fully neuter the United States military" and thus make the world "ripe for Soviet expansionism." The nuclear test ban movement was, in Teller's view, a woefully flawed concept that benefited everyone but us. The stalwart anticommunist thought such bans would ultimately make America more vulnerable because they made defensive weapons systems more difficult to design. It was a fascinating meeting to say the least.

Another fun meeting took place at the Hay Adams hotel in 1987 when former president Richard Nixon ate breakfast with me, Dinesh, and seven members of the current and former *Dartmouth Review* staff. *Wall Street Journal* editorial writer and *Review* founder Greg Fossedal arranged the gathering. Nixon talked about the importance of presidents pursuing a policy of "tough détente" wherein a president negotiates from a position of strength while keeping U.S. interests in mind. He was also somewhat critical of President Reagan (something that apparently had never changed over all those years). In particular, he viewed Reagan as too "idealistic" and not sufficiently realistic.

Dinesh reminded me of the awkward moment when Watergate came up in the discussion. Someone asked how it compared to Iran-Contra. Nixon quipped sarcastically that Reagan was getting away with Iran-Contra only because people thought he was dumb—the implication being that Nixon didn't have the option of playing dumb during Watergate because people considered him too smart. His comments seemed to confirm what I had long heard—despite Nixon's role as a conservative-populist pioneer, he had always harbored envy of Reagan for receiving the lion's share of credit for the populist movement's success.

The high point of my speechwriting experience came when Gary Bauer was transferred to the White House to work as assistant to the president for Policy Development. He couldn't bring his entire staff with him, so I was relieved—and honored—to make the cut. When I called my mother to tell her, she was over the moon. "I knew it!" she said, ever the proud parent. "So when are you going to talk to the president?"

Over the years, my mother would remind me how blessed I was to have had this experience. As usual, she was right. Later, friends told me she would brag endlessly that "my daughter worked with President Reagan," as if I was in and out of the Oval Office 10 times a day.

Whether she was right about every aspect of my job wasn't important. She got the most important part right. America is a place where a girl from Glastonbury, Connecticut, the daughter of a waitress and carwash owner, could end up working at the White House.

LESSONS FROM THE REVOLUTION

In his 1980 victory, Reagan converted Democrats not by adopting Democrat views but by convincing them that conservative-populist solutions offered the only hope for American renewal. We need to do that same thing again.

To be sure, Reagan wasn't perfect. Yes, he signed the Simpson–Mazzoli Act, granting amnesty to a limited number of "illegal aliens" (a term used by Reagan in his signing statement on the bill). But he did so in the expectation that, going forward, our laws would be enforced. They weren't. The Iran-Contra saga and his failure to shrink the size of the federal government also come to mind.

But then there are the historic achievements: some of the biggest tax cuts in American history, the creation of over 18 million jobs and unprecedented wealth, a renewal of American pride and patriotism, commonsense trade policies, the defeat of Soviet communism, and the winning of the Cold War.[62] His accomplishments were so great, Americans rewarded his legacy by electing his vice president as the nation's next commander in chief (no sitting vice president had been elected president since Martin Van Buren in 1836). Halcyon days, indeed.

For me personally, and for many of us who had entered the Reagan administration barely out of college, Ronald Reagan inspired us to devote our careers to the conservative movement. We were young and idealistic and loved President Reagan for having the courage and vision to wear down the Soviets and lift up the economy. We loved how he loved America—it was infectious. Looking back at photos of our 1984 college election night party at the Hanover Inn in New Hampshire, everyone seemed to glow. And it wasn't just the beverages we were imbibing. We realized we were blessed to be alive during one of the great moments in American history and to have a leader who understood that those three famous words—We the People—weren't just poetry, they were purposeful.

But Reagan's legacy only means something if we keep it alive by adhering to the principles that culminated in the largest-ever landslide presidential victory in American history. The same populist spirit that fueled Reagan's rise is finally back again today. That it was allowed to dim in his wake is an important cautionary tale of the fragility of movements and the need to maintain them, and it is a story that urgently needs to be told. Sadly, some conservatives took a dangerous detour during the next three presidents and thrust us into a bizarre world of globalization, wars based on idealism and nation-building, and intense hatred toward the very voters who accounted for the Reagan coalition in the first place. Indeed, it was only in the last several years that many of us who joined the movement in the 1980s and thought we were all fighting for the same cause learned that wasn't the case at all.

It is also important to remember that during Reagan's rise and presidency, he and those who followed and supported him were excoriated and ridiculed. Academia, the Establishment, media, the so-called "experts"—they all spent a lifetime trashing and attacking him and his supporters. The left's penchant for labeling anyone and everything they dislike as "racist" is hardly new. The race card has been their go-to move for decades. As early as 1976, Hubert Humphrey dubbed Reagan's governing philosophy a "disguised new form of racism."[63] Even at his death on June 5, 2004, some progressives vilely marked his passing with celebration. Progressive cartoonist Ted Rall said, "I'm sure he's turning crispy brown right about now." And a gay activist declared that he would "spend eternity in hell."[64]

Thankfully, the haters were part of a tiny minority. The rest of America mourned Reagan's death and celebrated his life. Many of us who were at Washington's National Cathedral that day were in tears for much of the 90-minute service. Saying good-bye to President Reagan meant so many different things to people, for different reasons. Thirteen years after Reagan's passing, conservatives in the United States and, indeed, across the globe still cite him as their compass. It may seem unkind to note, yet it is inescapably true, that few GOPers today run as "Bush Republicans."

Reagan's death didn't just mark the end of a political era, it marked the metaphorical end of our youth. The political memories of my own childhood included watching Dan Rather's reporting on the Vietnam War, long gas lines, 18 percent interest rates, and the Iranian hostage crisis. Reagan had felt like springtime after a bitter, long winter. By the time the horse-drawn caisson carrying Reagan's body was slowly making its way down Constitution Avenue to the U.S. Capitol, conservatism was entering a new season under George W. Bush, the son of his vice president.

History stops for no one—not even a giant like President Reagan. Technology advances, new issues arise, and those of us who were young in the 1980s felt the duty to help govern this nation in his wake.

As for me, after I left the Reagan administration in the fall of 1988, I headed to law school at the University of Virginia. My calling card on campus was the license plate on my little black 1983 Honda Civic hatchback. It read: FARRGHT. I knew President Reagan would appreciate the humor.

2.

KING GEORGE'S
NEW WORLD ORDER

The GOP Establishment Strikes Back

There are slogans—"Come Home America," "America First."
This is selfish! This is beneath the history of our great country.
—GEORGE H. W. BUSH

Two of the most dazzling and fun nights of my early career took place during the 1988 inaugural celebration for President George H. W. Bush. Being back in Washington, DC, if only briefly, for the inaugural festivities was a welcome break from my law school studies at UVA. My fellow young and single Reaganite pals and I threw on the best frocks our slender budgets could afford and headed off to the old convention center for one of the nine inaugural balls. Smiles and sequins lit up the place. We were seemingly one big happy Republican family. President Reagan had successfully passed off the presidential baton to George H. W. Bush, and now it was time to party.

The next night we were treated to an R&B concert like no other. President Bush's chief political strategist, the late great Lee Atwater, was a blues fan and a musician in his own right. Atwater assembled numerous music legends for an inaugural concert he called "a dream come true." Bo Diddley, Sam Moore, Percy Sledge, Willie Dixon, Koko Taylor, Carla Thomas, Joe Louis Walker, Ron Wood, Stevie Ray Vaughan—the lineup was a virtual who's who of R&B royalty. The diversity of styles and sounds had the gaggle of geeky but well-intentioned Republicans clapping out of time and rocking the night away. Eddie Floyd sang "Knock on Wood." Koko Taylor did "Wang Dang Doodle." And Stevie Ray Vaughn covered "Superstition." It was absolutely electric.

The press, of course, tried to racialize and politicize a beautiful night, but everyone, including the performers, was there without regard for politics. When Koko Taylor's manager tried to talk her out of playing for a crowd of Republicans, she replied, "I want to play for a president." Guitarist Joe Louis Walker agreed; the night was bigger than partisanship. "It's an honor for the blues to go all the way from the outhouse to the White House, no matter who the president is."[1] Classy.

At one point, Lee Atwater strapped on his guitar and ushered a tuxedo-wearing President Bush on stage holding an electric guitar with "Prez" emblazoned in red across its face. Lee shredded, Bush pretended to strum, and the crowd went nuts. It was an awesome capstone to my early days in Washington.

"INAUGURATION DAY MASSACRE"

Although the patriotic sparkle of the inaugural festivities presented a unified Republican front to the nation, a different scene was unfolding in the Bush transition. In fact, shortly after Bush's victory in November, I began hearing rumblings about the growing animosity between the Bush loyalists and the Reagan loyalists. Initially, I thought it all sounded a bit overblown and chalked it up to the normal growing pains all administrations experience during presidential transitions. It wasn't until I started hearing stories of the mass firings of some of my old pals in the administration—talented, committed conservatives—that I really began to believe it. A friend who worked at the Department of Justice in 1988 described how the Bush team chose to summarily terminate Reagan staff and replace them with career bureaucrats, rather than retaining them until the Bush appointees were in place.

Deb Garza, a counselor in the antitrust division, noted the fairly unusual scenario during the transition given that Bush had been vice president. "[M]any of us stayed in place to give President Bush and his AG time to find replacements—or, that was our thought." Sometime in February one of Attorney General Richard Thornburg's assistants (Murray Dickman) made a surprise visit to her office and asked (not very nicely), "What the hell are you doing here?" She explained that she was continuing to work until, at his pleasure, the attorney general accepted her resignation and asked her to leave. "He said, in effect, resignation accepted. Leave today."

The joke about the emissary living up to his last name will not disgrace this page.

"We always knew a stark division existed between the Bushes and the Reagans, but during the transition and its immediate aftermath, it became really clear," recalled another former Reagan administration official. "It was ugly and felt very personal." As one high-level official at the Department of Transportation put it: "The way we were treated, it might as well have been the transfer of power from a Republican to a Democrat administration."

In his book *Takeover*, longtime conservative activist Richard Viguerie recounted what came to be known as the "Inauguration Day Massacre" of the Reaganites. A well-planned purge of the Reagan conservatives who remained after the Bush victory in November 1988 was carried out even against those political appointees who were loyal to Bush.

For movement conservatives like Viguerie, this was an ominous sign of things to come:

> While Bush partisans argued that the new president was justified in putting his own people in place, the 1989 "Inauguration Day Massacre" firings were more akin to political executions; lists of those to be "executed" were drawn up, and they were fired before sundown of the first day of the new Bush administration in a well-planned agenda to replace conservatives (be they Bush supporters or not) with Establishment Republicans.
>
> While most conservative critiques of George H. W. Bush tend to focus on "Read my lips," and Bush's abandonment of his pledge not to raise taxes, the result of the "Inauguration Day Massacre"

firings was that with no conservatives left to say "hey, wait a minute," Bush quickly walked away from conservative principles on a
long list of policies and decisions.[2]

Reagan campaign manager Ed Rollins confirms that the Bush
team purged even loyal Reaganites who had helped with Bush's campaign. "That was the mentality of the new crowd," says Rollins. "Reagan was gone, so who needs him?" A few weeks into the new Bush
administration, Rollins ran into Bush chief of staff Jim Baker's right-
hand and alter ego, Margaret Tutwiler, at a party. "That evening she
made it clear to me that George Bush may have campaigned as Ronald Reagan's designated successor, but things would be different now."
According to Rollins, Tutwiler told him: "There are a lot of us who
had to suffer during the eight years of Reagan, and now it's our turn."[3]
We were Reagan people. They were Bush people. We all knew
what the differences were. Many of the GOP Establishment types who
behind closed doors scoffed at Reagan as a dim-witted former actor
with an "ultraconservative" outlook were now working in the Bush
administration.
They thought it was time to return the Republican Party to what
they believed was its more genteel, respectable roots. In effect, it meant
the return to power of the Rockefeller Republicans who had worked
to deny Reagan the presidency in 1976. This antagonistic dynamic between the populist, small government conservatism of Reagan, versus the more idealistic, big government conservatism of the Bushes,
would continue to surface in Republican politics over the three decades that followed.

"READ MY LIPS"

The Bush team's aggressive purge of the Reaganites had been unnecessary and exceedingly ugly. There was nothing wrong with wanting
to bring new talent aboard; every president does that. But this was
something different. The Bush people weren't just changing personnel,
they were changing the philosophy, principles, and policies that had
swept them into office. And there was a nastiness to it that signaled a

wholesale rejection of Reaganism. As even Bill Kristol, Vice President Dan Quayle's chief of staff (and later NeverTrumper), noticed, "a lot of Bushies were saying, 'We're not going to be like Reagan.' . . . 'Bush isn't like Reagan. He stays awake in meetings.'"[4]

Initially, the new Bush reality remained largely hidden from public view. Outside of political professionals and the well-connected, outward appearances seemed to indicate that George H. W. Bush intended to maintain and advance the Reagan coalition and its agenda. And why would the public doubt that? During the 1988 presidential campaign, Bush reassured the nation he would keep the country moving in the same direction Reagan had. His presidency wouldn't be so much a shift as a continuation.

"My friends, these days the world moves even more quickly, and now, after two great terms, a switch will be made," Bush told voters during his acceptance speech. "But when you have to change horses in midstream, doesn't it make sense to switch to the one who's going the same way?"[5] The eloquent line was inspired by President Franklin Delano Roosevelt's 1940 campaign slogan. President Reagan later said he felt it was Bush's clearest crystallization of the stakes involved and his best line of the entire campaign.[6]

Conservatives wary of Bush's moderate, Establishment background (he'd been a United Nations ambassador, an envoy to China, and CIA director) had also taken great solace in the now-infamous tax promise he made during his 1988 Republican National Convention acceptance speech. Speechwriter Peggy Noonan, who crafted the bulk of the speech, had asked conservative icon Jack Kemp for input during the drafting process. Kemp's advice: "Hit hard on taxes," he said. "Bush will be pressured to raise them as soon as he's elected, and he has to make clear he won't budge."

When Noonan turned in a draft of the tax portion of the speech to OMB director Richard Darman—one of Bush's most liberal and powerful advisers—he strongly opposed the tax promise and dismissed it as mere "populist posturing."[7] The famous passage read:

I'm the one who will not raise taxes. My opponent now says he'll raise them as a last resort or a third resort. When a politician talks

like that, you know that's one resort he'll be checking into. My opponent won't rule out raising taxes, but I will, and the Congress will
push me to raise taxes, and I'll say no, and they'll push, and I'll say
no, and they'll push again, and I'll say to them, "Read my lips: no
new taxes."[8]

The "read my lips: no new taxes" line was an oratorical masterstroke. In a single sentence, the Clint Eastwood–style tax promise
ameliorated long-standing criticisms that Bush was a "wimp" (he
wasn't; no World War II fighter pilot could be) and melted away concerns that he wasn't a rock-ribbed conservative committed to advancing the conservative-populist movement Ronald Reagan built (he
wasn't). What made the tax pledge infamous was not its boldness but
its betrayal.

Ultimately the buck stopped with Bush, but the man history cred-
its with convincing the president to go along with the politically catastrophic tax hike was Richard Darman.[9] As OMB director, Darman
wanted President Bush to strike a deal with Democrats to reduce the
budget deficit by a half-trillion dollars over several years. As usual,
Democrats outfoxed and out-negotiated Republicans. Back then, it
was Democratic majority leader George Mitchell doing the wheeling
and dealing. "As a precondition for entering the talks, however, Democratic Senate majority leader George Mitchell demanded that Pres.
George H. W. Bush renege, in writing, on his 'no new taxes' pledge,"
recounts OMB alum James Capretta. "The president did so at Darman's urging, and from that moment on, the president's standing and
leverage plummeted."[10]

(Can't you just see the Trump tweet, had Twitter been around in
1990? Total disaster. Worst deal—EVER! Bush + Darman = horrible
negotiators. SAD!)

Contrast this moment with that of Reagan's meeting with Gorbachev at Reykjavík. Reagan, too, had been tempted—promised a
"historic" achievement of ridding the world of nuclear weapons, if
only he would betray his commitment to SDI. But with the eyes of
the world watching—and with incredible scorn heaped on him by the
Establishment Media and the elites—Reagan said no dice, refused to

violate his principles, and walked away from the negotiating table. In so doing, he won the Cold War. Indeed, the principled example Reagan set over eight years only intensified the feeling of betrayal conservatives felt from Bush breaking his "no new taxes" promise.

The reason this matters goes well beyond historical finger-pointing; the worldview Darman and others in Bush World represented was sharply at odds with the conservative-populist coalition Reagan assembled and represents one of the first big GOP fissures that widened into a chasm decades later.

A close ally of Bush wise man Jim Baker, Richard Darman was a brilliant and seasoned bureaucrat who had worked in six U.S. Cabinet departments before going on to be partner and managing director of the powerful Carlyle Group. He was self-aware enough to admit that he possessed an "excessive regard" for his own "brainpower," and he had an almost cartoonish elitist demeanor.[11] His attitudes also stand in as a good summary of the views of the GOP Establishment, which was now poised to reassert its power after eight years of populist governance. Darman had served in the Reagan administration and witnessed the electoral power of Reagan's populism. He viewed it as a sort of rhetorical parlor trick linguistic legerdemain elites could use to get the rabble to pipe down and go along with the bureaucratic, big government policies conjured up by Ivy League elites like himself (two degrees from Harvard) who advocated for what he called the "sensible center."

In his book, *Who's In Control?: Polar Politics and the Sensible Center*, Darman explicitly stated his belief that for Bush to solve his political exigencies, the Bush team needed "to change our intended majority coalition" by eschewing a "hard-right, heavily populist, anti-government strategy" that believed in "financing a conservative vision with radical (not just substantial) reductions in existing government programs." Instead, said Darman, he favored "abandoning a portion of the right, building a deeper and wider base in the broad American middle, and financing market-oriented reforms and investments with a combination of a politically acceptable form of consumption tax and a serious, but selective, approach to spending reduction." Just in case he wasn't clear enough, Darman later stated: "I have suggested that where centrism is often sensible, populism is often (although not always) angry."[12]

Translation: toss the kooky right-wingers overboard and let the "adults" (liberal globalists) plan and manage the world economy.

Darman failed to kill the "read my lips" tax pledge in Bush's 1988 acceptance speech. But he was successful in getting President Bush to abandon it in 1990. On June 26, 1990, the White House tacked a statement to the pressroom bulletin board that Bush and a bipartisan group of congressmen had agreed to. The president's statement was short but only three words really mattered: "tax revenue increases." Conservatives were furious, Democrats were ecstatic, and the Establishment Media launched a years-long feeding frenzy that eventually devoured Bush's re-election chances.

The next day, the first line of the *New York Times* article on the tax betrayal read: "With negotiations on cutting the budget deficit stalled, President Bush today broke with his vow to oppose new taxes and said any agreement with Congress would require 'tax revenue increases.'"[13] The left had Bush in political checkmate, and they knew it. "President Bush's reneging on 'Read my lips: No new taxes' was the most famous broken promise in the history of American politics," said Bill Clinton campaign strategist James Carville.[14]

I remember feeling deeply disappointed and frustrated after the tax betrayal. I've always had immense respect for President Bush. It's hard not to. He had heroically served his country in World War II as the youngest naval pilot at the time and was awarded the Distinguished Flying Cross. He has always carried himself with dignity and decorum. Throughout his term in office, President Bush spent Christmas at Camp David because he worried about his Secret Service agents and their staffers being away from their families. My respect for the man only made my disappointment in his decision all the greater. As it turns out, the country felt the same way.

THE HIGHEST FALL

President Bush's approval ratings plunged after he raised taxes. Then Iraqi president Saddam Hussein invaded Kuwait, an act of aggression that sparked the short Persian Gulf War, which concluded on February 28, 1991. Bush's "telephone diplomacy" and broad-based coalition of international partners resulted in a quick routing that left Saddam Hussein crippled but in power (a huge mistake, as many saw at the time). In the end, a tragic but historically low 148 U.S. service members were killed in combat (24 percent of which were due to "friendly fire").[15]

As Americans welcomed home our soldiers, sailors, airmen, and marines, Bush experienced what political scientists and pollsters call the "rally around the flag" phenomenon, resulting in the highest-ever recorded approval rating (91 percent) for any American president since the creation of modern polling. Democrats and Republicans thought Bush's chances of reelection were a lock. "We were seriously in the doldrums," remembers James Carville. "We didn't have a chance. It was a really dismal time to be a Democrat."[16] But the soaring heights of Bush's popularity turned out to be a momentary political sugar high, one that could not overcome economic anxieties about the recession and the Bush policies many believed had put the world's interests above the people's.

It wasn't just Democrats who felt that way; conservatives and populists were frustrated by a Bush regime that in no way resembled the leadership they had been led to believe would be a continuation of Reagan. The violation of the tax pledge was just one of many decisions that angered the populists. Bush's actions on trade, his inability to connect with working Americans, and his patrician demeanor made the old Reagan coalition restless.

Enter Reagan speechwriter and conservative stalwart Pat Buchanan. I consider Pat a good friend and a man who has spent much of his career trying to keep Reagan's populist vision front and center in the GOP. The first time I met Pat Buchanan was in late March of 1982. When other college kids were going to Florida for spring break, we *Dartmouth Review* writers were making our pilgrimage to the Buchanan beachhead of populist conservatism. *Review* editor Dinesh D'Souza, publisher Keeney Jones, and I (a freshman reporter who happened to be dating the editor) drove 10 hours from New Hampshire to interview Buchanan at his McLean, Virginia, home. Buchanan was a member of our "advisory board" and stuck with us even during our most explosive controversies.

We immediately clicked. As an 18-year-old who was just beginning to understand the intolerance of the left at Dartmouth, I was drawn to Buchanan's pugnacious yet highly intellectual brand of nationalistic conservatism, and loved reading his syndicated column. The way he skewered the national press corps for its bias and intellectual snobbery was priceless. His take-no-prisoners approach was the same one we took at the *Review* toward the liberal tools on campus. Looking at all the political memorabilia Buchanan and his wife, Shelley, had on their shelves—framed photos of Nixon, Reagan, Confederate army pistols, awards—I was totally hooked. How exciting it would be, I thought, to have a career like his, to be in the national political fight every day. Embarrassing revelation: At this Buchanan meeting, I wore a corduroy skirt with whales on it, kneesocks, and a blue blazer. Tragic. It's a wonder the man ever spoke to me again.

As far back as his days working in the Nixon administration, Pat had witnessed the slow fusion of the Democrat and Republican parties into a singular ruling elite, a political class who sought above all else to maintain its own power.

Following Reagan's example from 1976, Buchanan decided to mount a primary run against an incumbent Republican president. But Buchanan would do so with an even more populist, nationalistic platform than Reagan—and he also was a well-established national figure in government, television, and print. In those days, he was, in effect, a political reality star.

With the Cold War won, Buchanan believed it was time to focus on the home front. He made his announcement on December 10, 1991, from the New Hampshire state capital. At the time I was seven months out of law school, living in New Haven, Connecticut, and clerking for federal appellate court judge Ralph Winter. I caught the replay at night on C-SPAN. Buchanan was on fire.

We must not trade in our sovereignty for a cushioned seat at the head table of anyone's New World Order.

The first challenge we face, then, is economic, presented by the rise of a European super state and a dynamic Asia led by Japan. The 20th Century was the American Century, but they intend to make the 21st, the century of Europe or the Century of Asia.

So, as we Americans congratulate one another on the victory for freedom that we, first and foremost, won, and won together for all mankind in the Cold War, we must begin to prepare for the new struggles already underway.

All the institutions of the Cold War, from vast permanent U.S. armies on foreign soil, to old alliances against Communist enemies that no longer exist, to billions in foreign aid, must be re-examined. With a $4 trillion debt, with a U.S. budget chronically out of balance, should the United States be required to carry indefinitely the burden of defending rich and prosperous allies who take America's generosity for granted as they invade our markets?

. . . [I]t is time to end these routinized annual transfers of our national wealth to global bureaucrats, who ship it off to regimes that pay us back in compound ingratitude. It is time to phase out foreign aid, and start looking out for the needs of the forgotten Americans right here in the United States.

So, today, we call for a new patriotism, where Americans begin to put the needs of Americans first, for a new nationalism where in every negotiation, be it arms control or trade, the American side seeks advantage and victory for the United States.

The people of this country need to recapture our capital city from an occupying army of lobbyists, and registered agents of foreign powers hired to look out for everybody and everything except the national interest of the United States.

On that day Buchanan, in essence, delivered a better, loftier version of Trump's "America First" speech. Of course, he was realistic; he knew his odds of victory were slim. Still, he wanted to help conservatives send a signal to the GOP Establishment that Bush's globalist designs for a "New World Order" stood in contradiction to the tenets of Reaganism. "President Bush wants to be president of the world," said Buchanan. "I want to be president of the United States."[17]

At first, the Bush campaign brushed Buchanan off as an irritating sideshow. Pat announced that his campaign theme would be "America First" (hmmm . . . where else have we heard that lately?), jabbed at the elitism of the Bushies, called the president "King George" (a royal version of "Low Energy" Jeb), and said he sought to put an end to "Skull and Bones International" (a reference to President Bush's membership in the Yale secret society club of the same name).

"Why is he being the way he is?" Bush asked his associates. "What the hell is he after? What does he want?"[18] The Bush people wanted conservatives to get in line. But Buchanan reminded the GOP Establishment that the party had strayed from its principles and demanded that conservatives have a seat at the table. Principled ideological pursuits like that were anathema to Bush World pragmatism.

"They had no real feeling for movement conservatism beyond the cosseting it required at election time," wrote campaign journalists Peter Goldman and Thomas DeFrank. "For them, the doctrinaire right was like a petting zoo where you showed up once every four years, stroked the animals for a while and then went home to the world of affairs."[19] But conservatives were in no mood for pat-on-the-head sessions. Americans were angry about the tax lie and fed up with President Bush's penchant for focusing on international affairs instead of the economic pain swirling in the heartland.

While out on the campaign trail in December 1991, Buchanan stopped by the James River Paper Mill in northern New Hampshire in a small town called Groveton. It was freezing cold and just before Christmas. That morning, the company had laid off 350 workers. When Pat arrived, many of the workers were picking up the free Christmas turkeys the company gave out and had their pink slips in hand. As Buchanan shook hands and greeted the workers, one man stood with his eyes toward the ground. When Pat shook his hand, the man looked up, stared him in the eyes, and said, "Save our jobs." The comment went through Pat like a spear. Later, inside the campaign van, Pat asked, "What do you do for a guy like that?" Pat's lovely wife, Shelley, started to cry. "We're going to come back here, and we're going to make things happen," Pat told her.[20]

Bush beat Buchanan easily, but not before Pat racked up three million votes. His respectable showing earned him some leverage within the party and a prime-time speaking spot at the August 1992 Republican National Convention in Houston, Texas. But the Old Guard remained tone-deaf to his populist message. When Pat's sister and campaign manager, Bay Buchanan, tried to get the 1992 GOP platform to include wording supporting a border wall ("structures," the Buchanan camp called them), Republican officials were stunned. Surely you don't mean a fence, they told her. "We're not talking about lighthouses," Bay replied.[21]

Predictably, the Establishment Media ripped Buchanan's speech for its focus on the culture wars and traditional Judeo-Christian values. "My friends, this election is about more than who gets what. It is about who we are," said Buchanan. "It is about what we believe, and what we stand for as Americans. There is a religious war going on in this country. It is a cultural war, as critical to the kind of nation we shall be as was the Cold War itself, for this war is for the soul of America."[22]

But Buchanan's speech was also about reminding Republicans that the little guy was hurting and in need of help. After recounting the story about the paper mill worker who told him to "save our jobs," Pat shared another story about a woman he met:

Then there was the legal secretary that I met at the Manchester airport on Christmas Day who came running up to me and said, "Mr. Buchanan, I'm going to vote for you." And then she broke down weeping, and she said, "I've lost my job; I don't have any money, and they're going to take away my little girl. What am I going to do?"

He then told the RNC crowd that even though working-class Americans may not have read the conservative canon, Republicans must embrace ordinary people and fight on their behalf:

My friends, these people are our people. They don't read Adam Smith or Edmund Burke, but they come from the same schoolyards and the same playgrounds and towns as we came from. They share our beliefs and our convictions, our hopes and our dreams. These are the conservatives of the heart. They are our people. And we need to reconnect with them. We need to let them know we know how bad they're hurting. They don't expect miracles of us, but they need to know we care.

Pat wasn't finished. He explained how the people of the small California town of Hayfork were now "under a sentence of death because a federal judge has set aside nine million acres for the habitat of the spotted owl—forgetting about the habitat of the men and women who live and work in Hayfork." He concluded by sharing a story about "the brave people of Koreatown who took the worst of those L.A. riots, but still live the family values we treasure, and who still deeply believe in the American dream."[23]

In the wake of Pat Buchanan's RNC address, Establishment Media did their best to paint the speech as a blight on Bush's candidacy. Not surprisingly, that was total bunk. Bush's numbers went up significantly after the convention, cutting Bill Clinton's lead over George Bush from 18 points to 2.

Buchanan's connection with working-class conservatives came easy. Attempts to try to humanize Bush or cast him as a pork rind-eating regular Joe often backfired. The quest for populist appeal is nothing new in politics, of course. In the early 19th century, congressmen roamed the Capitol in homespun outfits in deference to their rural constituents. Trying to "fit in" and be embraced by the masses is a time-honored political tradition. And as the old saying goes, in politics, perception is more important than reality. In the case of George H. W. Bush, his failed efforts to connect with regular folks were often the product of unfair media reports. Nevertheless, the gaffes were self-inflicted and had the effect of making Bush appear un-relatable to working-class voters.

On the campaign trail, for example, President Bush tried to quote a lyric from the Nitty Gritty Dirt Band. There was just one problem: he pronounced the band's name as the "Nitty Ditty Nitty Gritty Great Bird." A swing and a miss!

Then there was the unfortunate and devastating line Bush uttered during the 1992 presidential debate in Richmond, Virginia, while answering a question from a voter. A woman asked the candidates: "How has the national debt personally affected each of your lives? And if it hasn't, how can you honestly find a cure for the economic problems of the common people if you have no experience in what's ailing them?" The woman obviously meant to say "recession" instead of "national debt," but the question frazzled the president and left him fumbling to formulate a response.

"Well, I think the national debt affects everybody," said Bush. "Obviously, it has a lot to do with interest rates. . . ."

Debate moderator Carole Simpson interrupted the president.

"She's saying you personally," said Simpson.

"You, on a personal basis, how has it affected you?" the questioner pressed.

"Well, I'm sure it has. I love my grandchildren. I want to think that . . ."

The woman interrupted the president.

"How?"

"I want to think that they're going to be able to afford an education," said the president. "I think that that's an important part of being a parent. If the question—maybe I get it wrong. Are you suggesting that if someone has means that the national debt doesn't affect them?"

"What I'm saying . . ." the woman began.

"I'm not sure I get it," said Bush. "Help me with the question, and I'll try to answer it."

The debate moderator later clarified, "I think she means more the *recession,* the economic problems today the country faces rather than . . ."[24]

The question was wonky, and the woman seemed a tad too eager to try to score political points. But President Bush had uttered the phrase "I'm not sure I get it" while fumbling through an answer about his ability to empathize with voters' economic pain—a topic he should have been locked and loaded to nail and put to rest.

Even more devastating was the follow-up answer from the young Arkansas governor Bill Clinton. In a Southern accent, Clinton delivered a response brimming with emotional connection and populist appeal.

"Tell me how it's affected you again," Clinton said to the woman who had asked Bush the question.

"Um . . ." she replied.

"You know people who've lost their jobs and lost their homes?" Clinton asked her.

"Well, yeah, uh-huh."

"Well, I've been governor of a small state for 12 years. I'll tell you how it's affected me," said Clinton. He then launched into a pitch-perfect debate answer oozing with warmth and populist resonance:

Every year Congress and the president sign laws that make us do more things and gives us less money to do it with. I see people in my state, middle-class people—their taxes have gone up in Washington and their services have gone down while the wealthy have gotten tax cuts.

I have seen what's happened in this last four years when—in my state, when people lose their jobs there's a good chance I'll know them by their names. When a factory closes, I know the people who ran it. When the businesses go bankrupt, I know them.

And I've been out here for 13 months meeting in meetings just like this ever since October, with people like you all over America, people that have lost their jobs, lost their livelihood, lost their health insurance.

What I want you to understand is the national debt is not the only cause of that. It is because America has not invested in its people. It is because we have not grown. It is because we've had 12 years of trickle-down economics. We've gone from first to twelfth in the world in wages. We've had four years where we've produced no private-sector jobs. Most people are working harder for less money than they were making 10 years ago.

It is because we are in the grip of a failed economic theory. And this decision you're about to make better be about what kind of economic theory you want, not just people saying I'm going to go fix it but what are we going to do? I think we have to do is invest in American jobs, American education, control American health care costs and bring the American people together again.[25]

Clinton's answer was everything Bush's wasn't. He connected on a human level with a people-first response. His closing sentence advanced an America first strategy. Bill Clinton was many things, but stupid wasn't one of them. He understood populism's appeal and signaled that he would pursue an agenda based on American interests (which turned out not to be the case). In short, Bush hadn't just blown the debate moment, Clinton had seized it.

And of course who could forget the infamous grocery store scanner episode wherein the mainstream media reported that President Bush was fascinated and surprised in a checkout line by how grocery store scanners work—a metaphor for a president out of touch with everyday Americans. The truth is that the story was fake news. Bush was visiting the exhibition hall at the National Grocers Association and was seeing never-before-seen technology that had yet to be released to the public. "These weren't everyday grocery scanners; no one had seen these, the President and the press included," explained Bush campaign strategist Mary Matalin. But the media-created gaffe morphed into a "cultural stun gun." "The story was such a compelling metaphor to make their point, that it took hold in campaign mythology. From then on it was an article of faith with much of the public that Bush was out of touch."[26]

THAT "GIANT SUCKING SOUND"

In the remaining months of the campaign, President Bush took on Bill "Slick Willie" Clinton and a moderate Republican billionaire populist by the name of Ross Perot—one of the most eccentric figures ever to enter American presidential politics, and in retrospect, a harbinger not only of the rising populist movement, but of the kind of candidate these voters ultimately preferred.

Perot was short, quirky, had large ears and a squeaky voice, was pro-choice on abortion, and supported gun control. Perot's own campaign manager, Ed Rollins, later said, "Perot is insecurity incarnate" and that he would "have been a disaster in the White House."[27] Ouch.

So how in the world did a political novice like Ross Perot manage to win an impressive 19 percent of the popular vote and over 25 percent in nine states?[28]

Like Buchanan, Perot tapped into the vexation roiling the country, an economic anger that stunned President Bush the first time he saw it firsthand. The Bush campaign ran a series of taped focus groups with suburban voters who had voted for Bush in 1988 and then showed the president the sessions during a weekend at Camp David. President Bush was shocked by what he saw. "He doesn't get it," said one person. "Doesn't care," said another. "Out of touch." "Doesn't have a clue." Another stinger: "More interested in foreigners than America."[29]

Perot harnessed that economic outrage and honed in on the insanity of American leaders brokering trade agreements wherein we "get our pockets picked" and ship American jobs south of the border. "We own this country. It belongs to us," Perot said in his March 1992 speech at the National Press Club. "Government should come from us. . . . We have abdicated our ownership responsibility. . . . You've got to send them a message: you work for us, we don't work for you. Under the Constitution, you are our servants. . . . We've got to put the country back in the control of the owners. And in plain Texas talk, it's time to take out the trash and clean out the barn, or it's going to be too late."[30]

Perot then attacked a forthcoming trade treaty that President George H. W. Bush had worked hard to advance, something called the North American Free Trade Agreement (NAFTA)—this was another populist theme he co-opted from Buchanan:

The White House is all excited about the new trade agreement with Mexico. This agreement will move the highest paid blue-collar jobs in the United States to Mexico. This is going to create serious damage to our tax base during this critical period.

We have got to manufacture here and not there to keep our tax base intact.[31]

He may have been a kooky billionaire, but on NAFTA, Perot was a prophetic kooky billionaire.

NAFTA, of course, is the trade agreement between the United States, Mexico, and Canada negotiated by George H. W. Bush and signed into law by Bill Clinton on December 8, 1993.[32] A majority of Republicans supported it. Clinton strongly embraced it and lobbied Democrats hard to overcome objections from many in his party and its labor union base. NAFTA supporters like Clinton promised the trade deal would benefit America economically by removing tariffs, accelerating trade, boosting exports to Mexico, and generating U.S. jobs—a million in the first five years, Clinton promised.[33] Populists like Pat Buchanan warned NAFTA would create dozens of new bureaucracies, diminish U.S. sovereignty, mandate billions in foreign aid and loan guarantees, create reams of regulations, and ship hundreds of thousands of U.S. jobs and businesses to Mexico in pursuit of cheaper labor and bigger profits.[34] With Buchanan out of the race, Perot picked up the populist mantle and opposed NAFTA in memorable fashion.

In October, during the second presidential debate that included all three candidates, Perot hammered the folly of "one-way trade agreements," said "we have got to stop sending jobs overseas," and dropped his famous line.

> To those of you in the audience who are business people, pretty simple: If you're paying $12, $13, $14 an hour for factory workers and you can move your factory South of the border . . . pay a dollar an hour for your labor, have no health care—that's the most expensive single element in making a car—have no environmental controls, no pollution controls and no retirement, and you don't care about anything but making money, there will be a giant sucking sound going south.[35]

"A giant sucking sound." Perot hit a rhetorical home run. NAFTA wasn't signed into law yet, but Perot and millions of Americans—the kind who don't worship at the *Wall Street Journal*'s altar of globalism and internationalism for profit's sake—knew it was a raw deal for workers and bad for America. The biggest "tell" that NAFTA was going to be a boon for elites and a bust for everyone else was the fact that George H. W. Bush and Bill Clinton (as well as their Donor Class pals) all supported the monstrosity.

Ross Perot ran a disorganized and zany campaign. But the same working-class disgust with the political class that fueled Buchanan's run coalesced into Perot winning nearly one out of every five votes. In the four years since Ronald Reagan's presidency, people realized no one was looking out for them any longer. "Read my lips: no new taxes," the condescending elitism, a lopsided focus on international relationships to create a "New World Order," a looming NAFTA deal to cede even more American sovereignty and ship away even more American jobs . . . the people had finally had enough.

Personally, I found George H. W. Bush to be rather uninspiring, to put it politely. I had met him on a few occasions when he was vice president and thought he was a nice man but had little of the Reagan appeal. The Reaganites knew that while he was a loyal and patriotic man and a fine vice president, he wasn't one of us.

On Election Day, Bill Clinton captured 43 percent of the popular vote to Bush's 37 percent. The 19 percent Perot poached represented nearly 20 million votes. Clinton beat Bush by over 200 electoral votes (370–168). The wartime president who just two years earlier had hit the all-time high in presidential popularity lost the presidency to a draft-dodging, pot-smoking, serial philanderer.

A few months after his 1992 defeat, George H. W. Bush admitted that his decision to break the tax promise had been a colossal mistake. Bush had bought into the old Washington lie that if you'll just feed the government beast a crumb, it will be satisfied.

"I thought this one compromise . . . would result in no more tax increases," said Bush. "I thought it would result in total control of domestic discretionary spending. And now we see Congress talking about raising taxes again. If I had it to do over, I wouldn't do what I did then. . . . I did it and I regret it."[36]

In 2014, the John F. Kennedy Library Foundation gave George H. W. Bush a "Profile in Courage Award" for his decision to break his promise not to raise taxes. For the kids playing along at home, you know you've sold out conservative principles when progressives give you high-profile awards.[37]

While Bush apologized for shattering his tax promise, he remained defiant and nasty about Americans' opposition to NAFTA. During a 1999 speech in Canada, the former president blasted anyone who dared to criticize the trade deal:

> Some people are using uncertainty and ambiguity of the moment to create a momentum for turning America selfishly inward away from the world. And even though they deny it, they advocate policies that amount to protectionism and isolationism. There are slogans—"Come Home America," "America First." This is selfish! This is beneath the history of our great country. But it's out there and it worries me, this coalition of left and right. I simply think these views are wrong. On trade, that odd coalition that fought me early this decade—the far-left joined by the far-right—remains intact.[38]

That is an astounding statement, and one that did not receive much public attention at the time because Bush had been out of office for six years when he uttered it. But did you catch that? Anyone who wants to put "America first" is "selfish." Desiring Americans to have jobs instead of shipping them to other countries is "beneath the history of our great country." Anyone who dares to stymie rich elites from driving down labor costs so they can bag more cash, add another wing on their mansions, or park a new Bugatti in their garage is "far-right" and a mouthpiece for—wait for it—"isolationism" and "protectionism."

This is globalism in all its smug, know-it-all, "shut up, peasants!" ugliness. Globalism is fundamentally anti-American because it aims to raze American sovereignty by atrophying our ability to take independent actions that are in our nation's best interests. The elites declare mutiny on our national sovereignty by anchoring our ship to the lead weight that is the United Nations, allowing multinational trade deals to attach themselves like barnacles to slow our speed. They undermine and degrade our traditions and values by allowing nongovernmental organizations (NGOs) packed with radical activists to commandeer our ship of state in the name of international unity. When the ungrateful commoners start getting mouthy or overly empowered, globalists administer a verbal beatdown and trash the peasants as angry, "selfish," and xenophobic.

Is it any wonder Bush lost?

Is it any wonder that, after years of globalists deriding Americans for having the temerity to put working people's economic interests first, Donald Trump chose "America First" as his campaign slogan—a thumb in the eye to the bilge elites proffered for decades?

By the time Donald Trump arrived on the scene, the people were well past the point of no return with finger-wagging globalist lectures and faux moral superiority. Before the people reclaimed their power, however, the Establishment would continue heating the populist pressure cooker with disastrous policies that enriched elites and sacrificed millions of American working-class jobs on the altar of globalism.

In the end, George H. W. Bush stalled the conservative-populist engine that powered Reaganism. "George Bush was the beneficiary of the greatest baton pass in presidential history in 1988, and he and his people tossed it away," said Ed Rollins. "He did more than any other Republican to roll back the Reagan Revolution. Worst of all, he gave the country he loved to Bill Clinton."[39]

Why did it happen?

Pat Buchanan put it this way after Bush's defeat, "Republicans did not lose in 1992 because Pat Buchanan gave a blazing speech at Houston. They lost because Ross Perot walked off with one-third of the Reagan coalition. And Mr. Perot tore those voters away because Big Government Conservatives 'compromised' their principles, spent four years in an orgy of spending, raised taxes, and aborted a seven-year recovery."[40]

"Bush and his people never understood the coalitions that Reagan had handed down to them," said Rollins. "They did everything possible to piss them off."[41]

3.

CLINTON'S PERVERSE POPULISM

From Bubba to Barbra Streisand

I have to be a president beyond the borders.

—BILL CLINTON

On November 4, 1992, I walked into the Supreme Court cafeteria to order my usual breakfast of oatmeal with a side of scrambled eggs. But smelling the greasy sizzle on the grill, I felt a wave of nausea come over me. Clerking at the Supreme Court required long hours, but the night before was different. College friends and I were up late watching the election returns to see Arkansas governor and good-old-boy Bill Clinton beat George H. W. Bush by 202 electoral votes.

A fellow clerk and close friend met me in line with his tray. We looked at each other and didn't have to speak a word—he, too, was a strong conservative who worked for another justice. "This is going to be a long, long day," he said. "It's going to be a long four years," I answered glumly. A few more clerks from other chambers came behind us in line. One, a proud feminist, looked at me, flashed a big grin, and, giving a thumbs-up, chirped: "Happy Wednesday!" "Yeah, great," I responded sarcastically. "Congratulations on your guy winning."

As one of the more outspoken conservatives at the Court, I knew I was in for a day (or week) of serious ribbing by some of the young Democrats sprinkled through the chambers of Justices Harry

Blackmun, David Souter, and John Paul Stevens. Who could blame them? They were reveling in the fact that their long, twelve-year White House shut-out was finally over. After our one-year clerkship, many would be applying to work in the new administration, and they were excited. Still, I couldn't complain. Clerking for Supreme Court justice Clarence Thomas was as inspiring as it was educational. Against unrelenting and ugly attacks, he served with honor, worked vigorously, and made his judgments based on the Constitution as it was written. Who could ask for more?

Notwithstanding my deep philosophical difference with Bush, I supported him over Clinton. (Although I was ideologically more closely aligned with populist Ross Perot, I thought a vote for him was a vote for Clinton.) The morning after the election, I could not shake the dyspeptic feeling in my gut. And I wasn't just sick because of the money I bet on Bush. Mainly, I was sick for the country. I worried that everything that President Reagan had achieved—which had already been compromised by Bush—would be flushed down the toilet.

I would need an ocean of ink, a year's worth of your time, and a hazmat suit to trudge through the toxic sludge dump that is Bill Clinton's scandal-filled political career. Suffice it to say, there is a reason Bill Clinton is one of only two presidents in American history ever to be impeached.

Nevertheless, personal foibles aside, Bill Clinton was one of the most politically gifted politicians in modern times. And he was smart enough to know that having a populist appeal is key to winning elections. The everyman veneer included everything from his bad saxophone playing to his classic line "I feel your pain." He grew up in the small town of Hot Springs, Arkansas, not Hope, as he claimed (he even saw value in having a hometown with a populist name!).

One would think a kid who grew up middle class in middle America would have understood how important it was to keep the factories humming—those men and women who didn't have the grades or the money to go to an elite university needed to work, too. One would think he would have understood that the trade deals America negotiated would have to make life better for the everyday American. One might also think he would have understood that farming out health care reform legislation to his wife would go over like a glass of cold chardonnay at an AA meeting.

But despite campaigning as a "New Democrat" with a "Third Way" sensibility, Bill Clinton quickly evolved from a populist Southern governor into a globalist president. Instead of offering a course correction on Bush's New World Order, Clinton took globalism to new and disastrous heights. That Bush and Clinton's view of the world was closer than Bush and Reagan's is key to understanding the rise of today's populist movement. It also helps explain the chummy relationship between the two dynastic families, which has only become clearer over the years.

BUBBA GOES TO WASHINGTON

For most of Bill Clinton's first term, I worked as a litigation associate in the Washington office of Skadden, Arps, Slate, Meagher & Flom. My days were spent writing legal memos and doing witness interviews in various white-collar criminal matters. My mentor and boss was firm partner Bob Bennett, the liberal brother of Bill Bennett, the former Reagan education secretary and drug czar under Bush. (We joked that I was the only living human being to ever work for both Bennett brothers.) It didn't take me long to realize that big law firm practice wasn't for me. So I began writing freelance columns on politics for whatever newspaper would publish them.

The *Los Angeles Times*, *The Washington Post*, *The New York Times*, and *The Wall Street Journal* each gave me a byline and some ink from time to time. I covered a wide array of issues but constantly gravitated toward topics and themes connected to the populist outlook.

When the GOP Establishment began buzzing about recruiting Colin Powell as a Republican presidential nominee, I cowrote a *New York Times* piece with my friend and colleague Stephen Vaughn titled "Powell Is Bad for the GOP." Our anti-Establishment argument: if Republicans nominated a candidate who "agrees with Mr. Clinton on abortion, affirmative action and gun control, why nominate anyone at all?"[1]

Some of my other articles used humor to make serious points about presidential leadership. I published a fun *Los Angeles Times* piece contrasting Ronald Reagan and Bill Clinton on a host of issues. Under the section titled "Memorable presidential dialogue with repressive regimes," I wrote:

REAGAN (TO SOVIETS): "Mr. Gorbachev, tear down this wall.
CLINTON (TO CHINESE): "Cream or sugar?"[2]

Those early columns allowed to me to discuss current issues through a populist lens—an approach I later applied on the radio.

Throughout the 1992 election I was intrigued by Clinton's populist campaign style. During his five terms as Arkansas governor, Clinton had shown flashes of conservative populism that he cultivated into something he called a "New Democrat" philosophy—a break from the party's knee-jerk liberalism. He had supported welfare-to-work policies designed to break the cycle of government dependency—a position more in alignment with Republicans than members of his own party. He touted reducing his tiny state's welfare rolls by 17,000 people and maintained there was dignity in work. "I was always somewhat amused to hear some members of the press characterize [welfare reform] as a Republican issue, as if valuing work was something only conservatives did," said Clinton.[3] At a meeting of the nation's governors, Clinton brought a black Arkansas woman named Lillie Hardin to testify. He asked her whether able-bodied people should have to work to receive welfare benefits. "I sure do," she said. "Otherwise we'll just lay around watching the soaps all day." He then asked Hardin what was the best part of being off welfare. "When my boy goes to school and they ask him, 'What does your mama do for a living?' he can give an answer." Clinton beamed with pride. "It was the best argument I've ever heard for welfare reform," he said.[4]

His governorship had also contained moments that suggested he might be tough on crime; his support for the death penalty stood at odds with many Democrats, including failed Democratic presidential contender Michael Dukakis. One of the four inmates Clinton put to death was a black man named Ricky Ray Rector, who had shot and killed a white police officer and a civilian before shooting himself in the head, leaving himself mentally impaired. When Clinton ordered the execution of Rector during the presidential campaign, critics said he was doing so to project a "tough on crime" image. If so, it seemed to work. "You can't law-and-order Clinton," said former Arkansas prosecutor Jay Jacobson. "If you can kill Rector, you can kill anybody."[5]

But more than anything, Clinton understood that Reagan's conservative-populist revolution had rewritten the rules. Americans now viewed government as the problem, not the solution. In 1992, Clinton campaigned accordingly.

On welfare, for example, Clinton admitted that big government schemes had fostered a cycle of dependency. "For so long, government has failed us. And one of its worst failures has been welfare," Clinton said in a 1992 campaign ad. "I have a plan to end welfare as we know it to break the cycle of welfare dependency." Instead of asking hard-working middle-class taxpayers to fund cradle-to-grave social programs, Clinton vowed to make able-bodied citizens work and touted his Arkansas welfare record. "We'll provide education, job training, and childcare. But then, those who are able must go to work, either in the private sector or in public service," he said. "It's time to make welfare what it should be—a second chance, not a way of life."[6] It was a message with strong populist appeal.

He took a similar approach on crime. Clinton promised to put 100,000 more police on the street, "be tough on crime," create a national police corps that hired former members of the military to become cops, and make nationwide military-style boot camps like the one he had in Arkansas for nonviolent, first-time offenders to instill discipline. "We cannot take our country back until we take our neighborhoods back," Clinton declared. "It is the poor, it is the minorities, it is those who have been forgotten and left out who are most at risk to violent crime in America today."[7] One could almost hear echoes of Richard Nixon's populist promise to restore "law and order" for "forgotten Americans."

Positions like these resonated with conservative populists. Working people, by definition, value work. They don't mind giving people a hand up, but they know endless handouts breed dependency. Big government welfare policies also confiscate workers' money and hand it to those who are unwilling to work to support themselves. Similarly, populists support law and order policies because they protect the people and keep them safe. Communities wracked by crime force law-abiding citizens to become prisoners in their homes and to live lives of fear rather than freedom. Far from being "selfish" or "bigoted," conservative populists want a world where working people who play by the rules can get ahead and leave their children's lives a little better off.

Clinton's 1992 campaign pounded home these populist themes. "They're a new generation of Democrats, Bill Clinton and Al Gore— and they don't think the way the old Democratic Party did," started one of their political ads. "They've called to end welfare as we know it, so welfare can be a second chance, not a way of life. They've sent a strong signal to criminals by supporting the death penalty." The ad's tagline: "For people, for a change."

On Election Day, working-class voters and those in the all-important Rust Belt states rewarded Clinton handsomely. He won Pennsylvania, West Virginia, Ohio, Michigan, Illinois, Iowa, and Wisconsin. (The only Rust Belt state he lost was Indiana.) He also carried every region of the country save the South, where Bush narrowly edged him by two points.[8] After 1992, no Republican presidential candidate would ever carry Michigan or Pennsylvania again—until, that is, Donald Trump carpetbombed those states with his conservative-populist message. Trump would also win Wisconsin, something no Republican since Ronald Reagan had done.

But once Clinton got to the White House, things took a sharp left turn. During his first two years in office he drifted further from the populist platform he ran on and defaulted to big government schemes.

Less than a week on the job, President Clinton announced the appointment of Hillary Clinton to head a committee to overhaul America's health care system—a detail he had strangely forgotten to include in his campaign ads. The reason for choosing Hillary, said the president, was because "she's better at organizing and leading people from a complex beginning to a certain end than anybody I've ever worked with in my life." Plus, "we have a First Lady of many talents."[9]

As it turned out, one of those "many talents" involved creating Hillarycare, a 1,342-page government takeover of the nation's health care system. Early in the process then–Republican House whip Newt Gingrich warned Hillary not to fashion a comprehensive plan but instead introduce smaller reforms over time. He, like most conservatives, wanted to see the nation's health care system improved if possible. "It will fall of its own weight," Newt cautioned. "You won't be able to pass it." Hillary listened carefully "and promptly went off and did whatever she wanted."[10] The result: an unpopular bureaucratic behemoth that restricted patient choice and included individual and employer mandates. (Now where else have I heard that lately?) Far from empowering the people, Hillarycare was yet another big government Washington power grab—hardly the kind of people-centered leadership Clinton promised.

A precursor to the Obamacare nightmare, Hillarycare sought to seize control of the health care industry that, at the time, accounted for roughly one-seventh of the U.S. economy. "Not since Franklin Roosevelt's War Production Board has it been suggested that so large a part of the American economy should suddenly be brought under government control," wrote *The Economist*.[11] As the Heritage Foundation cautioned at the time, the Clinton health care scheme would raise costs, not lower them—constrict patient choices, not expand them:

> In effect, the Clinton Administration is imposing a top-down, command-and-control system of global budgets and premium caps, a superintending National Health Board and a vast system of government sponsored regional alliances, along with a panoply of advisory boards, panels, and councils, interlaced with the expanded operations of the agencies of Department of Health and Human Services and the Department of Labor, issuing innumerable rules, regulations, guidelines, and standards. But virtually all the perverse incentives of the current system are to be left in place.... This amounts to a stimulation of demand, combined with a constriction of supply. This is akin to turning up the heat on a pressure cooker, while clamping down on the lid. At some point, the lid will blow and the costs of the system will skyrocket in bigger deficits and even higher taxes.[12]

That Hillary would design a massive centralized health system that seized power and control over the people's health and well-being was a warning signal about the kind of president she would be. But at the time, all most people could focus on was seeing her health care boondoggle die as fast as possible, and thankfully it did.

Months later, Clinton nominated far-left judge Ruth Bader Ginsburg to replace Justice Byron White on the Supreme Court—a gift to his liberal base and elite Hollywood donors. (Don't let her long and in many ways touching friendship with the late Justice Scalia fool you.) Ginsburg may be a very nice lady but her record on the Court has been one of unbridled judicial activism. (Once, just once, it would be nice to see the left suffer the same fate as conservatives by picking a Supreme Court justice who turns out to be the opposite of what they thought they were getting.) Indeed, Clinton's first two years also included a second Court pick, Judge Stephen Breyer. Far from ruling in ways that protected the people's constitutional rights, Ginsburg and Breyer proved to be reliably activist judges.

And if any middle-class voters in rural America thought Bill Clinton's Southern roots might keep him from eroding gun rights, they were sorely mistaken as well. Instead of protecting the right to bear arms, Clinton signed gun control laws including the Brady Bill and the so-called assault weapons ban, decisions that rankled gun owners and Second Amendment supporters.

But Clinton's biggest populist betrayals came on trade and jobs. His campaign famously declared, "It's the economy, stupid!" Voters thought he understood they were electing him to foster and protect U.S. jobs. But once in the Oval Office, Clinton pursued the globalist trade policies the populist movement had warned about. The results were catastrophic for millions of workers and revitalized calls for an "America First" agenda in the years that followed.

BILL GOES FULL GLOBALIST & UNLEASHES THE NAFTA NIGHTMARE

Progressives have spent two decades waging a disinformation campaign to blur the lines of blame surrounding Bill Clinton and NAFTA. We saw it on display during the 2016 presidential campaign when the issue's toxicity threatened to splash onto Hillary Clinton's candidacy. Just weeks before the election, MSNBC's Rachel Maddow did her best to chop block for the Clintons. "Bill Clinton did not sign NAFTA," she said with her usual whiff of intellectual superiority. "George H. W. Bush signed NAFTA." The lie was so embarrassing that even the progressive publication Salon slammed Maddow. In a piece titled "Own Up to NAFTA, Democrats: Trump Is Right That the Terrible Trade Pact Was Bill Clinton's Baby," Salon wrote: "The usually whip-smart Rachel Maddow made a mind-boggling error the day after the Clinton-Trump debate. . . . Clinton *absolutely did* sign NAFTA."[13]

The history here matters, because the NAFTA disaster still haunts us—something Donald Trump wisely hammered home during the campaign and pledged to renegotiate as president. In December of 1992, after President George H. W. Bush lost reelection and was preparing to leave office, he signed the trade treaty between Mexico, Canada, and the United States. But before NAFTA could actually become law, it would first need to pass Congress.

Enter Bill Clinton. Far from a passive observer, the new president spent months working to ram the bill through Congress. He had an uphill climb. By the summer of 1993, Democratic House whip David Bonior, who fiercely opposed NAFTA, had all but killed the bill and claimed to have 218 "no" votes lined up against it—enough to defeat the measure. Undeterred, Bill Clinton kicked into high gear.[14]

"I was ready to go all out to pass NAFTA in the Congress," Clinton later said.[15] In his presidential memoir, *My Life,* Bill Clinton recounts that he and his vice president "had called or seen two hundred members of Congress, and the cabinet had made nine hundred calls" pushing NAFTA's passage. He also enlisted former president Jimmy Carter, who helped by "calling members of Congress all day long for a week."[16] During an intense, "table-pounding" Cabinet Room debate between Clinton and his advisers, Pulitzer Prize–winning Watergate veteran journalist Bob Woodward reported that the president punctuated the meeting with an ominous declaration: "I have to be a president beyond the borders."[17]

Clinton barnstormed the country and airwaves promising Americans that NAFTA would yield a jobs bonanza. "I believe that NAFTA will create a million jobs in the first five years of its impact," he said. "And I believe that that is more jobs than will be lost, as inevitably some will be, as always happens when you open up the mix to a new range of competition." Not to worry, however; Bubba assured the hard hats and factory workers that he had crunched the numbers and determined that they would be just fine, better even. "NAFTA means jobs, American jobs, and good-paying American jobs."[18]

Months out from the vote, the *Times*/CBS poll found that nearly half (49 percent) of Americans had never even heard of NAFTA. Of the ones who had, most believed it would result in fewer jobs.[19] Clinton continued selling the trade pact. Although the president's marketing megaphone was much louder, a small but influential handful of populists rose up and spoke out.

Pat Buchanan made the populist case in the pages of *The Washington Post* in a hard-hitting piece titled "America First, NAFTA Never." "NAFTA epitomizes all that repels us in the modern state" and represents "the architecture of the New World Order," Pat wrote. Furthermore, the trade agreement was "part of a skeletal structure for world government" and "would supersede state laws and diminish U.S. sovereignty."

Buchanan then appealed directly to conservatives:

> The battle over NAFTA is also a struggle about what it means to be a conservative in 1993. Who defines the term in the post-Reagan era?
>
> To "conservatives of the heart," even if NAFTA brings an uptick in GNP [Gross National Product] it is no good for America. No matter the cash benefits, we don't want to merge our economy with Mexico, and we don't want to merge our country with Mexico. We don't want to force American workers to compete with dollar-an-hour Mexican labor. That's not what America is all about.
>
> Of late, some of our brethren on the Right have come to exhibit a near-monomaniacal obsession with economics, an almost religious faith in its ability to solve the crisis of the spirit and the dilemmas of the heart. But there are higher things in life than the bottom line on a balance sheet, or being able to buy Hong Kong

suits at the cheapest possible price. Community and country are two of those things.[20]

Buchanan wasn't the only former presidential candidate battling NAFTA; Ross Perot also went on offense against the trade deal. He published a book titled *Save Your Job, Save Our Country: Why NAFTA Must Be Stopped—Now!* Perot then held dozens of anti-NAFTA rallies throughout the country warning that NAFTA was a jobs killer. At the events, which sometimes drew crowds of 3,500 people or more, Perot delivered his usual mix of facts and down-home witticisms. "Money is going to chase cheap labor. That's as simple as the law of gravity," Perot told a Lansing, Michigan, crowd. The key, he said, was to "work together like the spokes within a wheel." "There are so many Americans who don't think this is a good idea, if we get organized [NAFTA] is dead on arrival before it hits Congress. . . . Do you think it's right for these companies to move your jobs to Mexico?" he asked the crowd. The Establishment "don't think you have any sense."[21]

Perot's most high-profile anti-NAFTA moment came during his 90-minute CNN *Larry King Live* debate with Vice President Al Gore on November 9, 1993. Clinton was short 25 votes in the House; the administration believed Gore debating Perot could tip the balance in the remaining weeks before the vote.

"This is a good deal for our country," said Gore.

"The problem is, this is not good for the people of either country," Perot said.

Both men then whipped out graphs and photos as visual aids. Gore was his usual obnoxious self, talking to the nation like he was reading a storybook to children.

"Every Nobel Prize winner" and "every past president" supports NAFTA, Gore said.

Perot turned to the camera and spoke directly to the people.

"A good deal will sell itself, folks—just plain talk. Four former presidents came out for it and couldn't sell it. All of the secretaries of state came out for it and couldn't sell it. . . . This dog just didn't hunt. . . . They all tried to sell it to you and the fact that they couldn't demonstrates that this deal is not good for our country," said Perot.

"This is a fork in the road. The whole world is watching," Gore declared. "This is a major choice for our country of historic proportions. If we give in to the politics of fear and make the wrong choices, the results will be catastrophic." (If this sounds exactly like the left's reactions to Donald Trump's decision to pull out of the Paris Climate Accords, that's because globalists always use the same "our way or DOOM!" hyperbolic rhetoric.)

Perot fired back. "If we have to, we the people, the owners of this country, will clean this mess up in 1994," said Perot. "Working people all across the United States are extremely angry—there's no way to stop them. They are not going to tolerate having their jobs continue to be shipped all over the world. We have to have a climate in this country where we can create jobs in the good old U.S.A."

The Perot-Gore debate on *Larry King Live* became the highest-watched regularly scheduled show in CNN history at the time.[22]

Importantly, there was another populist back in 1993 who warned NAFTA would be a disaster—and he did it at a conference that featured Presidents Ford, Bush, and Carter. At that conference, Bush declared that "our future lies south of the border."[23] The lone voice disagreed. "The Mexicans want it, and that doesn't sound good to me." He explained that NAFTA "would only benefit Mexico," was "poorly crafted," and that "we never make a good deal." He "was the only speaker swimming against the NAFTA current," reported the *Fresno Bee*. The speaker's name: Donald Trump. Records of his prophetic 1993 NAFTA warning were unearthed in February 2016 by none other than that right-wing rag BuzzFeed.[24]

Despite the populists' best efforts, the Establishment got its way. In the House, 132 Republicans voted for NAFTA and 43 against. House Democrats voted 102 for NAFTA and 156 against it.[25] The Senate passed the trade deal 61–38, with 27 Democrats and 34 Republicans voting in favor of NAFTA.

At the December 8, 1993, signing ceremony, President Clinton made bold promises and heralded the dawn of a new "economic order" that would "remake the world." "In a few moments, I will sign the North American Free Trade Act into law," said Clinton. "NAFTA will tear down trade barriers between our three nations. It will create the world's largest trade zone and create 200,000 jobs in this country by 1995 alone. . . . When I affix my signature to the NAFTA legislation a few moments from now, I do so with this pledge: To the men and women of our country who were afraid of these changes and found in their opposition to NAFTA an expression of that fear . . . the gains from this agreement will be your gains, too."[26]

Clinton not only lied, he made a "pledge" to the American working class who opposed NAFTA that they would receive "gains."

They received pink slips instead.

The populists' NAFTA predictions proved painfully prescient. Between 1993 and 2013, the U.S. trade deficit with Mexico and Canada went from $17 billion to $177.2 billion.[27] Those figures aren't from some right-wing think tank or Donald Trump shill. Those are the findings of Robert E. Scott, founder of the progressive Economic Policy Institute (EPI), an organization that frequently and strongly condemns Trump.

The effects on American workers have been even more catastrophic. EPI data concluded that in just 10 years, NAFTA was responsible for displacing 851,700 American jobs. To put that in context, that's more people than live in Columbus, Ohio.[28] "All of the net jobs displaced were due to growing trade deficits with Mexico," stated the EPI. "Growing trade deficits and job displacement, especially between the United States and Mexico, were the result of a surge in outsourcing of production by U.S. and other foreign investors. The rise in outsourcing was fueled, in turn, by a surge in foreign direct investment into Mexico, which increased by more than 150 percent in the post-NAFTA period."[29]

The destruction of nearly one million American jobs and the implosion of American manufacturing—*that's* Bill Clinton's NAFTA legacy.

Now that Donald Trump is president and progressives are losing their collective minds, Democrats have suddenly discovered newfound support for NAFTA. *President Trump says it's a disaster, so it must be good!* they reason. A Gallup poll taken at the end of February 2017 found that Democrat support for NAFTA far outnumbers Republican support. Sixty-seven percent of Democrats now believe

NAFTA has been good for America, a huge leap from 2004 when only 39 percent of Democrats supported it. And all this despite the fact that by 2008, even Hillary Clinton and Barack Obama were calling for NAFTA to be renegotiated.

Whether President Trump can make good on his promises to renegotiate NAFTA and stanch the flow of American jobs to Mexico remains to be seen. The highly complex deal was negotiated a quarter-century ago and failed to take into account modern issues like digital trade and intellectual property rights. Renegotiating NAFTA will involve making sure that scores of variables tilt in America's favor. The good news is that Trump wisely selected Robert Lighthizer as his U.S. trade representative—President Reagan's deputy U.S. trade representative and one of our nation's smartest trade experts. And at Lighthizer's side as USTR general counsel is Stephen Vaughn, my brilliant former Skadden Arps colleague and one of my closest personal friends. These men are as good as it gets on trade and will serve our nation well. The other bright spot: it's encouraging to know that the only president who wisely foresaw NAFTA's fatal flaws way back in 1993 now occupies 1600 Pennsylvania Avenue.

1994–1996: BUBBA GETS SHELLACKED, POPULIST RESULTS ENSUE

When the 1994 midterm congressional races rolled around, Americans were fed up. Despite his promises of governing as a new kind of populist Democrat, Clinton had delivered an unpopular liberal agenda, tried to foist Hillarycare on the country, signed NAFTA into law, and had failed to "end welfare as we know it" like he had promised. The country was ripe for a wave election.

Leading the conservative charge would be the brilliant former college-history-professor-turned-congressional-backbencher Newt Gingrich. Newt's adherence to conservative principles—combined with his unrivaled intellectual firepower—made him Clinton's nemesis. He also understood populism's power. Even before entering Congress, as a history professor at West Georgia College, Gingrich kept a file in his office titled "Populism," where he would collect news articles about Americans whom Washington elites had failed. One headline read: "Why People Are Mad at Washington."[30] As James Pinkerton put it, "By 1989, [Gingrich] was the *de facto* leader of the House Republicans, and then, in 1994, he led a nationwide populist rebellion—the signature of which was the famous 'Contract with America.'"[31]

Six weeks before the 1994 midterm elections, Newt Gingrich introduced the Contract with America—a list of 10 bills Republicans promised to bring up for a floor vote if they took back Congress. Reagan biographer Lou Cannon said over half of the Contract included language from Ronald Reagan speeches.[32] The document contained popular proposals designed to shift government power back to the people through greater accountability, openness, and by placing limits on federal authority.

Making laws apply equally to members of Congress, auditing the Congress for waste, fraud, and abuse, placing term limits on committee chairmanships, introducing a three-fifths majority rule for tax hikes—the Contract with America's populist appeal and over 60 percent plus approval rating made it a winner.[33] Indeed, 367 GOP House candidates signed the Contract.[34] The House ended up passing all of the plan's proposals except for the constitutional amendment on term limits (which required a two-thirds vote).[35]

On the night of the 1994 midterm election, I cohosted a party at then-conservative David Brock's townhome in Georgetown (while Brock and I had appeared on the 1995 cover of *The New York Times Magazine* in an issue on young conservatives, Brock would later go on to become a leftist leader and create Media Matters). The party was a raucous affair, with great music and multiple TVs blasting the latest election returns. Everyone was there to celebrate what we knew was going to be a big night for conservatives.

Meanwhile, the scene over at the Clinton camp was dire. Top Clinton aide George Stephanopoulos said he "was in pain" and "more anxious than ever" about the election. When the results came in, voters had repudiated Clinton's liberal agenda:

Democrats everywhere were defeated, but not a single Republican incumbent running for governor, House, or Senate lost. The

Republicans won back the Senate, captured a majority of the governorships for the first time since 1970, and took control of the House for the first time since 1954. Our nemesis Newt Gingrich was now Speaker—two heartbeats away from the White House.[36]

It was an exciting time to be a young conservative professional in Washington, especially after the GOP takeover shocked the Establishment. I found that the best way to pop the Establishment's bubble of pomposity was through irreverent humor. One of the Clintons' favorite events was a gathering of power players and influencers called Renaissance Weekend, an elite confab that still exists today and bills itself as the "grand-daddy of ideas festivals." The whole thing struck me as a hubristic conclave of snobby know-it-alls and made me want to gag, so I decided to do something about it.

In response, lawyer Jay Lefkowitz and I cofounded our tongue-in-cheek counter-event—Dark Ages Weekend.

We held the first three-day gathering in 1994 over the New Year's holiday, and a few hundred conservatives attended. One of the highlights was when Judge Robert Bork got up and gave one of my favorite speeches ever with an address he cheekily titled "A Defense of the Dark Ages." He covered the historical innovations that occurred during the time period as only he could. By the end of his talk everyone was on their feet and clapping.

The following year, we upped the ante and sent out 3,000 invitations with a black dragon logo to conservatives and held the event at the Doral Golf Resort in Miami, complete with a "William the Conqueror Golf Tournament." Our steering committee included William Bennett, Arianna Huffington (before she became a leftist and the creator of the Huffington Post), Jeb Bush, and Armstrong Williams. Speaker Newt Gingrich was our keynote speaker, and panel discussions included topics like "Life After the Welfare State: What Replaces It?" and "Health Care: Can the Industry Heal Itself?" The whole thing was a blast and a way for conservatives to show we could laugh at ourselves while advancing serious ideas about limited government. Dinging the Establishment's self-important stuffiness made it extra sweet.

Beyond the fun, the two years between the midterm election and the 1996 presidential election also produced major conservative policy victories. After twice vetoing welfare reform legislation, and with his reelection chances now in jeopardy, the president was forced to support the reforms he'd abandoned. He would never survive a third veto politically, especially not after his populist 1992 campaign promise to "end welfare as we know it." On August 22, 1996, the president signed the Personal Responsibility and Work Opportunity Reconciliation Act of 1996. House majority leader Dick Armey said Clinton's decision to finally support welfare reform was reminiscent of the old saying, "When you're being run out of town, jump up front and act like it's a parade."[37] Indeed, Clinton's greatest successes occurred when conservatives dragged him back to his populist roots.

Progressives spread scare stories that the welfare reform act would spawn mass poverty and force children to live on the streets. "If, in 10 years' time, we find children sleeping on grates, picked up in the morning frozen, and ask, Why are they here, scavenging, awful to themselves, awful to one another, will anyone remember how it began?" said Democrat senator Daniel Patrick Moynihan.[38]

Instead of creating Generation *Les Misérables,* the law brought poverty rates for black children and single-parent homes to record lows, sent employment for unskilled single moms soaring, and slashed the welfare rolls by over 50 percent.[39] It was a strong populist achievement that empowered people to break free of government dependency and live independent lives.

The Republican Congress also passed and Clinton signed an immigration law toughening border enforcement and strengthening deportation for illegal aliens. The left hated it, which of course meant it was great for the American people. It broadened the list of reasons illegal aliens could be deported and made it harder for progressive judges to find loopholes to keep them in the country. It also placed important restrictions on legal immigration.

The GOP Congress pulling Clinton back toward commonsense conservative-populist positions redounded to his benefit. In 1996, Clinton sailed to reelection, beating Republican Bob Dole 379 electoral votes to 159. After the 1994 Democrat drubbing, Clinton seemed to have learned his lesson and supported some Republican proposals to break the cycle of welfare dependency and crack down on illegal immigration.

But as was his way, Clinton strayed in his second term in more ways than one. There was, of course, the Monica Lewinsky scandal that consumed much of his second term and led to his impeachment. But for American workers, his greatest sin—a globalist trade scheme even worse than NAFTA—was yet to come.

BUBBA'S SECOND ACT

During Bill Clinton's second term I worked as a political analyst for CBS *Evening News* (don't laugh). Needless to say, my politics didn't align with Dan Rather's. But most weekends the network featured my on-air commentaries, which I introduced and wrapped from the anchor desk. The job took me across the country and out of the dead space of Washington. In October 1997 I traveled to California near the U.S.-Mexican border to report on a Clinton effort to curb illegal immigration.

Operation Gatekeeper was implemented in 1994 with bipartisan support, under the direction of Clinton attorney general Janet Reno. It included the construction of a five-and-a-half-mile-long double border fence from the Pacific Ocean eastward. Congress also added money to double the number of border patrol agents and improve biometric scanning to detect repeat offenders and criminals at weak spots along the border. News flash: The fencing worked; it choked off the entry point for thousands of lawbreakers. Although critics note that it merely pushed the illegal crossings eastward.

Driving on the dusty border road with the chief officer from U.S. Border Patrol Chief Johnny Williams, I heard his story about the old days, pre-Gatekeeper, when illegal immigrants would swarm right past the San Ysidro checkpoint and into the United States. California governor Pete Wilson, who himself had taken a bold and popular stand against the explosion of illegal immigration, told me a federal focus on securing the southern border was long overdue. Wilson had supported proposals the people overwhelmingly supported, like

Proposition 187 to ban illegal aliens from using social services, Proposition 209 to prevent racial preferences in state hiring, and Proposition 227 to ensure English education in schools. The people were with him, but the elites labeled the measures "racist."

Yet whatever populist inclination Bill Clinton had toward immigration enforcement was diluted by the economic punch he delivered to the nation's gut during his second term. Indeed, he saved the best (worst) for last. If NAFTA had unleashed a flood of dangerous economic currents crashing into the American working class, his decision to pave the path for China's entry into the World Trade Organization (WTO) by giving it Permanent Normal Trade Relations (PNTR, now known as Most Favored Nation) status swelled into an outsourcing tidal wave. Millions of American manufacturing jobs were washed out to sea—the South China Sea, that is.

Like any good elitist, Bill Clinton heralded loudest the policies that hurt regular working people the most. In *My Life,* Clinton says he believes that "clearing the way for [China's] entry into the WTO" would "prove to be one of the most important foreign policy developments of my eight years."[40] Technically, that is a true statement. It is "one of the most important foreign policy developments" if you want to understand the destruction of American manufacturing. It is also "one of the most important foreign policy developments" for understanding how millions of U.S. manufacturing jobs were vaporized in record speed, even as China grew at a steroidal rate of muscular economic growth.

Let's start with the basics. The World Trade Organization was officially created during Bill Clinton's presidency in January 1995, but it had existed in other forms since 1948. On paper, the WTO claims its purpose is to act as a sort of "trade referee" between its 164 member nations. The WTO is supposed to help countries hammer out trade agreements, iron out legal contracts between nations seeking to buy and sell things to and from each other, and resolve disputes. So-called Most Favored Nation status means all WTO members agree to treat each other equally. If you lower tariffs for one country, you agree to extend the same tariff cut to all the other WTO members, as if they are all a "most favored" trading partner.

Clinton sold the China trade deal just as he'd sold NAFTA. He enlisted an all-star cast of globalist elites to help get the China trade bill through the Congress, including: Presidents Gerald Ford and Jimmy Carter, President George H. W. Bush's globalist alter ego James Baker, and President Nixon's brain trust Henry Kissinger.

In total, Clinton's behind-the-scenes jawboning resulted in over 100 face-to-face or group meetings with members of Congress and dozens more over the phone.[41]

He made sweeping promises more grand than those he had made with NAFTA. "Economically, this agreement is the equivalent of a one-way street," Clinton promised on March 8, 2000. "It requires China to open its markets—with a fifth of the world's population, potentially the biggest markets in the world—to both our products and services in unprecedented new ways. All we do is to agree to maintain the present access which China enjoys." It would be an economic dream come true, Clinton vowed. "We'll be able to export products without exporting jobs."[42]

"We do nothing," President Clinton said bluntly. We take and the Chinese give, he explained. "They have to lower tariffs. They open up telecommunications for investment. They allow us to sell cars made in America in China at much lower tariffs. They allow us to put our own distributorships over there. They allow us to put our own parts over there." He then doubled down on how beautiful and glorious America's New World Order would be. "This is a hundred-to-nothing deal for America when it comes to the economic consequences."[43]

All of Washington's usual poker players anted up and played their strongest hands. Deep-pocketed Establishment forces like the United States Chamber of Commerce and the Business Roundtable dropped their biggest-ever campaign for a bill at the time with a $10 million ad blitz—peanuts in comparison to the cash multinational corporations stood to gain in the form of outsourcing high-wage American jobs and gaining greater access to cheap Chinese labor and over one billion potential customers.[44]

Big Labor pushed back. "This is a betrayal of workers' interests," said the then-president of the United Steelworkers of America George

Becker. "This is about moving factories from the U.S. so they can export back here."[45]

Meanwhile, libertarians over at the Cato Institute were busy being, well, libertarians—rambling on about theoretical mumbo-jumbo while looking down their noses at the dum-dums who just didn't get the need to worship trade agreements. "It is primarily U.S. exporters who will benefit," declared Cato Institute senior fellow Doug Bandow. Furthermore, he said, "the silliest argument against" giving China permanent Most Favored Nation status "is that Chinese imports would overwhelm U.S. industry." Most Favored Nation status for China "would create far more export opportunities for American than Chinese concerns," the libertarian scholar explained.[46]

"If we vote for this, 10 years from now we will wonder why it was a hard fight," Clinton said. "And if the Congress votes against this, they'll be kicking themselves in the rear 10 years from now because America will be paying the price."[47]

Clinton's China trade campaign worked. On May 25, 2000, the Congress voted 237–197 to give China permanent Most Favored Nation status. Clinton's cheerleaders at *The New York Times* heralded the vote as a "stunning victory" and said the president considered it a "crowning foreign policy triumph."[48] Clinton took his victory lap using words that send a shiver up the spine today. "This is a good day for America. In 10 years from now we will look back on this day and be glad we did this," said Clinton. "We will see that we have given ourselves a chance to build the kind of future we want."

Seventeen years hence, it is difficult to overstate the economic destruction wrought by China's entry into the WTO and Congress and President Clinton's decision to grant the Chinese permanent Most Favored Nation status. A 2016 analysis published in the *Annual Review of Economics* concluded that between 1999 and 2011, America lost between 2 and 2.4 million jobs.[49] Others, like the left-leaning Economic Policy Institute, put the American jobs loss figures even higher at 3.2 million jobs, when calculated between the years 2001 and 2013.[50]

The brutal economic reality was a cruel reversal of Clinton's promises: all the gains were on the Chinese side, all the losses and devastation were America's. American manufacturing jobs were eviscerated. From 2001 to 2011, U.S. manufacturing jobs plunged from 17.1 million to 11.8 million.[51] That's a loss of 5.3 million manufacturing jobs, a figure that's nearly the population of the entire state of Minnesota.[52]

The narrowing of the trade deficit between the United States and China never materialized either. To the contrary, it exploded. In 2000, the annual trade in goods deficit with China stood at a towering $84 billion. After Clinton ushered China to the front of the line, the trade deficit more than *quadrupled* to a jaw-dropping $367 billion by 2015.[53] The year before America let China join the WTO (1999), the United States accounted for 25.78 percent of world GDP. By 2014, that figure had dropped to 22.43—the lowest it has been in government records going back to 1969, according to the Economic Research Service of the U.S. Department of Agriculture. In 1999, China's annual GDP was $1.094 trillion. In 2015, it was more than $11 trillion. In 1999, the U.S. national debt was $5.7 trillion (the good ol' days!). Today, after the big government globalist policies of the last several presidents, U.S. national debt stands at a mind-bending $20 trillion.[54]

HOW THE ELITES BLEW UP THE WORLD

Everything Bill Clinton, the global business elites, and both Republican and Democratic members of Congress said in support of giving China permanent Most Favored Nation Status turned out to be wrong and untrue. The numbers that should have gone down went up, and the numbers that should have gone up went down. And all those claims about greater trade with China sparking some sort of human rights "renaissance" of religious freedom and democracy? Tell that to the Christians who have seen their churches pushed underground, the crosses stripped from the rooftops, and their pastors summarily imprisoned. By almost any measure, the United States became weaker while China, our chief geopolitical adversary, grew stronger. This decline was not inevitable—certainly no major U.S. policymakers predicted it. Instead, it is the result of a series of foolish mistakes that have consistently undermined our position while making life easier for our rivals. NAFTA sent our jobs to Mexico, and facilitating China's rise shuttered American factories and incinerated millions of American jobs.

What the globalists don't understand—or don't care about—is that because of the enormous anti-American sentiment around the world, it's almost impossible to create a multinational organization where U.S. interests don't become compromised or harmed.

This was true of the United Nations, of NAFTA, of the WTO— and it would have been true of the Trans-Pacific Partnership (TPP) as well had President Trump not wisely killed its prospects. NATO may have advanced our interests during the Cold War—because so many elites in Western Europe were genuinely afraid of the Soviets. But those days are gone.

The best strategy for the United States is to preserve its own independence as much as possible—thus leaving ourselves free to pursue our own interests. Otherwise we will be stuck in international organizations where we will always be unloved and outvoted.

Again, remember how we got here. By the late 1980s, the United States stood on a pinnacle of success and prosperity unmatched by any country in history. The Reagan voters, thinking that their political problems had been solved, quit paying so much attention to life in DC—so the American political system was left to the Bushes, the Clintons, and their donors. And what they decided to do with all of the power and money bequeathed to them by Reagan was to create a New World Order.

Their plans, of course, depended on an all-powerful United States, which would solve everyone's problems. When there was a lack of jobs in Latin America, people from Latin America could simply move here and find work. When Asian companies built too much capacity for steel, automobiles—or anything, really—the United States would run massive trade deficits to buy up the surplus and keep Asian factories humming.

When Europeans wanted to take longer vacations, or spend more money on welfare programs, the United States would find the money and troops needed to protect Europe from its enemies. After all, we could afford it. And if the countries of the Middle East were stuck with flawed political systems, we would spend trillions of dollars—and thousands of lives—to give them better ones.

These trends continued for years under the leadership of both parties. As a result, the United States no longer has the money or the resources to do all of the tasks that the Clintons and the Bushes assigned to it. And so the New World Order is falling apart. China is throwing its weight around in Asia, while Russia does the same in Syria, because we are not strong enough to push back.

As we've seen, U.S. foreign policymakers on both sides of the aisle made a series of disastrous blunders. They believed that NAFTA would promote better relations in North America and reduce concerns over illegal immigration. They were wrong. Instead, illegal immigration from Mexico to the United States surged, while relations between all three NAFTA countries have generally deteriorated.

Leaders believed that the World Trade Organization would serve as a bastion of support for market economies, and would encourage countries like Japan to give up their mercantilist practices. They were wrong. Instead, the WTO has targeted the United States in an attempt to force us to change our laws to better suit their preferences.

The elites believed that facilitating the rise of China would lead to a freer and safer world. They were wrong. The relentless dictators in China are using their newfound wealth to consolidate their power, both inside China and around the world. If current trends continue, we will soon be driven from Asia, and a communist dictatorship will replace the United States as the world's largest economy.

The globalists believed that giving away our manufacturing base and welcoming illegal immigrants from around the world would lead to a happier and more prosperous America. They were wrong. The U.S. economy has performed so poorly that experts like Larry Summers now suggest we have entered a period of permanent "secular stagnation."[55] Meanwhile, U.S. politics are riven by the utter mistrust that many voters feel for the elites who govern them—and by the contempt many of those elites feel for voters.

History is not kind to fools, and the United States is paying an enormous price for throwing away the strategic advantages we enjoyed after the collapse of the Soviet Union. As President Reagan taught us, we have to be willing to say things the Establishment doesn't want to hear.

A final note: Immediately after Congress passed the China trade deal and President Bill Clinton began his victory lap, a governor issued a congratulatory statement. "Passage of this legislation will mean a stronger American economy, as well as more opportunity for liberty and freedom in China." His name: Texas governor George Walker Bush.

4.

ENDLESS WAR & SHAMNESTY

"W" Is for Waste

*We will be changing the regime of Iraq
for the good of the Iraqi people.*

—George W. Bush

My radio callers were in full panic mode.

I was hosting the 6:00 p.m. election night coverage on WABC in New York City. The date was Tuesday, November 2, 2004. Establishment Media had done what they always do: talk up the Democrat presidential candidate—in this case liberal Massachusetts senator John Kerry—using tones of triumphalism and inevitability to quash Republican hopes and turnout. As early as May 2004, political analysts like Chuck Todd had begun running stories with titles like "A Kerry Landslide?" wherein he explained to all us dolts that "it seems improbable that Bush will win big. More likely, it's going to be Kerry in a rout."[1]

By election night, my radio listeners were in a tizzy. Media exit polls dribbled out across the internet and elsewhere suggesting a big win for Kerry. An election postmortem determined that the 2004 exit polls were the most inaccurate out of any in the last five presidential contests.[2] But that realization wouldn't come until later. There, that night, all people were hearing were snippets of the fatally flawed exit poll results.

"Either the exit polls are completely wrong or George Bush loses," said Democrat strategist and FOX News analyst Susan Estrich.[3] Television anchors also ginned up a cloud of Republican doom. President George W. Bush "appeared subdued," said NBC News's David Gregory. Bush portrayed a "rare sense of doubt," reported ABC News's Terry Moran.[4]

On air, I chose calm over alarm. I told my radio listeners to hang on, breathe, and not to believe the media hype. Something was off and I knew it. I was getting inputs from several trusted sources; the statistical inconsistencies were too great to believe the early exit numbers bouncing through the echo chamber. When the votes were finally tabulated, the so-called "political experts" were, as usual, proven wrong. (Is there any profession where you can be so wrong so often and still be paid so much?) Bush garnered over 62 million votes and won the popular vote for the first time in 16 years (50.2 percent). It was an impressive victory with strong populist support—just as he enjoyed in 2000—and one Establishment Media had all but rendered impossible.

The next day I was reading *The Wall Street Journal* and saw my name mentioned in Peggy Noonan's *Journal* column. Amid the Election Night "flurry of worry," I had dashed off an email to Peggy telling her the exit polls were junk and not to be believed. I was so blurry-eyed the next morning I had all but forgotten about the email. Noonan, who had apparently been alternating between listening to me, Sean Hannity, and Rush Limbaugh throughout the day and night, reminded me of my email by graciously noting the exchange in her column:

> Oh, another last note. Tuesday I heard three radio talkers who refused to believe it was over when the ludicrous, and who knows but possibly quite mischievous, exit polls virtually declared a Kerry landslide yesterday afternoon. They are Rush Limbaugh, Sean Hannity, and Laura Ingraham. The last sent me an email that dismissed the numbers as elitist nonsense and propaganda. She is one tough girl and they are two tough men. Savor them too.[5]

I was happy George W. Bush was reelected and even happier that John Kerry and John "Silky Pony" Edwards lost. In August 2004,

President Bush's campaign team had asked me to serve as master of ceremonies for their 15,000-person Minneapolis rally at the Xcel Energy Center in St. Paul. I was glad to do so. A Republican president hadn't won the state of Minnesota since 1972, but I liked the fact that Bush wasn't about to concede it to Kerry. I helped prime the audience with a red meat, patriotic set-up for the main attraction. The place was packed, and when Bush finally drove into the arena aboard his campaign bus, the place went wild. "The other day, my opponent said he thought you could find the heart and soul of America in Hollywood," Bush told the crowd. "I think you can find it right here in this hall. I'm proud to be with the heart and soul of America tonight!"[6]

Sadly, President Bush's second term veered wildly off course and produced disastrous consequences for America, the Republican Party, and the conservative movement. A war-weary nation with a floundering economy soured on the president. Voters were impatient for policies that bolstered the home front, but instead Bush supported legislation that would have granted mass amnesty to millions of illegal immigrants. This served merely to divide his own base and pave the way for the election of the most radical president in American history.

"ENDING TYRANNY IN OUR WORLD"

The first year of George W. Bush's presidency started on solid populist ground with the first of two tax cuts (the second in 2003) reminiscent of Ronald Reagan's. On June 7, Bush signed into law the Economic Growth and Tax Reconciliation Act of 2001, a massive $1.35 trillion tax cut phased in over 10 years. The plan included an across-the-board tax cut, dropped the lowest tax rate from 15 percent to 10 percent, and reduced the top rate from 39.6 percent to 35 percent. It also provided tax relief for married couples, doubled the child tax credit, and saved the average family of four $1,825 annually.[7] These were real results that put money in people's pockets and allowed workers to keep more of what they earned. "Across-the-board tax relief does not happen very much in Washington, DC," said Bush. "In fact, since World War II, it has happened only twice: President Kennedy's tax cut in the '60s and President Reagan's tax cut in the '80s. And now it's happened for a third time, and it's about time."[8]

On social issues, Bush thoughtfully navigated the difficult ethical question of federal funding for embryonic stem cell research. Proponents argued the research would yield life-saving cures for people with diseases like Alzheimer's and Parkinson's. Opponents countered that taxpayers should not be forced to pay for research that destroys embryos (human life) and accelerated science down the path of human cloning. On August 9, President Bush delivered a nationally televised speech to announce his decision. "As a result of private research, more than 60 genetically diverse stem cell lines already exist," he said. "I have concluded that we should allow federal funds to be used for research on these existing stem cell lines, where the life and death decision has already been made." Bush said his policy would allow scientific advancements "without crossing a fundamental moral line" that would "encourage further destruction of human embryos that have at least the potential for life."[9] The president also said the government would spend $250 million on adult and animal stem cell research. While there were still critics on both sides, Bush's policy maintained a respect for human life while also allowing science to explore ways to save future lives. It was a morally prudent compromise most people could live with.

And then four weeks later, the world changed.

On September 11, 2001, 19 Islamic terrorists hijacked four airplanes and turned them into missiles to knock down the Twin Towers, crash into the Pentagon, and down a plane outside of Shanksville, Pennsylvania, killing in all nearly 3,000 people. The following month, the United States invaded Afghanistan, then 17 months later invaded Iraq. The nation and Congress rallied to both causes, with a few prominent exceptions in both politics and the media. I wholeheartedly supported both interventions, and believed Saddam Hussein had weapons of mass destruction. (The political WMD that blew up in the face of the Republican Party turned out to be faulty U.S. intelligence and a neocon crusade to "export democracy" to the Middle East.)

The post-Bush years have been a time of soul-searching and reflection for conservatives. Most of us stuck with the president and supported him for the first couple years of the Iraq War. But it was striking how Bush's policies were at odds with his populist campaign rhetoric.

Here's then-candidate Governor George W. Bush during the 2000 campaign:

- " . . . we can't be all things to all people in the world. . . ."[10]
- "I'm worried about over-committing our military around the world. I want to be judicious in its use."[11]
- " . . . we've got to be humble, and yet project strength in a way that promotes freedom."[12]
- "I think one way for us to end up being viewed as the ugly American is for us to go around the world saying, 'We do it this way. So should you.'"[13]
- "I don't think our troops ought to be used for what's called nation-building. I think our troops ought to be used to fight and win war."[14]
- "I think what we need to do is convince people who live in the lands they live in to build the nations. . . . Our military is meant to fight and win war. That's what it's meant to do. And when it gets overextended, morale drops."[15]

Then these from President Bush:

- "So it is the policy of the United States to seek and support the growth of democratic movements and institutions in every nation and culture, with the ultimate goal of ending tyranny in our world."[16]
- "We will be changing the regime of Iraq for the good of the Iraqi people."[17]
- "The survival of liberty in our land increasingly depends on the success of liberty in other lands. The best hope for peace in our world is the expansion of freedom in all the world."[18]
- "We must stand up for our security, and for the permanent rights and the hopes of mankind. By heritage and by choice, the United States of America will make that stand."[19]

- " . . . we will help you to build a new Iraq that is prosperous and free."[20]

President Bush's statements contained more than poetic sentiments, they represented a clarion call for the nation-building policies he once rejected as unwise and inappropriate. Moreover, Bush's call in his second inaugural address for "ending tyranny in our world," while a sweet notion, took us one step closer to becoming a reality version of *Team America: World Police*. So much for the "humble" foreign policy.

As for his promise to avoid costly nation-building, Bush later said, with his usual self-reflective profundity, "[A]fter 9/11, I changed my mind."[21]

In February 2006 I traveled to Iraq to see things firsthand. While in Baghdad with the army's 4th Infantry Division, I watched a young female lieutenant who had graduated from West Point in a meeting with a local mayor where she was being asked to play the roles of soldier, diplomat, and reconstruction coordinator simultaneously. She was a total professional, and I felt a sense of deep pride and gratitude for her impressive skills. At the same time, it was obvious to me that we were turning the world's deadliest fighting force into unwitting Peace Corps volunteers.

In hindsight, our military response to the Taliban in Afghanistan made sense given that 9/11 was planned there by Osama Bin Laden. But Iraq was an entirely different matter altogether. By the end of 2007, the country had turned against the war. The Gallup poll found that 60 percent of Americans thought the Iraq War was a mistake, but the Bush neocons wanted a surge and got it.[22] Today, we're still in Iraq, but with far fewer troops, and facing a new enemy—ISIS. To date, our Middle East adventures in Afghanistan and Iraq have cost taxpayers an estimated $4 trillion to $6 trillion with 6,757 American lives lost.[23]

Meanwhile, there were a few prominent Americans who opposed the war in Iraq on the principle that it wouldn't advance America's interests: columnists Patrick Buchanan, Robert Novak, and a certain Fifth Avenue billionaire with a populist instinct began to express serious doubts. Over a month before the Iraq invasion in March 2003, Fox Business anchor Neil Cavuto asked Donald Trump how much attention Bush should devote to the economy versus Iraq. "Well, I'm starting to think that people are much more focused now on the economy," said Trump. "Perhaps he shouldn't be doing it [Iraq] yet." He added: "The Iraqi situation is a problem, and I think the economy is a much bigger problem."[24] Less than a week into the Iraq invasion, Trump called the war "a mess."[25] Although it later became a point of contention between Trump and the liberal press, as FactCheck.org reported "[b]y 2004, Trump's opposition to the war was well documented."[26] He cited his preference for the money to be spent on the home front, and in a March 2004 *Esquire* interview posited: "Does anybody really believe that Iraq is going to be a wonderful democracy . . . ?"[27] Unlike the interventionists that dominated the GOP, Trump the populist saw storm clouds on the horizon. The American people, by the end of the Bush presidency, would catch up with him.

HARRIET MIERS SUPREME COURT FIASCO

After issues of war and peace, few decisions a president makes are as consequential as Supreme Court nominations. Populist conservatives believe that crucial in their quest to return power to the people is a federal judiciary that sees its role as limited under Article III of the Constitution. Federal judges enjoy life tenure, a fat pension, and have little accountability to the people beyond impeachment (which is rare). When they begin to operate as super-legislators, they harm the underpinnings of our representative democracy.

At various times during the 2000 campaign, Governor Bush invoked the names of Justices Antonin Scalia and Clarence Thomas as jurists whose philosophy he admired. During one of his fall debates with Al Gore, he told moderator Jim Lehrer: "I don't believe in liberal activist judges. I believe in—I believe in strict constructionists."[28] That sounded pretty good, but the proof is always in the pudding.

This is especially the case because Republican presidents have had a less than stellar record in selecting the type of judicial nominee Bush described. The list includes John Paul Stevens (Gerald Ford), Anthony

Kennedy (Ronald Reagan), Sandra Day O'Connor (Ronald Reagan), and David Souter (George H. W. Bush). As a law clerk for federal appellate Judge Ralph K. Winter Jr. and later for Supreme Court justice Clarence Thomas, I know firsthand the intelligence and personal fortitude necessary to interpret our laws and uphold the Constitution, while avoiding the temptation to rewrite them.

"The best approach is for President Bush to nominate an unquestionably solid judicial conservative," I wrote in 2003. "No one who waffles at the thought of a negative mention in *The Washington Post.* No one who believes the Constitution must 'evolve with the times.'" I also warned against Bush appointing someone solely on the basis of gender or ethnicity. "Nominating someone for purely political reasons—such as Alberto Gonzalez, White House Counsel, and a prominent Latino—would be a mistake of Souterian proportions."[29] It never occurred to me that I needed to warn against nominating a justice based on personal friendship and loyalty alone.

Yet on October 3, 2005, President George W. Bush nominated his longtime personal friend and political ally Harriet Miers to fill the seat of retiring justice Sandra Day O'Connor. This was a Texas pal who had worked for his 1994 governor's race and whom he had appointed to be head of the Texas Lottery Commission. (If that doesn't scream Supreme Court material, I don't know what does.) As soon as I learned the news, I knew we were headed for trouble. "This is a disaster!" I said to a conservative legal friend on the phone when the news broke. An hour later I began my radio show with the same line and was the first well-known conservative to oppose the nomination of the president for whom I had campaigned.

President Bush had put cronyism above qualifications. Personal loyalty over loyalty to the Constitution. This decision sparked one of the first major populist and conservative uprisings against the Bush administration. By all accounts Miers was a decent and loyal person. Beyond that, she was woefully wrong for the job by any serious standard.

Former Bush press secretary Tony Snow (who departed this earth far too young) appeared on my radio show in an attempt to change my mind on the Miers nomination. The interview didn't go well for him—the Bush folks seemed totally unprepared for the heat they were taking from the right for this decision. My radio listeners were initially in rebellion against me but later came around to see that I was right.

Miers did have her fans, however. Democrat senator Harry Reid praised her, saying, "I like Harriet Miers. . . . [S]he was a trailblazer for women as managing partner of a major Dallas law firm and as the first woman president of the Texas Bar Association." Reid added that she possessed "relevant non-judicial experience" that "would bring a different and useful perspective to the Court."[30] Just what conservative populists want in their nominee!

More significantly, Judge Robert Bork (a conservative hero) called the Miers nomination "a disaster on every level" and noted that she possessed "no experience with constitutional law whatsoever." The pick, said Bork, was a "slap in the face" to conservatives.[31] Charles Krauthammer called the Miers pick "scandalous." "There are 1,084,504 lawyers in the United States. What distinguishes Harriet Miers from any of them, other than her connection with the president?"[32]

I kept pounding away on air and pointed out that the stakes were too high for conservatives to gamble on an unqualified lawyer with no constitutional track record. The White House lined up people to call me, in order to put my mind at ease (and get me to ratchet down the decibel level). One of the people the Bush administration had call me was a former top lawyer in the White House counsel's office. He said he was confident Miers was a fine pick and would be loyal to Bush. I wasn't worried about loyalty to Bush; I wanted what all conservatives wanted: someone loyal to the Constitution. All the past Republican picks had been nice individuals, too. But many of those "nice people" turned out to be conservatives' worst nightmare once on the Supreme Court. A person's past judicial rulings and writings are the strongest predictor of their future decisions. Miers had neither. The little we did know about her was far from reassuring. "Legislating religion or morality we gave up on a long time ago," Harriet Miers said in a speech at an Executive Women of Dallas event.[33] In another, she said her views on abortion and school prayer had been shaped by the idea of "self-determination." How is that distinguishable from what Sonia Sotomayor would say today?

The White House finally realized it was fighting a losing battle.

On October 27, 2005, Harriet Miers withdrew her Supreme Court nomination. Bush and Harry Reid were unhappy.

"The radical right-wing of the Republican Party killed the Harriet Miers nomination," said Harry Reid. You're welcome.

As for Bush, he tried to cast us Miers critics as the elitists. "How could I name someone who did not run in elite legal circles?" he queried. "Harriet had not gone to an Ivy League law school."[34] It was a ludicrous charge raised by a guy who went to Yale and Harvard, and whose entire family lineage defines the term "political elite." Miers had gone to Southern Methodist, a good school. Her educational pedigree wasn't the issue—her lack of experience and writings on constitutional issues were. In the end, even Bush admitted that if he had it to do all over again, he "would not have thrown Harriet to the wolves of Washington."[35] A typically imperious reaction.

After the Miers saga, I never felt the same about the Bush administration. A true conservative doesn't pick his pal to sit on the highest Court of the land over literally hundreds of eminently more qualified individuals across America. Thankfully, the GOP grass roots summoned the courage to defy their own president and demand a course correction. Bush selected Samuel Alito, a man of extensive judicial experience, to replace Miers. On the day of his confirmation, my mind drifted back to Reagan's failed nomination of the brilliant Judge Robert Bork. If there had been talk radio, the Drudge Report, and Fox News in 1987, Bork might have survived—and the course of history changed. The Miers fight was populist activism at its best. But there were more battles ahead.

THE 2006–2007 "SHAMNESTY" WARS

This period of time was among the most alarming and hopeful of the Bush presidency. "Alarming" because never in my life had I seen political leaders display such contempt and indifference toward the people they claimed to represent; "hopeful" because working Americans mounted a brave and tireless uprising and crushed the Establishment's attempts to force immigration amnesty on the nation.

In March 2006, hundreds of thousands of pro-amnesty activists took to the streets of major cities to demonstrate in support of granting amnesty to millions of illegal aliens. As they marched, hundreds of activists waved Mexican flags and chanted "Mexico! Mexico!" Others held signs that said "You stole our homeland!" and "I'm in *my* homeland!" At Montebello High School in California, a group of 1,000 students engaged in a pro-amnesty class walkout, commandeered the school's flagpole, turned the American flag upside down in the distress position, and hoisted the Mexican national flag above it on the flagpole.[36] The image was an infuriating, if poignant, symbol. As even George W. Bush later conceded, the national spectacle of Mexican flag-waving and Reconquista-style rhetoric was an "in-your-face display that offended many Americans."[37]

Then on May 15, 2006, the president delivered the first-ever prime-time presidential address on immigration to build support for the Senate to pass a "comprehensive immigration bill." Bush lectured the country that deporting millions of illegal aliens was "neither wise nor realistic" (even though minutes prior he said his administration had rounded up and sent home six million illegal aliens over five years). He tossed out buzzwords about adding "surveillance systems" and "infrared cameras" to the border but said "the United States is not going to militarize the southern border."[38] The president then claimed he was against "amnesty" but for allowing millions of illegal aliens to become citizens, provided they filled out some paperwork and paid a fine. Or, as the rest of the sentient world calls it, "amnesty."

For good measure, he threw in a classic "Bushism"—an empty catchphrase used to sell globalist policies the people didn't want: "[E]very human being has dignity and value no matter what their citizenship papers say." *Okaaaay* . . . so what's your point exactly? There are seven billion people on the planet. Thankfully, most of them are good, decent, and wonderful souls. Bush's comment subtly hinted that populist opposition to amnesty was somehow motivated by small-minded bigotry and prejudice against these good people. But saying that "every human has dignity and value" is irrelevant to resolving the question of whether millions of people should be allowed to illegally enter another country, drain its resources, and defy its laws. It's also misleading to ascribe angelic intentions to all who enter America illegally. According to the Federal Bureau of Prisons, 21.8 percent of all federal prison inmates are not U.S. citizens—and that's just for federal prisons, which house only a portion of America's inmates.[39]

Here's another humdinger of a Bushism: "The longest and tallest fence in the world would not stop those determined to provide for their families." Okay, now seriously, where does one even begin to deconstruct this paragon of mawkishness? Not to be indelicate, but in point of fact, the "longest and tallest fence" in the world would likely stop most people determined to do just about anything. But the strawman argument that the only reason illegal immigrants enter America is to "provide for their families" is, while gushing with sentimentalism, just not accurate. Again, over one out of five people in America's federal prison system are noncitizens. Not all those who break the law to enter America are cherubs.

If anyone should know the facts about crime and illegal immigration, you would think it would be a former Texas governor like Bush. The Texas Department of Public Safety says that between June 1, 2011, and June 30, 2017, a staggering 225,000 criminal illegal aliens (redundant, I know, because technically *all* illegal aliens are criminals) were booked into Texas jails. The charges vary and include: 1,227 homicide charges; 71,374 assault charges; 17,291 burglary charges; 71,790 drug charges; 729 kidnapping charges; 41,814 theft charges; 46,526 obstructing police charges; 3,962 robbery charges; 6,450 sexual assault charges; and 9,016 weapons charges. "According to DPS criminal history records, those criminal charges have thus far resulted in over 269,000 convictions," says the Texas Department of Public Safety.[40]

And remember: that's just for Texas.

But why let "facts" and "logic" get in the way when you can instead use emotional language to sell a disastrous amnesty scheme that would destroy the nation?

The day after Bush's immigration speech to the nation, Vice President Dick Cheney appeared on Rush Limbaugh's radio show. Rush read Cheney an analysis by populist Republican senator Jeff Sessions that showed the "compromise" bill proposed by Senators Chuck Hagel and Mel Martinez would grant between 110 and 217 million immigrants legal status over the next 20 years. Cheney seemed surprised and unfamiliar with the report. "One of the big concerns here is the strain this would put on an already stretched social safety welfare net," Limbaugh told the vice president. "I don't think we can handle that financially and certainly not in an assimilation way."[41]

The Establishment didn't care. Ten days after Bush's speech, the Senate passed the Hagel-Martinez bill that the president said "conformed" to the comprehensive immigration plan he outlined in his speech. Thankfully, the bill bogged down in the House and couldn't get finished before the November 2006 midterm elections.[42] But the push for amnesty was far from dead.

After over three and a half years of George W. Bush's neocon Iraq adventure, a war-weary public repudiated the president's party at the polls. On November 7, 2006, Democrats swept the House (net +31 seats), Senate (net +6 seats), and a majority of the nation's governorships and legislatures. It was 1994 in reverse, and it gave the nation Speaker of the House Nancy Pelosi and Senate majority leader Harry Reid. The Gallup poll found that the number one issue on voters' minds was the Iraq War.[43] CBS News exit polls revealed only 41 percent of voters approved of the war. Of those who disapproved, a whopping four out of five voted for a Democrat House candidate.[44]

After a historic drubbing like that, one would think Bush and the GOP Establishment would reverse course and return to the populist agenda Americans were promised. But no. Bush said that while "many Americans voted last night to register their displeasure with the lack of progress" in Iraq, "we cannot accept defeat."[45]

Translation: it's my fault, but deal with it. Nothing's changing.

Other Republican wizards like John McCain claimed the historic loss wasn't so much a referendum on the war as a rebuke for failing to grant amnesty to illegal aliens. "We didn't pass immigration reform," said McCain. "We could have and should have."[46] The truth was exactly the reverse: the more Bush and the Establishment talked up their amnesty scheme, the less conservatives and populists supported Republicans. But instead of learning their lesson and relinquishing their amnesty dreams, Bush and the GOP Old Guard linked arms with Democrats. "Comprehensive immigration reform" is "an issue where I believe we can find some common ground with the Democrats," Bush said in a press conference the day after his party's historic defeat.[47]

Bush ignored the lesson of the election. Americans hadn't stayed home because Republicans were too conservative. They stayed home because Bush betrayed his populist promises. Instead of the Reagan-style foreign policy pragmatism he promised in 2000, Bush pursued interventionism and nation-building. On issues like illegal immigration, instead of pursuing conservative policies, Bush embraced Democratic ones. Worse, he declared war on his own populist base in a brazen attempt to impose amnesty on the people.

In 2007, with President George W. Bush's strong and vocal support, the House and Senate debated and considered a flurry of amnesty bills. They didn't call them "amnesty bills," of course. That would have been too honest and transparent. Instead, they marketed the plans using the poll-tested, focus-grouped "comprehensive immigration" nomenclature.

For Democrats, amnesty represented a way to turn millions of mostly poor, uneducated people into voters who could power Democrat victories for decades to come. For Bush and the Establishment, passing an amnesty bill would allow them to placate the GOP's corporatist, country club crowd. Guaranteeing a thriving pool of low-wage workers would drive labor costs down and corporate profits up. It would also reduce legal exposure. Corporate officers who hire illegal aliens can face civil and criminal charges. As *The Hill* noted, "calls for 'comprehensive immigration reform' would absolve the corporations of their civil and criminal liability for employing illegal aliens," a benefit that "is potentially worth billions in profits, billions in uncollected civil fines by the US Government, eliminating the potential of criminal charges of managers and the billions in criminal forfeiture under the RICO statutes."[48]

Yet noticeably missing from all this were the wishes of the people. Americans had seen their communities ravaged by an influx of illegal immigrants who took their jobs, strained city budgets and services, and added economic and human costs in the form of increased drugs, gang activity, and crime. Pro-amnesty forces claim illegal aliens are economically advantageous because they pay sales taxes and provide cheap labor that lowers the price of products. What they don't mention are the staggering costs illegal aliens impose on taxpayers for things like social services, law enforcement, and education that dwarf whatever marginal economic benefits pro-illegal immigration groups claim.[49]

President Bush was relentless in his advocacy for amnesty. He said his "first partner on immigration reform was President Vicente Fox of Mexico." Stop right there. Why would Bush's "first partner on immigration reform" be a Mexican president hostile to the American rule of law and the demands of a fed-up American working class?[50]

Bush also held an Oval Office meeting with lawmakers, including the late Democrat senator Ted Kennedy, a longtime advocate and sponsor of unrestricted mass migration to this country. The president pulled Kennedy aside to discuss resuscitating amnesty. "I think this is something we can get done," Bush told the liberal legend. "Let's prove the skeptics wrong again." Needless to say, Kennedy was game.

This collusion between the Establishment leaders of both parties had me doing three hours of straight immigration shows day after day by the spring of 2007. My listeners and legions of conservatives melted Capitol Hill phone lines and flooded congressional in-boxes demanding that their members of Congress oppose amnesty. As my old boss Ronald Reagan used to say, "When you can't make them see the light, make them feel the heat."[51] And boy did we ever.

Teddy Kennedy teamed up with Republican senators John McCain and Jon Kyl to establish a "path to citizenship" for illegals. The McCain-Kennedy amnesty sham placed the fate of our country on the line and everyone knew it. It was general quarters, all hands on deck. The president was incensed that we ungrateful populist rabble-rousers weren't willing to sit in silent obeisance while he and the nation's leaders conspired to subvert the rule of law, thwart the people's will, and further erode the American workforce.

Talk radio hosts and TV commentators warned of a "third world invasion and conquest of America," groused Bush in his memoir. "The mood on the airwaves affected the attitude in Washington. Congressmen pledged, 'We will not surrender America,' and suggested that supporters of reform 'wear a scarlet letter A for 'amnesty.' "[52] Bush added that when senators went home they were met with "angry constituents stirred up by the loud voices on radio and TV." Bush echoed Republican amnesty proponent Senator Lindsey Graham, who also complained about "the loud folks" opposing the open borders agenda—as though we were fomenting this populist outrage rather than reflecting and voicing it. We were "loud" because our country was being led by an out-of-touch elite who openly and brazenly defied the people's will. Nevertheless, Bush persisted and continued conspiring with Kennedy.

"At the height of the frenzy," says Bush, "I got a call from Ted Kennedy after I'd finished delivering a speech at the Naval War College in Newport, Rhode Island. 'Mr. President,' he said, 'you need to call Harry Reid and tell him to keep the Senate in session over the weekend.'" Bush says he honored Kennedy's request because "we believed we were within a vote or two of getting the comprehensive reform bill passed." Thankfully, the last-ditch effort failed and amnesty was dead (for the time being).

The Bushes believed that mass illegal immigration was an "act of love," as Jeb Bush infamously dubbed it. In his presidential memoir, *Decision Points,* George W. Bush reveals that one of his inspirations for "comprehensive immigration reform" (amnesty) was Paula, the sweet and hardworking Mexican housekeeper his parents hired when he was a teenager. Bush says she received a permanent work visa and "became like a second mother" to him and his siblings. Then, like a verbal habit he just couldn't shake, Bush punctuated his touching paragraph about Paula the housekeeper with a golden oldie Bushism: "Family values don't stop at the Rio Grande." (What does that even mean? Can't the same be said for just about anything at any time?)

I have no doubt that Paula was a wonderful, hardworking housekeeper. And what's not to like? According to Bush, she followed the rules and worked in the United States legally. But, as usual, Bush used emotional non sequiturs like flash-bang grenades to distract from the catastrophic effects of illegal immigration on American workers, communities, and taxpayers.

FROM POPULIST APPEAL TO GLOBALIST ZEAL

Thankfully, Bush's attempts to substitute gauzy language for logic failed. But top Bush administration officials had a long memory regarding those conservatives like myself who dared to oppose them. After the amnesty flop, the White House didn't even bother trying to defend its policies on conservative talk radio. In fact, the president never once appeared on my radio show, despite all that my listeners and I did to help get him elected. This was self-defeating, robbing himself of chances to defend his policies and advance his agenda directly to millions of Americans.

The pettiest of the Bush snubs occurred during the 2008 papal visit to the White House. Thousands of Catholics from the Washington, DC, area were invited for the occasion—but not I. Later I was told that my name was removed from the list of invitees by someone in the West Wing. Very Christian of them.

By the end of the president's second term, the country had grown tired of endless war in the Middle East. Then a cascade of crashing financial dominoes set off a chain reaction that resulted in one of the worst global financial crises in history. In September 2008, the subprime mortgage disaster culminated with the government seizing control of Fannie Mae and Freddie Mac while Lehman Brothers filed for bankruptcy protection. The highfliers on Wall Street had flown too high and leveraged themselves to the hilt in search of ever-bigger profits. On September 24, 2008, Bush delivered a chilling speech to announce to the nation the dire circumstances. "We're in the midst of a serious financial crisis," the president said. "Financial assets related to home mortgages have lost value during the housing decline, and the banks holding these assets have restricted credit. As a result, our entire economy is in danger."[53] The following week, the Congress passed and the president signed the Troubled Asset Relief Program (TARP), a $700 billion bank bailout.

As far as populists were concerned, this corporate welfare was proof positive that big government and big banks will always be in bed together. In announcing the bailout, Bush said he was a "strong believer in free enterprise" and that his "natural instinct is to oppose government intervention." He added: "I believe companies that make bad decisions should be allowed to go out of business." Taxpayers and their families had struggled, too—but no one bailed them out. Instead, their hard-earned dollars were used to dig Wall Street out of its self-imposed jam.

The bailouts became a flashpoint for populists on both the right and the left that would reverberate across the next decade of politics. For socialists like Bernie Sanders and the Occupy Wall Street (OWS) crowd, it was evidence that America needed to engage in radical redistribution of wealth and throw away its economic history. But for conservative populists, the financial crisis and the globalist policies that followed were proof that America had allowed the incestuous relationship between big business and big government to spiral out of control and rob the people of their power.

In the short run, however, eight years of George W. Bush had left Americans ready for a change. Bush's approval rating in January 2009 was an abysmal 22 percent. Americans were desperate to try a new approach.

The Bush years were tragic—for the party, for the conservative movement, and for the country. Bush's populist campaign promises got buried in the sands of Iraq. Instead of a prudent foreign policy rooted in realism, Bush launched a neocon crusade built on disastrously flawed intelligence to spread democracy around the globe. Trillions of dollars and thousands of lives later, conservatives were left with a simple question: how can the president ask Americans to defend the borders of other countries when he is unwilling to defend our own?

Bush's decision to aggressively pursue amnesty after his unpopular war had just cost Republicans the Congress was another insult to the millions of conservative-populists who had worked so hard to put him in power.

Because of Bush, conservatives lost everything.

We lost the House.

We lost the Senate.

And we lost the White House to the most far-left radical ever to step foot in the Oval Office.

One month before the nation went to the polls to choose George W. Bush's replacement, CNN's Wolf Blitzer asked Donald Trump to assess the Iraq War and Bush's performance.

"The war is a total disaster. It's a catastrophe, nothing less. It is such a shame that this took place," said Trump.

"Who do you blame?" Blitzer asked.

"Well there's only one person you can blame and that's our president," said Trump. "It's just very sad. I don't know if they're bad people. I don't know what's going on. I just know that they got us into a mess the likes of which this country has probably never seen. It's one of the great catastrophes of all time."

"How does the United States get out of this situation?" Blitzer asked.

"You know how they get out? They get out! That's how they get out. Declare victory and leave. This country is just going to get further bogged down. They're in a civil war over there, Wolf. There's nothing that we're going to be able to do with a civil war."

Blitzer asked Trump for his assessment of Washington.

"Look, everything in Washington has been a lie. Weapons of Mass Destruction—it was a total lie," said Trump. "Everything's a lie. It's all a big lie. . . . If the Democrats get their act together, they're going to have a big victory. . . ."[54]

For Trump, it was a rare moment of understatement.

5.

THE GREAT GOP UNIFIER

Barack Obama Unites Conservatives, Inspires the Tea Party

We are five days away from fundamentally
transforming the United States of America.
—BARACK OBAMA

Call me a party pooper, but I don't like conventions. You're either the kind of person who enjoys the sport of elbowing your way through a crowded room of people or you're not. I'm not. But when the organizers of the 2008 Conservative Political Action Conference (CPAC) asked me to introduce former Massachusetts governor Mitt Romney to the thousands gathered in Washington, DC, at the Omni Shoreham Hotel, I was delighted.

CPAC is the Woodstock of the right, a mix of young activists and conservative stalwarts who come to hear presentations by candidates and media stars. I had supported Romney, an old friend going back to his days as governor of Massachusetts, over the globalist moderate Senator John McCain. Unlike McCain, Romney was receptive to populist arguments on trade—especially regarding China. And although he was hardly an immigration hawk, Romney rejected the idea of granting blanket citizenship to illegal immigrants and had criticized the Bush amnesty deal.

When Romney and his entourage walked backstage where I was putting the final touches on my remarks, one of his aides pulled me aside and said, "The Governor needs to talk to you." As Romney walked toward me, I knew something was wrong—his face looked ashen. "Sorry to tell you so late, but I'm dropping out of the race here," he said. The room stopped. McCain, despite having come out ahead of Romney after Super Tuesday, was still wildly unpopular with conservative voters, especially the party's base. Convinced Romney had made a huge mistake, I was crestfallen. McCain would never beat the Democrats given the frustration and impatience of the American electorate over GOP business as usual.

Somehow, in the five minutes remaining, I hastily redrafted my speech to fit the occasion, delivered my remarks, and exited the stage feeling like I had just taken a roundhouse kick to the stomach.

Romney, as usual, struck a gracious note of gratitude.

"It's such an honor to be introduced by Laura Ingraham," said Romney through a nervous smile. "You know, we have all the fun. The people in our party, they're gorgeous, they're brilliant. Thanks to her and all of talk radio for what they do to keep the conservative movement strong and alive and vibrant. And I appreciate her generous introduction."

Then Mitt dropped the bomb.

"This isn't an easy decision. I hate to lose," he said. "I entered this race because I love America. And because I love America, in this time of war, I feel I have to now stand aside for our party and for our country."[1]

"No! No!" the audience yelled.

When he referenced John McCain, the crowd booed. I groaned.

Just the year before, things were looking up for Romney. He had won the CPAC straw poll, and six months earlier, he won the Ames (Iowa) Straw Poll (which I emceed; and which is now discontinued).

Over the course of the primary season, I had many conversations on and off the air with both Mitt Romney and his close confidantes, urging him to take a more populist stance on key issues such as trade and immigration. Part of my appeal focused on how he needed to differentiate himself from John McCain on the Iraq War. The nation didn't want to elect another Bush, and McCain was close to it. Romney seemed to get it—especially after he lost the Iowa caucuses to

Mike Huckabee and finished behind him in South Carolina. Romney needed to cap Huckabee's popularity among blue-collar conservative voters—in other words try to "out-populist him." He hit the former Arkansas governor's record on immigration hard in negative ads, including his policy on in-state tuition for illegal immigrants. But for Romney it was too little, too late.

Huckabee himself was stronger than Romney on the issues I cared about, and we also matched up on most social issues. In retrospect, I probably made a mistake in not supporting him. In addition to his strong pro-life stance, Huckabee opposed fast-track trade authority and globalist trade deals. But at the time, I thought Romney had the money, the name ID, and the credibility within the Establishment to pull off a win and beat whomever the Democrats offered up. Following its tried-and-failed pattern of presidential primogeniture, the GOP tapped the next elder statesman in line, John McCain, to run against the most dynamic, charismatic Democrat since JFK, Barack Hussein Obama.

Old versus new, the past versus the future, analog versus digital—the media script wrote itself. After eight long years of Bushism—filled with costly wars, an unpopular amnesty push, and a financial collapse—the last thing voters wanted was a pro-amnesty, pro-NAFTA moderate like McCain, who was a war hawk on foreign policy and a neophyte on economic policy. As McCain admitted, "the issue of economics is not something I've understood as well as I should."[2] Not surprisingly, Obama crushed McCain by over 9.5 million popular votes and 192 electoral votes (Obama's 365 to McCain's 173).

Several of us in the conservative movement warned throughout the 2008 election that Obama was the real deal, a true leftist radical. In February 2008, *Newsweek* ran a cover story called "There Will Be Blood: Why the Right Hates McCain," with a photo montage of prominent conservatives Rush Limbaugh, Sean Hannity, Ann Coulter, James Dobson, and myself. We were all in open rebellion against the McCain nomination because we knew where it would end up—in defeat. At the time, McCain was up six points over Huckabee, but had been trounced by him in the Kansas caucuses. The former preacher and Arkansas governor was comfortable with my talk radio audience—warm and engaging, a social conservative who believed blue-collar Americans were getting treated like dirt by a government that didn't give a damn. My radio audience was not enamored of the GOP front-runner and the feeling was probably mutual. "I don't even listen to Rush. I'm not a masochist," McCain sniffed to *Newsweek*. When asked if he would reach out to social conservative Focus on the Family founder James Dobson to find common ground, he said simply, "I know what it takes to unite a party."[3]

Meanwhile, another fellow who thought he could bring people together (and was actually good at it) was on the move. Barack Obama had been trained in the dark political arts by adherents of Saul Alinsky. But he cast himself as a populist everyman, even calling himself a "mutt," a little bit of everything. But like the Bushes and Clinton, Obama was a populist poseur with a radical bent who ended up governing as a globalist. Indeed, he had served alongside Weather Underground terrorist Bill Ayers on a Chicago board. Ayers and his wife, Bernardine Dohrn (who was also a Weather Underground member with a prison record), hosted a political gathering in their home with Obama when he ran for the Illinois state senate. And Obama considered the radical, anti-American Reverend Jeremiah Wright—a man who officiated Obama's wedding and baptized his daughters—his spiritual mentor.[4] Yet the full weight of these associations would have little impact on voters precisely because they received scant attention. The Obama team's razzle-dazzle marketing, knack for demonizing critics, and their eloquent candidate made Obama's run against McCain an electoral cakewalk.

A big part of the problem was McCain's disastrous decision to assure voters that Obama was harmless. During a McCain event in Minnesota, a voter voiced sincere concerns held by millions of conservatives: "My wife and I are expecting our first child, on April 2nd, next year," the voter said. "And frankly, we're scared. We're scared of an Obama presidency." McCain shook his head disapprovingly at the man's comments and rushed to Obama's defense. "I have to tell you, he is a decent person and a person that you do not have to be scared of as President of the United States," said McCain.

An elderly military veteran at the event also stood up. "We would like you to remain a true American hero. We want you to fight." Once again, McCain chastised his own voters. "I will fight, but we will be respectful," the candidate lectured. "I admire Senator Obama and his accomplishments and I will respect him. I want everyone to be respectful and let's make sure we are because that's the way politics should be conducted in America."[5]

The Republican crowd booed and howled at McCain's anemic responses. Voters understood that spouting politically correct bilge instead of hard-hitting facts about Obama's radicalism was a surefire formula for defeat. The McCain camp's hypersensitivity to charges of racism (the obligatory smear Democrats have hurled at every conservative since Barry Goldwater) belied what GOP voters already knew: Republican opposition to Obama had nothing to do with his race and everything to do with his progressive radicalism. McCain's unctuous comments only served to annoy and exasperate conservatives who were already fed up with the dictates of political correctness and the GOP Establishment's weak-kneed strategies.

One person who didn't boo McCain's comments was Obama's top hired gun and chief political strategist, David Axelrod. As Axelrod later wrote in his political memoir, "this one moment, when [McCain] stood up to the ugliness instead of feeding it, would be McCain's finest of the campaign."[6]

How touching. Imagine that—an act of political suicide by a Republican presidential candidate is christened an act of gallantry by a liberal operative from Chicagoland. Democrats and their Establishment Media allies prefer their GOP opponents polite, compliant, and cowed by identity politics. (Is it any wonder that after years of the GOP's wimpy obedience to politically correct pabulum conservatives finally went with a loud, politically incorrect New York brawler?)

Grassroots voters were shocked that for years Obama sat at the feet of his radical spiritual mentor Rev. Jeremiah Wright in Chicago. Wright's influence over Obama was so profound that he titled his memoir *The Audacity of Hope* after a line from one of Wright's sermons. Before McCain's defeat, the radioactive contents of Wright's sermons became public. "The government gives them the drugs, builds bigger prisons, passes a three-strike law and then wants us to sing 'God Bless America.' No, no, no, God damn America, that's in the Bible for killing innocent people! God damn America for treating our citizens as less than human! God damn America for as long as she acts like she is God and she is supreme!"[7]

In response, John McCain's ad man, Fred Davis, prepared a devastating 30-second television ad on the issue with the walkaway tagline: "Character matters, especially when no one is looking."[8] But it never ran. According to McCain's aides, the candidate decided "he did not want to touch" the Reverend Wright issue. His running mate, Sarah Palin, said she was forbidden from even mentioning Wright or his radical roots. Palin added: "The brainiacs in the GOP machine running John McCain's campaign at the time said that the media would eat us alive if we brought up these things."[9]

When the second presidential debate rolled around on October 7, McCain didn't even mention Ayers. In the closing weeks of the campaign, Sarah Palin tried to resurrect the Ayers controversy by referring to Obama "palling around with terrorists." But again, it was too little, too late. "That McCain waited so long to launch this line of attack helped us immeasurably," said Obama campaign manager David Plouffe. "Voters tend to treat attacks late in campaigns with a high degree of skepticism. 'If this is so important,' they asked, 'why is this the first time we are hearing about it seriously?' "[10]

In the end, neither the Jeremiah Wright nor Bill Ayers associations made a dent in the Obama campaign even though most of us hosts in conservative talk radio pounded them daily. It turned out that John McCain preferred to turn his anger on his own supporters rather than against his opponent. Instead of unloading on the untested senator from Chicago, McCain celebrated Obama's inherent goodness and lauded his nonexistent achievements.

I wanted to scream. Why bother even going through the formality of voting, with a GOP candidate this weak? With McCain's refusal to throw Obama to the mat, his doubling down on two unpopular wars, his inability to see Americans' desire for homeland security and investment, his unconvincing performance at the debates, and his obvious disdain for conservative media outlets, he didn't stand a chance. The result: America elected the most inexperienced, untested, and liberal president in U.S. history. (After a brain cancer diagnosis in

July 2017, McCain would disappoint and infuriate conservatives once again by casting the decisive vote to kill the repeal of Obamacare—he had voted *for* repeal just two years earlier. A favorite of the elite media and the most anti-populist politician in the GOP, McCain cemented his legacy with the left. Some maverick.)

One week before Obama's inauguration, President Bush worked with him to fill the bailout fund with the second half of the $700 billion TARP cash. "Acting at Barack Obama's behest, President George W. Bush on Monday asked Congress for the final $350 billion in the financial bailout fund, effectively ceding economic reins to the president-elect in an extraordinary display of transition teamwork," reported CBS News. For conservatives, it was an infuriating case of insult to injury. Not only had Republicans lost the White House, Bush was now working in tandem with Obama to further betray conservative principles.[11]

To his followers, Obama represented a messianic figure, who at times sounded like a left-wing populist. He was going to bring our troops home, focus on schools and health care, on good jobs for the downtrodden. Heck, back then he even claimed to support traditional marriage! (He even tried to con Pastor Rick Warren, in a nationally televised forum, that he favored traditional marriage, citing the Bible!)

Let's face it—Obama came across as cool, hip, and historic, while McCain appeared old, boring, and prehistoric. When Obama trounced the Arizona "maverick," the conservative post-mortems began almost immediately. The GOP base was down, but not out. In the midst of the political wreckage, populist forces were beginning to organize.

TEA PARTY UPRISING

After the GOP's crushing loss to Obama, many wondered whether conservatism was dead.[12] The Republican Establishment and its coterie of crackerjack consultants had run a sputtering campaign that failed to present a strong case for conservative ideas and to call out Obama's true agenda. With McCain's stubborn refusal to attack Obama, and his squishy consultants enabling him, the junior senator waltzed to victory.

Faced with the prospect of four to eight years of Obama, and with an ineffective and bumbling GOP Establishment still running things, everyday Americans decided to do something distinctly American: they took matters into their own hands and began to plot a revolution. Despite the damage to our nation, Obama's presidency served to unify conservatives and galvanize a powerful grassroots movement, a populist rebellion known as the Tea Party.

One of the sparks that set off the Tea Party inferno was Obama's cramdown of the ironically titled "American Recovery and Reinvestment Act." After Congress passed this $787 billion "stimulus bill," a blogger named Liberty Belle (Keli Carender) had had enough. In desperation, she organized a protest, quickly dubbed a "tea party," in Seattle.[13] On the day of the party, she dashed off the following note on her blog: "Make no mistake, the president will be signing that bill tomorrow; I have no illusions that he will actually listen to us. But, maybe, just maybe we can start a movement that will snowball across the nation and get people out of their homes, meeting each other and working together to redirect this country towards its truly radical founding principles of individual liberty and freedom. Maybe people will wake up slowly at first, and then quickly when they realize the urgency needed."

I celebrated this effort on the radio. Carender was doing exactly what I had called on citizens to do in my 2007 book, *Power to the People*—don't wait on others to solve your problems. I wrote that book during Bush's second term when I saw how the GOP Establishment had begun turning against its own conservative-populist base. My solution to the problem was to get involved locally, stir things up, and take the fight straight to the Establishment.

Two days after Carender's blog, on February 19, 2009, CNBC cut to analyst Rick Santelli on the floor of the Chicago Mercantile Exchange. He was critiquing Obama's mortgage bailout and the stimulus boondoggle (which the Congressional Budget Office later revised to $830 billion in actual cost).[14] Suddenly, in the middle of his analysis, on live television, Santelli turned to the traders on the floor all around him: "This is America. How many of you people want to pay for your neighbor's mortgage, that has an extra bathroom and can't pay their bills? Raise their hand." "Boo," the traders responded. "President Obama, are you listening?" Santelli, exasperated, yelled. "We're thinking of having a Chicago tea party in July. All you capitalists that want to show up at Lake Michigan, I'm going to start organizing!" Roars rang out all around him from the trading floor. A powerful, organic, grassroots movement was born.

Nancy Pelosi called this new political force "astro-turf by some of the wealthiest people in America."[15] "The Tea Party Movement: Deluded and Inspired by Billionaires" blared a headline in *The Guardian*. The theory on the left was that the evil billionaire Koch brothers, who had donated to groups that support the Tea Party, had secretly conspired and created the grassroots group. *New York* magazine asked David Koch about the left's conspiracy theory. "I've never been to a Tea Party event," he said. "No one representing the Tea Party has ever even approached me."[16]

For its part, the White House pretended they weren't even aware that there was anything called the Tea Party. During a White House briefing on February 9, 2010, Obama press secretary Robert Gibbs mocked the town-hall protests that the Tea Party had organized across America.

> QUESTION: How closely did the White House monitor the tea party convention this weekend? Do you have any reaction to it?
> ROBERT GIBBS: I didn't watch it at all. (smile)
> QUESTION: Do you see the Tea Party movement as a real political force this year?
> ROBERT GIBBS: Look it seems to be a very successful private enterprise. I would say that there appear to be fewer speech makers that are unemployed in this economy than what might have previously been reported.

The next day on radio, I suggested that Gibbs keep his day job and leave the comedy to the professionals.

Democrats were doing what McCain and the GOP Establishment had done in 2008—they were misconstruing, misrepresenting, ignoring, dismissing, and even ridiculing the views of regular, everyday Americans.

Believe me, I spoke at two large Tea Party events, including one in Richmond, Virginia. There was nothing "astro-turf" about them. Basically, the gatherings consisted of thousands of patriotic, politically aware Americans who believed the Obama administration was driving us off an economic cliff. They featured conservative speakers from a wide range of backgrounds who addressed issues ranging from government spending to Obamacare.

In December of 2009, I spoke at an event in Washington called the Code Red Rally to stop Obamacare. On a blustery cold day, we amassed a great crowd of Tea Partiers and others on the Senate side of the Capitol. When it was my turn to speak I said we should all stop pretending that the Obamacare debate was about "helping the uninsured" or "giving the people what they want." It was none of those things. "It's about amassing as much power in a central government as humanly possible," I said. "It's about wealth redistribution. It's social engineering at its absolute worst." (In other words, it was the old progressive dodge of statism packaged as populism.) "The American people must take this political system back from those who have hijacked it in one of the most abhorrent power grabs that we the voters have ever seen."[17] We came up short but in the middle of the day, in the busy run-up to Christmas, we turned out a great crowd—and my entire radio crew even had fleece jackets made for the occasion!

At all the Tea Party events I attended, I never saw the racism and hatred the media promised. Instead I saw a lot of American flags, a lot of baby strollers, and heard a lot of John Philip Sousa playing over loudspeakers. They also picked up after themselves, something so-called "environmentalist" protestors seldom do.

Soon, Tea Party members began organizing and attending town halls with their members of Congress. Everyday people, some who had never been all that politically active before, began showing up and holding elected officials to account for profligate government spending. The Founding Fathers would have been proud. The people put so much heat on the Establishment that some members of Congress refused to attend town halls with their own constituents because they knew they would be humiliated and held to account. "I had felt they would be pointless," said Democrat New York congressman Tim Bishop. "There is no point in meeting with my constituents [to] listen to them and have them listen to you if what is basically an unruly mob prevents you from having an intelligent conversation."[18] What a profile in courage!

Tea Partiers also held demonstrations and rallies to oppose oner-ous taxation. They had been just as offended by George W. Bush for the $700 billion TARP bailout during the subprime mortgage crisis as they were at Obama's $830 billion "stimulus" plan, automobile industry bailouts (which ended up losing taxpayers over $9 billion), Obamacare, and mass amnesty. Yes, they were conservative-popu-lists, but they held both Democrats and Republicans accountable.[19]

Not surprisingly, the left and their backers in the commentariat scrambled to kill the Tea Party in the crib by trashing its members as racists or worse. Politico warned of "the Tea Party's terrorist tactics."[20] The *New York Times*'s Joe Nocera alleged the Tea Party was "waging jihad on the American people" and had declared "war on America."[21] Former MSNBC host Keith Olbermann growled that "If racism is not the whole of the Tea Party, it is in its heart, along with blind hatred, a to-tal disinterest in the welfare of others. . . ."[22] (A swing and a miss by Mr. Baseball Expert.) CNN's Anderson Cooper and others began making vulgar references to a particular sex act. "It's hard to talk when you're tea-bagging," quipped Cooper.[23] To call it frat house humor would be an insult to the Greek system. *Washington Post* columnist Colbert King wrote a piece titled "The Tea Party Resurrects the Spirit of the Old Con-federacy."[24] No one ever accused progressives of being subtle.

When none of their charges stuck, they tried new tactics. Web-sites like www.crashtheteaparty.org sprung up to organize progres-sives to "act on behalf of the Tea Party in ways which exaggerate their least appealing qualities (misspelled protest signs, wild claims in TV interviews, etc.) to further distance them from mainstream America and damage the public's opinion of them."[25]

Not to be outdone, *The New York Times* was busy running Tea Party profiles that attempted to portray its membership as crazy doomsday preppers who may or may not be militia terrorists. "Some have gone so far as to stock up on ammunition, gold and survival food in anticipation of the worst," the *Times* reported in breathless tones. "A popular T-shirt at Tea Party rallies reads, 'Proud Right-Wing Extremist.'" Irony appears to be totally lost on these people. The article then turned to a recent Department of Homeland Security report "warning that recession and the election of the nation's first black president 'present unique drivers for right wing radicalization.'" The *Times* helped spread the Obama administration's fake news further by citing its finding that "Historically, domestic right wing extremists have feared, predicted and anticipated a cataclysmic economic collapse in the United States" based on "antigovernment conspiracy theories."[26] Worse, they singled out American veterans as likely sources for terrorist radicalization. The strategy by Obama and his servants in the Establishment Media was clear: use the hyperbolic DHS "report" to destroy the reputations of Tea Party members by portraying them as crazy, paranoid, dangerous, racist, domestic terrorists. It was a classic case of psychological projection—promoting a stereotype that applied to the radical members on the left rather than everyday Americans showing up to wave American flags and signs opposing big government.

The left's full-scale war against the Tea Party was good in one respect: it was proof positive that Democrats feared its power. In trying to define the movement as a radical and racist force, progressives unwittingly revealed themselves to be the real radicals. Millions of working-class Americans gathering peaceably to voice their desire to see the nation's laws obeyed, fiscal discipline restored, and individual freedoms protected wasn't radical. To the contrary, such views are inherently American—principles our Founders instantiated in the Constitution. "We the people" tell the government what it can do, not the other way around.

The left isn't stupid; they know all that. They also know that populist uprisings like the Tea Party imperil Democrats' electoral odds and produce wave elections. That's why progressives raced to deploy their creaky strategy of smearing conservatives as bigots and homegrown terrorists, or as tools of the nefarious Koch brothers.

Months before the November 2010 midterm elections, I appeared on *The Today Show* with Matt Lauer to challenge the left's Tea Party calumnies head-on. At the time, Democrats had been targeting Tea Party favorite Sarah Palin. A Palin Super PAC social media graphic used surveyor symbols on a congressional district map to denote hotly contested races in the upcoming midterm elections. Democrats said the survey symbols looked like crosshairs. In progressives' fevered imaginations, this, of course, meant Palin was calling for the assassination of Democrats. The following year, progressives would dredge up the episode in a cynical attempt to blame Palin for the shooting of Democrat congresswoman Gabby Giffords.

Right before my segment with Lauer he ran a news story by now-retired NBC reporter George Lewis dishonestly linking Palin and the Tea Party to threats of violence and vandalism. Lauer and I went live immediately after the segment. I was in no mood to play NBC's games and immediately launched into some on-the-spot fact-checking.

LAUER: Alright George Lewis in Arizona, this morning. George, as always, thanks very much. Laura Ingraham is a Fox News contributor and a radio talk show host. Hi Laura, good to see you.

ME: Hey, Matt. Can I just say something? George Lewis' report— and I love George Lewis, I think he does a great job. How do you go from Sarah Palin giving a speech to saying, 'did she rile up the people too much' and then talk about death threats? I think that kind of reporting really is what drives people crazy about the dinosaur media.

Matt seemed rattled and a little taken aback.

LAUER: Well, there have been some people who say that, that some of her, her comments and, and some of her graphics that she's used over the last couple of weeks have, have, perhaps, incited some people. And maybe . . .

ME: Well yeah, I know they say that.

LAUER: —and maybe misrepresented her thoughts. She cleared it up herself. So, why wouldn't you connect the two?

ME: Yeah well, well why wouldn't I connect the two? For the same reason that the media didn't connect the film *The Assassination of George Bush* to any, any threats against the President. Look, free speech is supposed to be alive and well in the United States of America. Condemning violence, condemning vandalism, absolutely. We all do. But to say that Sarah Palin and the Tea Party movement is responsible for vandalism or threats is just a way to dismiss the American people and their dissatisfaction with this health care bill.

Matt apparently didn't like my answer; he quickly shifted the discussion elsewhere. Toward the end of the segment, however, he circled back around to the issue to see if I'd bite.

LAUER: When you look at what's going on right now, the vitriol, the comments, the intimidation, vand-, and I'm not talking about from one side. It's happening both directions. Vandalism, threats to violence. Can you compare it to any other time in your experience?

ME: Well I think that what we're seeing now is that the people feel like they, the people in Congress don't have their consent to govern them. They keep doing things that are incredibly unpopular. And so when that happens, folks get angry. And there's gonna be freaks in every movement, Matt. I mean we have the anti-WTO protestors throwing stuff. We have Code Pink camping out at George Bush's ranch during his time. We have people on, frankly, your cable channel saying really hateful things about conservative commentators and politicians. And I say more speech not less, but no vandalism. No threats.

For the next several months leading up to the election I appeared on Fox News and elsewhere to defend the Tea Party. I supported their general mission to reduce taxes, reduce the debt, and reduce spending. They wanted to end the bailouts and the crony capitalism that rips off taxpayers to reward the well-connected. There was an earnestness and moral component to this movement that drove the left nuts, and that sent them into a frenzied attempt to ridicule, humiliate, and dehumanize Tea Partiers. The Democrats and their media allies fell into their familiar pattern of avoiding a debate on the issues—refusing to engage their opponents on the merits—and instead decided to make it personal. But their demonization of the millions of voters who love their country only served to further energize the Tea Party.

Ever since Richard Nixon attacked big media for their elitist attitudes and coverage, populists had viewed the press suspiciously. But during the Obama years, Establishment Media were now maliciously maligning average everyday working people whose only crime was wanting a government that returned power to the people. If you want to understand why Trump's war against big media has been so successful, just look at the way the press treated the citizen patriots during this period.

Nevertheless, Tea Partiers wore the slings and arrows as badges of courage and soldiered on. Their adherents have "a sour, narrow-minded defensiveness against any possible threat of income redistribution," wrote Steve Fraser and Joshua Freeman in Salon.[27] New York Times columnist Charles Blow pondered the question of just how racist the Tea Party was, describing it as "a Frankenstein movement."[28] As one Tea Partier's rally sign put it, "I may be a redneck, but I know how to balance a checkbook." Others drew solace from the sense of community fostered at rallies. "This is really encouraging," one woman told The Washington Post at a Tea Party event. "In Portland, Oregon, where we're from, we feel like we are a little minority. It's nice to know we are part of something bigger."[29]

As Election Day neared, campaign chroniclers Mark Halperin and John Heilemann observed that "the more Obama learned about the Tea Party candidates poised to win in November, the greater his incredulity—and disgust." Obama turned to one of his aides and said, "If people vote for this [the Tea Party], they deserve it."[30] This was the same condescending attitude he had expressed in April 2008 when he described small-town Pennsylvania.

> You go into these small towns in Pennsylvania and, like a lot of small towns in the Midwest, the jobs have been gone now for 25 years and nothing's replaced them. And they fell through the Clinton administration, and the Bush administration, and each

successive administration has said that somehow these communities are gonna regenerate and they have not.

And *it's not surprising then they get bitter, they cling to guns or religion or antipathy toward people who aren't like them or anti-immigrant sentiment or anti-trade sentiment as a way to explain their frustrations.*[31] (italics added)

Obviously, the presidency hadn't taught him much.

On Tuesday, November 2, 2010, Tea Party patriots stormed the voting booths and repudiated Obama at the polls by delivering Republicans the biggest landslide victory by either party since 1948. In the Senate, Republicans scored a net gain of six seats. In the House, the GOP picked up a jaw-dropping 63 seats, more than enough to replace Speaker of the House Nancy Pelosi. Just as impressive were Republicans' gains at the state level. There, the GOP added six governorships and a whopping 680 seats in state legislatures.

In a rare moment of honesty, Obama perhaps summed up the sea-change election best: he and Democrats had received a "shellacking."

ROMNEY'S CAUTIOUS RUN

The 2010 Tea Party–led Republican landslide portended good things for GOP chances in the 2012 presidential election. The Republican primary pitted Establishment favorite Mitt Romney against populist insurgent Pennsylvania senator Rick Santorum, with former Speaker of the House Newt Gingrich and libertarian Texas congressman Ron Paul in tow.

Picking up where populist Mike Huckabee left off in the 2008 Republican primary, Santorum branded himself a "blue-collar conservative" throughout the primary season—and found more success. He said his campaign was powered by "the same people that President Obama talked about who cling to their guns and their Bibles—thank God they do."[32] In addition to calls to reduce the size of government, Santorum also argued for a pro-manufacturing agenda that would end corporate income taxes on manufacturers. Donning a signature red sweater-vest, Santorum managed to rack up wins in 11 states, including Minnesota, Missouri, Alabama, and Mississippi. With a tiny fraction of the campaign war chest of Romney, he relied on family and friends to help his dedicated volunteers.

Few took Rick Santorum seriously. He was ridiculed for his Christian values and dismissed by many of the same people on the right and left who would laugh off Donald Trump four years later. These self-appointed political soothsayers should have spent more time examining why Santorum performed so well when the traditional campaign deck was stacked against him. The "experts" should have taken notice of Romney's razor-thin victory over Santorum in Ohio and small victory over him in Michigan, despite the hometown advantage. Both states were receptive to Santorum's tough trade message since both had been adversely affected by decades of globalization.

It wasn't difficult to see where this was going—without Santorum and Newt Gingrich forming an alliance against Romney, there was no way they'd overcome his money advantage. (And even then it would have been a stretch.) On the day before the Iowa caucuses, the former House Speaker appeared on my radio show, and I floated the idea of a Gingrich-Santorum coalition to stop Romney:

> ME: Can you see a scenario under which the two of you would align together to try to defeat the Establishment candidate Mitt Romney?
>
> GINGRICH: Absolutely, of course. Rick and I—you know, we have a 20-year friendship. We were both rebels. We both came into this business as reformers. And the thing that's interesting is if you take the votes that you add from [Rick] Perry and [Michele] Bachmann, you begin to see the size of the conservative vote compared to Romney. But if you take, you know, Santorum and Perry and Bachmann and Gingrich, you get some sense of what a small minority Romney really represents.[33]

The national media picked up on the idea, so a few days later, to keep the momentum going, I asked Santorum the same question. But he proceeded to throw a bathtub of cold water on the coalition concept: "Campaigns aren't about alliances, campaigns are about ideas. . . . I believe that the conservative movement will align behind us. It hasn't done that yet."[34]

It never did. Despite Santorum's impressive strength against Romney, the conservative vote remained splintered—some opted for Gingrich and still others for libertarian Ron Paul. While there are inherent tensions between libertarians and populists over things like trade agreements and immigration, the two can and have coexisted within the same coalition, such as during the Reagan Revolution. But the simple fact is that even when libertarians run their own presidential candidates on a libertarian ticket, like they did with Gary Johnson in 2016, it doesn't tend to affect Republicans.

Had Santorum and Gingrich combined forces they might have been able to win key battleground states, and pull off an upset of the more Establishment-friendly Romney. It was very frustrating to watch because I knew how it would end.

As I mentioned at the beginning of this chapter, I've always liked Mitt Romney. His smarts and business savvy impress me, and I consider him to be a genuinely good and decent family man. I also believed that the time might be right for his political star to finally rise on the national stage. The failed "stimulus," 8 percent unemployment, sky-rocketing health care costs, the $2.6 trillion Obamacare disaster, an explosion of the nation's debt, Benghazi—Obama's first-term failures were piled sky-high. The moment was ripe for a referendum on his abysmal four years in office. If the GOP candidate ran a strong campaign and laid out a conservative agenda for the future, he could win.

That did not happen. I think there are three main reasons why Romney lost. First, I believe he was badly served by his expensive team of Establishment consultants. This, mind you, was the same group of geniuses who produced the massive "fail whale" known as Project ORCA, a digital turnout and poll-watching "app" that Team Romney heralded as a technological miracle that was "unprecedented" and would help "win the 2012 presidential election."[35] It was precisely the kind of slick, expensive, mumbo-jumbo product the Consultant Class loves to pitch to nervous candidates and their donors seeking an electoral edge.

ORCA was the Romney campaign's attempt to shrink the data gap between them and the Obama campaign's impressive data mining operation, Project Narwhal. ORCA wasn't even an acronym; the Romney whiz kids named it that because the only known predator to a Narwhal is an Orca killer whale. The only problem was, this ORCA was toothless—heck, it couldn't even swim!

The plan on paper was that 37,000 Romney volunteers were supposed to use the get-out-the-vote app to track voters on Election Day and send alerts and reminders to those who hadn't voted yet.

The night before Election Day (nothing like the last minute!), the 37,000 volunteers finally received a 60-page instruction manual (why not 70 pages?) emailed in .pdf form explaining how to use ORCA. "They expected 75–80 year old veteran volunteers to print out 60+ pages on their home computers? The night before election day?" asked John Ekdahl, a volunteer and popular blogger known as Ace of Spades.[36] He says the Romney campaign didn't turn ORCA on until 6:00 a.m., "so people couldn't properly familiarize themselves with how it worked on their personal phone beforehand." Volunteers then experienced system crashes, malfunctioning usernames and passwords, and an unresponsive telephone help line.[37]

There was also this inexplicable fact: the Romney consultants never beta-tested Project ORCA to fix the tech bugs before launching it on Election Day.[38]

"The end result was that 30,000+ of the most active and fired-up volunteers were wandering around confused and frustrated when they could have been doing anything else to help," said Ekdahl. "Like driving people to the polls, phone-banking, walking door-to-door, etc."[39] After the election, Romney consultants—eager to protect their next paydays—did their best to minimize Project ORCA's importance and suggested it wasn't the humiliating disaster everyone said it was.

Breitbart senior editor Joel Pollak crunched the numbers and found that had ORCA volunteers instead just brought 20 voters to the polls in key states, "Romney would have won the election. . . . There was, in fact, massive suppression of the Republican vote—by the Romney campaign, through the diversion of nearly 40,000 volunteers to a failing computer program. There was no Plan B; there was only confusion, and silence."[40]

Still, elections are ultimately won by candidates, not computers. A second reason Romney lost was because rather than defining himself as the champion of everyday Americans who felt estranged by both parties, he allowed himself to be victimized by the Democrats' smart and cynical use of identity politics.

Enter what the Obama campaign branded "the war on women."

Democrats created a star in Sandra Fluke, the Georgetown University Law School student who, in late February 2012, was invited to appear at an "unofficial hearing" by House Speaker Nancy Pelosi to testify before Congress about her need for free contraceptives at the Jesuit institution.

Many religious institutions believed that Obamacare's "contraceptive mandate" violated their religious liberty. Fluke was plucked out of obscurity to make the Republicans look mean, uncaring, and hostile to the needs and desires of poor innocent women like Fluke. She claimed some of her fellow students spent $1,000 a year on contraception. (Why it is our obligation to subsidize their sex life is beyond me.) After Fluke's political performance on Capitol Hill, Rush Limbaugh went on a rip-roaring rant about the stunt, and used the words "slut" and "prostitute" to refer to her. He initially doubled-down on his comments, smashing back at his critics' "phony" outrage, adding: "Well, what would you call someone who wants us to pay for her to have sex? What would you call that woman? You'd call 'em a slut, a prostitute or whatever."

Media Matters, NOW, and a bevy of irate Democratic congresswomen fanned the flame into a firestorm. Activist groups targeted Rush's advertisers for boycotts, and basically tried to use the incident to run him off the airwaves. President Obama took time out of his busy schedule to call Fluke personally. Rush later apologized to Fluke "for the insulting word choices." But damage was done to radio advertising across the board. If the left could knock Rush back and hurt "the people's medium" of conservative talk radio with the "war on women" theme, they knew they could keep the drumbeat going all the way to Election Day. If the Republicans' favorite radio host has such little regard for women, the Republicans must be guilty, too. The exploitation of the incident was both predictable and disgusting—the last thing the GOP needed was to give away female votes to Barack Obama.

More trouble was stirred up on this issue when two GOP Senate candidates, Missouri Rep. Todd Akin and Indiana state treasurer Richard Mourdock, both made what can only be described as cringe-inducing comments about abortion during the campaign. Akin tried to explain why he opposes abortion in all cases—even rape: "It seems to me, first of all, from what I understand from doctors, that's really rare. If it's a legitimate rape, the female body has ways to try to shut that whole thing down."[41] Mourdock's gem? At an October debate against his Indiana opponent Rep. Joe Donnelly, he also tried to explain why he favored life instead of abortion in cases of rape, arguing that "even when life begins in that horrible situation of rape, that is something that God intended to happen."[42] When pressed to distance himself from Mourdock, Romney said he "disagreed" with his comments, but didn't pull his endorsement. Nor did Romney demand an ad be taken off the airwaves in which he appeared in support of the candidate.

The lovelies at *The Atlantic* took great joy in the moment with a piece titled: "Richard Mourdock, Mitt Romney, and the GOP Defense of Coerced Mating."[43] An ABC News headline read: "Richard Mourdock Rape Comment Puts Romney on Defensive." You can almost see the editors high-fiving one another for landing "rape" and "Romney" in such close proximity in the headline.

In the end, Obama beat Romney among women by 11 percentage points (McCain lost women to Obama by 13 points). Among single women, Obama blew Romney out by winning 67 percent of the vote compared to Romney's 33 percent.[44]

The lesson in all this for conservatives is: fielding bad candidates affects the rest of the field. The gender gap is nothing new. Conservatives can begin narrowing it—smashing through the left's phony narrative frames—by speaking to women voters in ways that are personally relevant. Economic and physical safety for women and their families should be key messages aimed at female voters.

I had taken to the radio and made waves by blasting Romney's consultants for what I saw as a campaign whose message and focus had veered dangerously off course.

"If you can't beat Barack Obama with this record, then shut down the party," I said. "Shut it down. Start new, with new people. Because this is a gimme election, or at least it should be." I was disgusted by the "millions and millions and millions of dollars that are paid to these political consultants election after election." I pointed out that we hire people who have lost past elections to run future ones. That made no sense to me. Why hire people with proven track records of crafting messages that fall flat and fail to connect with ordinary people?

I felt that Romney had been ill-served by the GOP hucksters with whom he had surrounded himself. His chief media adviser, Eric Fehrnstrom and campaign chief Stuart Stevens were total disasters. Fehrnstrom was the communications maestro who used the phrase "Etch A Sketch" in a CNN interview during the primary to describe how Romney would pivot into the general election. "Everything changes," Fehrnstrom said. "It's almost like an Etch A Sketch. You can kind of shake it up and restart all over again."[45] An avalanche of mocking tweets and memes quickly ensued. Fehrnstrom handed Romney's critics and opponents a visual metaphor to portray him as a wishy-washy candidate whose principles and convictions were as permanent as an Etch A Sketch doodle. Best of all, they didn't even have to pay Fehrnstrom his consulting fee. He'd given away the idea for free—to the detriment of his own candidate.

Stuart Stevens—who would later become a die-hard Never-Trumper—is reportedly the man behind Romney's flimsy and unpersuasive campaign strategy.[46] He had worked on the successful Bush 2000 campaign, and thus was considered "an expert." As the *Wall Street Journal*'s Kimberly Strassel put it: "In the la-la land where adviser Stuart Stevens presides, Mr. Romney wins by never saying a single thing, ever, that might rock a single boat, ever. Just keep the focus on Mr. Obama. After all, no president has ever won with an economy like this. One problem: Mr. Obama is winning."[47] I was glad to see others ringing the alarm bells. Conservatives needed to do their part to jolt Romney's campaign into undergoing a course correction before voter sentiments calcified.

Then, one week after my on-air comments, a videotape emerged of Romney speaking at what he thought was a private fund-raiser at a Boca Raton mansion. What later became known as the "47 percent" flap would be the third factor that doomed the Romney candidacy. Obama deftly fanned it into a firestorm.

On the surreptitiously recorded video, Romney was heard saying:

> There are 47 percent of the people who will vote for the president no matter what. All right, there are 47 percent who are with him, who are dependent upon government, who believe that they are victims, who believe that government has a responsibility to care for them, who believe that they are entitled to health care, to food, to housing, to you name it. . . . These are people who pay no income tax; 47 percent of Americans pay no income tax. So our message of low taxes doesn't connect. And he'll be out there talking about tax cuts for the rich. I mean, that's what they sell every four years. And so my job is not to worry about those people. I'll never convince them that they should take personal responsibility and care for their lives. What I have to do is convince the 5 to 10 percent in the center that are independents, that are thoughtful, that look at voting one way or the other depending upon in some cases emotion, whether they like the guy or not, what it looks like.[48]

Unbeknownst to Romney or his consultants, a bartender named Scott Prouty had secretly recorded his remarks. Initially, Prouty anonymously posted a different snippet of the video online. James Carter IV, the grandson of President Jimmy Carter, saw the video, tracked down its source, obtained the full version, and handed it off to progressive *Mother Jones* Washington bureau chief David Corn.[49] When *Mother Jones* released the hidden video on September 17, 2012, the story immediately engulfed national media and became the lasting and dominant frame to communicate how Romney's mega wealth and aristocratic roots had made him loathe, not love, the working-class people whose votes he sought to win. The video torpedoed any hope Republicans had of igniting the populist spirit that had powered Reagan and George W. Bush to their two-term victories.

Contrary to what many have contended, New Jersey governor Chris Christie's embrace of Barack Obama post–Hurricane Sandy did not cost Mitt Romney the election. Christie was dealing with one of the worst natural disasters to ever befall his state. Was he supposed to push Obama away when he came in for a hug? Or tell the president to stay home when the state was in such distress? The truth is: Romney never led Obama in any poll. Obamacare, one of the major issues animating the campaign and exciting the base, was the one issue Romney could not fully exploit. Repeatedly on my show I asked him if he regretted his own version of universal care in Massachusetts. Repeatedly he demurred.

One of the most disturbing parts of Obama's reelection was knowing that the unprecedented radicalism of his first term would only intensify in his second. Even beyond the obvious outrages like Obamacare and the reckless running up of the national debt, among Obama's most pernicious actions were his anti-populist attempts to pulverize the little guy. It was everything conservatives had cautioned against and feared for over a generation—vicious and vindictive federal abuses of power designed to enforce a radical ideology.

Under Obama, the government sought to force the Little Sisters of the Poor—an order of Roman Catholic nuns who serve the elderly and impoverished—to pay for contraceptives, sterilization, and abortion pills as part of its Obamacare contraception mandate. Such a policy was, of course, in direct violation of the Little Sisters' religious faith—not to mention absurd. But it took a years-long legal battle and a unanimous Supreme Court victory for the Little Sisters to finally get the federal government off their backs so they could return to nurturing the needy and dying, instead of being bullied by Washington bureaucrats enforcing ideological edicts.

When Obama wasn't legally roughing up nuns, he was busy sending armed federal agents to bust in and raid the Gibson guitar company's Nashville, Tennessee, headquarters to seize pallets of imported wood. Gibson said the Obama DOJ "suggested that the use of wood from India that is not finished by Indian workers is illegal, not because of U.S. law, but because it is the Justice Department's interpretation of a law in India."[50] The company vehemently denied any wrongdoing. But the Obama administration spent two years strong-arming the legendary guitar company into a settlement deal to avoid criminal charges. Human Events reported that during the ordeal, Gibson's CEO "was told by government agents he could make his problems go away if he used foreign labor for manufacturing."[51] After the administration got the company to fork over more than $300,000 (and make a $50,000 donation to an environmental group), the feds ultimately ending up returning the imported wood and allowed Gibson to use it. It was an outrageous abuse of power against an American manufacturer and its workers.

Then there was the administration's use of the IRS as a political weapon to systematically target conservative groups and deny them their tax-exempt status. Hundreds of conservative charities seeking IRS approval were forced to endure extra and costly scrutiny that progressive groups were never subjected to. Their crime? The conservative groups contained words like "patriot" or "Tea Party" in their names.[52] The IRS scandal was yet another example of the Obama administration using the incredible power of the federal government to crush citizens whose only goal was helping Americans voice their most deeply held beliefs and values. After Obama's 2012 victory, I knew Americans would be forced to face another four years of federal abuses and outrages.

Romney's 2012 loss was demoralizing for conservatives. Many said it was the last straw for conservatism. Ann Coulter appeared on my show the morning after the election and by the end I joked that I might need to do an intervention. "If Mitt Romney cannot win in this economy, then the tipping point has been reached," Ann said grimly. "We have more takers than makers and it's over. There is no hope." "Pep up, chin up," I told Ann. "Dust yourself off. Move forward, girl."[53]

I understood and sympathized with the bleak outlook, but I'd been around long enough to know that conservatism's obituary has been written and ripped up myriad times. After hosting several more interventions with friends, I started to feel like the chief psychologist for conservatives. Dejected voters needed to remember it was only after Barry Goldwater's landslide loss to LBJ that the conservative movement rose from the ashes—a movement that led to the Reagan Revolution.

THE GRASS ROOTS TACKLES COMMON CORE

In 2009, governors and school superintendents from 46 states created a set of K-12 education math and English standards they said should apply to every student in the United States. The plan's originators, the Council of Chief State School Officers and the National Governors Association Center for Best Practices, claimed the "root cause" of America's failing education system was "an uneven patchwork of academic standards that vary from state to state and do not agree on what students should know and be able to do at each grade level."[54] To fix this, they hatched a top-down, one-size-fits-all policy detailing the textbooks, teaching aids and materials, and tests all teachers must use to be in accordance with Common Core standards. Advocates claimed that because the Common Core was state-led, the federal government would not have a hand in it. (Spoiler alert: that was a total lie.)

In the wake of Romney's loss to Obama in 2012, Common Core emerged as a galvanizing issue for conservative populists and libertarians who saw big government encroachment into education policy as a threat to how their children are taught.

The driving force behind Common Core was the globalist Bill and Melinda Gates Foundation. (Gates is an ardent proponent of globalization and opposed Brexit, issuing a warning before the vote that Britain exiting the EU would make it "significantly less attractive" for businesses.[55]) His charity pumped over $230 million into creating and selling the education scheme.[56] Big business groups like the Chamber of Commerce also supported it and spent millions promoting it. Big government Republicans like Jeb Bush loved it, too—as did Obama and most liberals. (As any good globalist knows, education curriculum is the surest path toward shaping the values and attitudes of the next generation.)

In 2009, Obama launched his "Race to the Top" initiative that doled out $4.35 billion in "stimulus" money in the form of grants to states if they agreed to adopt common standards. If that sounds like the federal government was trying to coerce states into Common Core by dangling billions of dollars in front of them in the middle of a recession, that's because it was. Supporters claimed states' adoption of Common Core was voluntary and not required to win Race to the Top cash. But once again, that wasn't true: the grant application process awarded extra points to states that adopted Common Core.[57] "The program was $4.35 billion dollars of carrots swinging in front of fifty hungry rabbits," said Hayden K. Smith of the anti–Common Core group FreedomWorks.[58]

By 2012, conservative groups like the Heritage Foundation, FreedomWorks, and the American Principles Project had mounted an aggressive campaign to educate voters on the centralized educational planning scheme and to whip up grassroots and Tea Party opposition. They understood that local control of curriculum is a must—otherwise we have *government* schools, not public schools. The people also knew that local control sparks experimentation and innovation in teaching methods. The key, they said, was giving parents influence on curriculum decisions, not a faraway panel of "experts" and bureaucrats feeding from Bill Gates's and the federal government's money troughs. "The elites in the Republican Party and the Democratic Party don't get this," American Principles Project lawyer Emmett McGroarty said.[59]

But the populist movement forced them to begin getting it. The people hit the streets, held rallies, organized state and congressional calling campaigns, and urged elected officials to abandon Common Core so their states could return power to the people. Their efforts got the attention of decision makers. "We didn't see it coming with the intensity that it is, apparently all across the country," said Republican Georgia governor Nathan Deal.[60]

In 2013, the anti–Common Core grassroots movement was big and growing. Still, according to Gallup two-thirds of Americans had never even heard of Common Core.[61] Conservatives had their work cut out for them. Like-minded patriots pressed on, spoke out, educated the public, and took the Establishment to task on their children's behalf. For their efforts they were ridiculed. Establishment figures like

Obama education secretary Arne Duncan dismissed them as "white suburban moms who all of a sudden—their child isn't as brilliant as they thought they were."[62] He also smeared them as paranoid kooks. "It's not a black helicopter ploy and we're not trying to get inside people's minds and brains," Duncan sneered.[63]

The snobbery was bad enough, but Common Core's results were even worse. Test scores were down and teacher frustrations were up. Even the teachers' unions that had previously supported it were now in an uproar. American Federation of Teachers chief Randi Weingarten, a well-known progressive, said education officials dumped stacks of sloppily produced Common Core materials on teachers and said, "Here's 500 pages. Just do it." Weingarten added: "You think the Obamacare implementation is bad? The implementation of the Common Core is far worse."[64]

Not surprisingly, student test scores plunged, dropping as much as 30 percent in New York. As parents began seeing the Gates and Obama education brainchild up close, they realized conservatives were right after all. Indeed, in a stunning public relations victory, the same American public who in 2013 had never heard of Common Core opposed it by a whopping 60 percent just one year later.[65] Indeed, in the years ahead, opposition to the centralized education scheme would be a key issue for Republican presidential candidates and an albatross around the necks of candidates like Jeb Bush and John Kasich who supported it.

But in 2013, Common Core supporters like George W. Bush's education secretary Margaret Spellings began realizing that the populist fire against their education power grab might have grown too big to contain. "What might have been a brush fire is now a more substantial fire," Spellings said.[66]

The Establishment was worried. The peasants were getting too powerful. A beatdown was just around the corner.

SCHUMER-RUBIO 2013 AMNESTY BILL

Finally the GOP Establishment decided it needed to take back control of the party—and the narrative—from the populist insurgents.

In March of 2013, a gaggle of Establishment figures including RNC chairman Reince Priebus unveiled a 97-page autopsy of the election. Tellingly both *The Washington Post* and *The New York Times* praised the effort—never a good sign. The document found that the party hadn't paid enough attention to working-class voters (big shocker there). "We should speak out when CEOs receive tens of millions of dollars in retirement packages," they wrote, "when middle class workers haven't had a meaningful raise in years." To be "welcoming and inclusive" the autopsy suggested downplaying social issues, including support for traditional marriage. And predictably the autopsy singled out Romney's "self-deportation" comments as alienating Hispanic voters. Zoraida Fonalledas, a GOP committee woman from Puerto Rico, advised at the report's unveiling, Republicans "must embrace and champion comprehensive immigration reform."

Enter the Gang of Eight. In 2013, former Tea Party darling Marco Rubio and liberal New York icon Chuck Schumer joined forces to craft the mother of all immigration amnesty bills: S.B. 744. I along with 150 conservative leaders and groups signed a letter opposing it. Our reasons included the fact that the bill would legalize millions of illegal immigrants, fail to secure the border, cede control to an Obama administration that had repeatedly proven untrustworthy on immigration. It would also grow government with new spending and regulations, and crush job opportunities for low-skilled American workers.

The party decided to roll the dice on the entire GOP coalition by ignoring the plight of working Americans. But at least *The Washington Post* was happy. In case you've forgotten, here are the notorious members of the Gang of Eight:

- Senator Chuck Schumer (D-NY)
- Senator Marco Rubio (R-FL)
- Senator John McCain (R-AZ)
- Senator Lindsey Graham (R-SC)
- Senator Richard Durbin (D-IL)
- Senator Robert Menendez (D-NJ)

- Senator Jeff Flake (R-AZ)
- Senator Michael Bennet (D-CO)

Back when Rubio was running in his senate primary challenge against liberal Republican Charlie Crist, I was one of his early supporters. I even did a campaign event with him in Orlando. The first time he came on my show he was 23 points behind, and mine was one of the first national appearances he had done. No one at that time thought he had a chance, but he exposed Crist for what he was—an ineffective, Establishment figure more interested in maintaining his tan than cutting taxes. The fresh-faced candidate with Cuban roots became a quick favorite of libertarians and conservatives alike. He won one of the first "Tea Party" victories of the 2010 midterms.

But what a difference three years made. In 2013 he appeared on my show once to sell his amnesty bill and it wasn't pretty. His attempts to promote it as a "border enforcement first" plan failed. The fact is, legal status for illegal aliens was immediate with a promise of later enforcement. My listeners were irate and wondered what had happened to the man in whom they had placed so much hope. This deeply disappointed me because I believed that had he listened, he might have found more success in 2016. The blowback was so fierce that Rubio had to back away from his own bill. He did lasting damage to his career by throwing in with the corporatists and the open borders crowd. During the bill's negotiations, Republican analyst Niger Innis said that Marco Rubio "got his butt handed to him."[67]

I knew few if any members of Congress would actually read the 847-page Schumer-Rubio monstrosity, so I decided to do it myself. Every. Single. Page.

The Schumer-Rubio bill was riddled with provisions that made it even worse than the original 2007 Kennedy-McCain shamnesty act on which it was modeled. Like the facts that border agents didn't really have to be hired until 2017 and that it gave Homeland Security Secretary Janet Napolitano the discretion to nix any part of the border wall she deemed unnecessary. There was also this little gem: the bill not only forgave *past* visa overstays, it also forgave some *future* visa overstays as well.

The first week of June 2013 I appeared on *Fox & Friends* with Rubio. He tried to reassure viewers that the Gang of Eight's amnesty bill was "nowhere near being done" and that, in its current form, lacked the 60 votes it needed in the Senate to move it to the House. "People don't trust the Department of Homeland Security to do the job or to come up with a plan that will do the job," said Rubio.

"People, you're right, have no faith in this border actually being enforced," I said. "They know that when Chuck Schumer, Dick Durbin, and Bob Menendez are giddy over the passage of a bill—Republicans, conservatives, most people in the middle class who are seeing their wages stagnate or go down, have something to worry about. So, they are looking to you for leadership, Senator Rubio. And I can tell you from my radio listeners, they think it's time to stop dividing the Republican Party on this issue. With all your good intentions—and I know you have them—you're a terrific person. But people want us to focus on jobs, the economy, and raising the middle-class lifestyle and wages here."

Media outlets framed my comments as me "confronting" Marco Rubio over the immigration bill. In reality I was only posing the same questions and concerns to Rubio that my radio callers had shared with me. I knew that if conservatives went the wrong way on this issue, all the other issues that we care about would be undermined.

Just days after Rubio and I appeared on Fox together, Rubio went on the Spanish television network Univision and said, "First comes legalization. Then comes the measures to secure the border. And then comes the process of permanent residence."[68] It was the kind of thing voters hate: a politician who seems to be saying one thing to one group and another thing to another group. That Rubio's statement was made in Spanish only heightened the perceived pandering.

In a last-minute maneuver, an amendment to the Schumer-Rubio bill was added to reassure skeptics about enforcement. The amnesty bill easily cleared the Senate with 68 votes for and 32 votes against. This despite the position of the voters that Senator Rand Paul shared with my radio audience: "Eighty percent of our phone calls have been against this immigration reform bill."[69]

The people got it. When the Tea Party Patriots polled their local coordinators to gauge support for the Schumer-Rubio amnesty bill,

85 percent said they opposed the measure. "There is zero support within the tea-party movement for the Gang of Eight's initiatives," said Michael Johns, a Tea Party pioneer. Tea Party Nation founder Judson Phillips agreed. "The weight of the amnesty bill is greater than the weight of the Obamacare bill, and we know how that one turned out. I don't know anybody who's involved in the tea-party movement at any level who thinks that the Gang of Eight plan's a good idea."[70]

Days before the Senate passed the bill I issued the GOP this warning: "To all the Republicans who supported this . . . you're writing your own political obituary," I said. "I hope you know that you've just participated in the political equivalent of a one-night stand. Once the Democrat leadership has had their way with you, they are not going to love you in the morning."[71]

All eyes turned to the House, where thankfully the bill languished. But not before Speaker John Boehner mocked conservatives who were opposed to passing amnesty. "Here's the attitude. 'Ohhhh. Don't make me do this. Ohhhh. This is too hard,'" Boehner told the Middletown Rotary Club in 2014. "We get elected to make choices. We get elected to solve problems and it's remarkable to me how many of my colleagues just don't want to. . . . They'll take the path of least resistance." Boehner added: "I've had every brick and bat and arrow shot at me over this issue just because I wanted to deal with it. I didn't say it was going to be easy."[72]

It would have been nice if John Boehner had been as tough with Obama as he was with conservatives who were fighting to keep American wages from flatlining due to illegal immigration. The GOP Establishment's amnesty obsession was infuriating. What was the point of having a Republican Congress if they refused to listen to their own constituents? I held out hope that John Boehner would stand up for Americans first. Both American citizens and legal immigrants deserve the opportunity to earn market wages—not wages artificially depressed by an unending flood of cheap labor.

If the GOP Establishment wouldn't hear the people on immigration, the people would find other, more dramatic ways to get their attention.

CANTOR GOES DOWN IN FLAMES

As I explained in the introduction to this book, the defeat of Republican majority leader Eric Cantor was not only historic (no sitting majority leader had ever lost in a primary), it also sent an undeniable message to GOP members of Congress that conservatives would no longer tolerate the Establishment's amnesty shenanigans. My decision to campaign for a little-known economics professor, Dave Brat, against Cantor was not without its risks. I figured, if we were ever going to get good people to challenge the failed Establishment, we would need to give them a platform and a fair hearing. So I gave Brat a platform and a bigger microphone.

In a speech before the American Enterprise Institute Cantor said, "It is time to provide an opportunity for legal residence and citizenship for those who were brought to this country as children and who know no other home."[73] It was pure emotion masquerading as policy. Worse, it was dishonest emotionalism, because its true aim was doing the bidding of the mega donors who filled GOP campaign coffers. Outside groups like the pro-amnesty big spender American Action Network (which spent millions of dollars on ads), for example, shared office space with Karl Rove's Crossroads GPS/American Crossroads. Then there was former Republican Mississippi governor Haley Barbour's "Americans for a Conservative Direction." The group was funded by Facebook founder Mark Zuckerberg's pro-amnesty group FWD.us, which spent millions promoting the measure.[74] As the *Times* reported, FWD.us "has been running ads in Iowa lately that implore those watching to 'stand with Marco Rubio to end de facto amnesty.'"[75]

When I made the decision to campaign for Brat at the Dominion Club in Virginia a week before his primary election, I knew the odds were stacked against him. In the weeks prior, Eric Cantor had dropped $1 million advertising his candidacy. In April and May, he spent $370,000 on ads, $120,000 on campaign mailers, $30,000 on polling, and $13,000 on yard signs.[76] Brat? He had about $100,000 left in campaign funds. Still, I knew we needed to take a chance and fight. "Don't forget," I said in my speech at the Brat rally, referencing his opponent, "the first four letters of his name spells *Can't!*"

In the end, money mattered much less than communicating a populist message that respected the wishes of ordinary Americans. When Dave Brat beat Cantor by 11 points, some media outlets credited me with having "claimed the scalp of Representative Eric Cantor, the third most powerful Republican in the House of Representatives, by headlining a massive rally that helped to propel his obscure opponent to a shock victory."[77] But the truth is, the victory belonged to the people and the candidate who had the courage to stand against seemingly impossible odds and fight.

Following his defeat, Eric Cantor did a few ho-hum Sunday interviews to soften his post-historic upset landing. Listening to him and watching him made me wonder how he hadn't been tossed out of office sooner. I had previously joked that Obama should have considered trading Cantor for Sgt. Bowe Bergdahl, and now he was sore about it. It was as if nothing of consequence had happened on June 10—except that seven days earlier, Laura Ingraham made a wiseass joke about him. Embarrassing.

As for it being "personal," let me say this: I had high hopes for Cantor a decade ago, and I never thought it would come to this. How could a supposedly conservative House majority leader coauthor the House immigration principles, support the DREAM Act and ENLIST Act "in principle," and then claim that Dave Brat was to his left on the issue? Did Cantor think his multimillion-dollar ad campaign would make his lies go down more smoothly? To the extent that talk radio helped level the playing field of PAC ads and biased coverage, the people benefited. But make no mistake about it, this was a stunning victory for the grass roots, the people who said "oh no you won't" to a House GOP itching for amnesty in order to please big business interests who wanted cheap labor no matter the damage.

I hoped to cross paths with Representative Cantor at ABC's *This Week* following his defeat. We were both booked on the show. But he scooted out before we could have a word. What would I have said? "It's not personal, but what we do take *personally* is the decline of the country that we love. We also take it personally when our 'leaders' fail the people year after year, only to cater to big business and illegal immigrants. We take it personally when you take our support for granted despite the fact that your policies make the American working class weaker year after year. Plus, 13 years is a good run." And unlike most 52-year-old men that get fired in America today, Cantor won't have any trouble getting a higher-paying job. In fact, he already has. After his defeat, Eric Cantor cashed in on Wall Street and joined a major hedge fund to help grease deals with Congress.[78]

In November, Dave Brat won his seat in Congress, as the GOP picked up a net 13 seats in the House of Representatives. Republicans also picked up nine seats in the Senate and gained the majority. I wish I could say that the GOP Establishment thanked its conservative base by getting its act together and learning from its mistakes. Sadly, that wasn't the case. Less than a month after the GOP 2014 midterm victory, the Republican House leadership backed the $1 trillion "Continuing Resolution-Omnibus," which some people dubbed the "cromnibus." I simply called it "a 1,600-page bad joke." The flab-filled spending bill made no attempts at cutting spending, basically gave Democrats what they wanted, and also included $2.5 billion to accommodate illegal immigrants and refugees. Republicans were funding the next border wave. What was the point of winning the election if this was the kind of slapdash fiscal approach Republicans planned to take?

It was mind-boggling to me that on the heels of a major Republican electoral victory, John Boehner and his gang decided to push a bloated budget to a vote so quickly. What they should have done was pass a short-term continuing resolution and then advance a real budget plan in February or March. That would have given them time to work department by department to slash spending. Instead, Boehner had essentially engaged in the same kind of rush job he criticized Barack Obama for with the stimulus. "Here we are with 1,100 pages not one member of this body has read," said Boehner in 2009. "What happened to the promise we are going to let the American people see what's in this bill for 48 hours?"

John Boehner and the GOP Establishment had basically thumbed their noses at the conservative base who had just given them an impressive midterm victory. Boehner had pledged there would be transparency once the Republicans were firmly in control—that it would be a new dawn for the way we spend taxpayers' money. I was livid. So were my listeners. I went on air and told the hard, painful truth.

"This is not representation on Capitol Hill right now, this is mis-representation. . . . Right now I think the Republican leadership is pretty giddy . . . they're drunk on their own power. . . . We will not forget this betrayal," I said. "And there will come a time when you will come calling on us. You will need us to help you. When that day comes, don't be surprised if many of those rock-ribbed conservatives across the country will not answer the call to help you because you've beaten them down so badly. You've betrayed them so terribly . . . you're not going to betray them a third time."[79]

The Republican Congress passed the cromnibus betrayal two weeks before Christmas on a vote of 219–206. For conservatives, it was Charlie Brown's football all over again—you take a run to kick the football, and they yank it away and let you crash to the ground. The battle between conservatives and its GOP Establishment over-lords is exhausting but essential. It would be nice if the tug-of-war over political power and policies were just between conservatives and progressives, Republicans and Democrats. But as we've seen, the GOP Establishment will never relinquish its grip. The only choice for grassroots conservative-populists is to do the heavy lifting that his-tory requires by organizing, mobilizing, and fighting a two-front war against progressivism on the one hand and the same Establishment that dismissed and defied Ronald Reagan on the other.

Infuriating? You bet. Worth it? Definitely.

A POPULIST CURRENT GATHERS
ON A DISTANT SHORE

In 2014 I began introducing my radio listeners to an important, if ignored, voice from across the pond—Nigel Farage, the leader of the United Kingdom Independence Party (UKIP). Farage caught my eye when his small, populist rebel party began swelling into a movement to give voice to the British working class. Farage seemed to be de-scribing political forces and scenarios that paralleled America's. Even though most Americans knew very little about him at the time, I wanted to expose American conservatives to his populist ideas.

During a September 2014 interview, I asked Farage what he saw as the evolution of elite politics in the United Kingdom. He explained that in his lifetime he had seen Parliament go from being a place where real people with real life experiences served to a place dominated by Oxford-trained elites who lived lives divorced from the realities of most everyday Britons. "They lack authenticity," he explained:

> I'm deeply flawed . . . should I hide that? . . . No, there's no point, and that's what the rest of them do. The rest of them try and make out they are different human beings than they are. And I think, that, actually, voters know, voters actually quite like people who have got a few flaws because the voters are flawed themselves too. So this sort of, shiny, bright, perfect, image that a politician tries to give, and the picture of him with the wife and the kids, I don't think people need that. I think what they want to know is why are you in politics? Are you in politics because you actually want to do something? Or are you in politics for rank and position?[80]

Farage was on to something. Voters in the UK, like those in America, were looking past inconsequential "flaws" and seeking confident leaders who would fight for their principles. The next wave of conservative leadership need not be "shiny, bright," or "perfect" so long as they would be true to their ideals and keep their promises.

Then Farage identified the core problem facing working people: "The key battle today is about community and identity. Who are we as nations? Who are we as communities? How do we want to live? This stuff is all being threatened directly by excessive immigration and by things like how small businesses are being closed down and our community is changing. The politics of the future is about community and identity."

He was talking about the United Kingdom, but he might as easily have been speaking about America. As it turned out, the populist wave he was describing in the United Kingdom would soon crash onto America's shores.

6.

THE RISE OF TRUMP

The Republican Presidential Primary

I love America. And when you love something, you protect it
passionately—fiercely, even. We are the greatest country the
world has ever known. I make no apologies for this country, my
pride in it, or my desire to see us become strong and rich again.

—DONALD TRUMP

I know I told you I hated conventions, but somehow I can't seem to avoid them. Speech notes in hand, I walked on stage across the massive red backdrop with the large banner, "Conservative Action Starts Here." The runway-style dais jutted straight out into the crowd, flanked on either side by hundreds of conservatives who had made the annual pilgrimage to CPAC.

Everyone knew this confab would be especially important. Held in late February 2015 at the Gaylord National Resort and Convention Center in National Harbor, Maryland, CPAC was the first chance for conservative activists to see the Republican presidential candidates in one place, jockeying for position.

I felt strongly that it was important CPAC not devolve into a "coronation" for any one particular candidate. I decided my speech would address the issue everyone in the grass roots was buzzing about—the one GOP elites hoped would remain unspoken. After a few introductory pleasantries, and just hours before Jeb Bush's CPAC appearance, I scanned the audience and posed the question.

"How many of you in the room are skeptical of another Bush term?"

Hundreds of hands shot up, as hoots and whistles filled the air. Days earlier a story had broken about Jeb Bush's wife, Columba, and her South Florida shopping extravaganza. She reportedly took out a loan to purchase over $42,000 worth of jewels in a single day.[1] Working off the news, I pressed on.

"I think you have to look on the bright side; I think Jeb could really explode the gender gap," I said. "I think women could actually turn out in droves for Jeb Bush. I mean, what woman doesn't like a man who gives her a blank check at Tiffany's? Diamonds are a girl's best friend—that would be a great theme song for Jeb Bush." The crowd laughed.

"We could dispense with this whole nomination process altogether. It's kind of inconvenient running for president. Why don't we just call it quits? And Jeb and Hillary can run on the same ticket," I said to chuckles from the audience. "I mean, go through the list of things they agree on: Common Core, amnesty, giving Obama fast-track trade authority, a lot of new trade deals with China, the surveillance culture. So I'm designing the bumper sticker. It could be, 'CLUSH 2016.'" Then, in my best Hillary Clinton Benghazi hearings voice, I added the tagline: "What difference does it make?!" The audience howled and cheered.

Immediately, the usual suspects, who eventually became ardent NeverTrumpers, took to Twitter to defend the Bush royal family—and trash me.

"As a woman, I find it particularly distasteful that Ms. Ingraham's anti-Jeb obsession, turned into a swipe at Columba Bush at CPAC. Unseemly," tweeted GOP Establishment NeverTrumper and CNN commentator Ana Navarro, who is close to the Bushes.[2] *Washington Post* blogger Jennifer Rubin growled in displeasure: "A distasteful personal attack on jeb [sic] by Laura Ingraham . . . an embarrassment for her and CPAC," she tweeted just minutes after I delivered the line.[3] "Ingraham apparently doesn't think anyone can beat Bush so she will do it. . . ."[4] (Well, since that was before Donald Trump entered the race, she was right about the last part.)

I then offered my diagnosis of what ailed our country and the party, which tracked pretty closely to what Donald Trump would say just four months later at Trump Tower:

I'm tired of the airbrushed talking points; I'm tired of the backroom deals. We've seen what happens when the elites are in charge without the people's input—they fail, and fail, and fail more. We already know that the media and much of the Donor Class is hostile to conservatism. Guess what? That's been true for a very long time. The idea that we should be conducting any type of coronation in the Republican Party today because 50 rich families decide who they think would best represent their interests? No way, José!

Each time we've listened to the elites, we're sorry we did so.

They said Reagan couldn't win. They were wrong.

They said the Soviet Union couldn't be defeated. They were wrong.

They said inflation and high interest rates, high unemployment were permanent things; they couldn't be eradicated. We had to learn to deal with a new era of scarcity, and they were wrong. . . . The elites said we could raise taxes and no one would read our lips, but the American people did.

And the elites said we couldn't win control of Congress and that Newt Gingrich and his revolution were a doomed failure, but the American people thought otherwise. The elites said we couldn't run the table in 2014 and that Obamaism was the wave of the future—that women and minorities and single moms would never turn out for conservatives—and they were wrong. The people thought otherwise.

The elites said that unless conservatives embraced and passed comprehensive immigration reform, i.e., amnesty, after 2012, that conservatives and Republicans could never win in 2014—the elites were *spectacularly* wrong. . . . American citizenship is not something that should be so easily bargained away. American citizenship is ours.

As I closed my speech, the CPAC faithful gave me a standing ovation. All the right people were furious, and I had accomplished what

I set out to do by warning conservatives about nominating another Republican who would offer the same warmed-over big government solutions that have failed before. Jeb Bush was set to appear at CPAC for a question-and-answer session with my friend Sean Hannity just hours later. The reception Bush received was polite. But a sign of trouble ahead came when Jeb discussed his support for driver's licenses and in-state tuition for illegal aliens. The crowd booed.

It was hardly a secret that I opposed Jeb Bush. As early as 2013, in the wake of Mitt Romney's defeat, I began warning that the Bushes were gunning for a comeback, another do-over. I met with my old Reagan administration pal Bill Kristol in his office at *The Weekly Standard* and told him that if we didn't rally around a single conservative alternative to Jeb, that's who we would get. One of the ideas I raised was having a "conservative convention or primary" to winnow down the field. Kristol shrugged it off, saying, "I think it's the more the merrier" in the primary field. Other Bush devotees would express the same sentiment. They knew that more was merrier all right—for the guy with all the money and name recognition. It was my firm belief that the only way to beat Bush was for one strong, conservative populist to emerge, around whom the grassroots voters would coalesce. In that scenario, the moderates would cannibalize each other's share of the vote, making it more likely that the populist would win.

After CPAC 2015, some suggested Bush had a "talk radio" problem. (We cruel, heartless conservative "talkers" just weren't willing to give him a fair shake.) Nothing could be further from the truth, I told Politico. Jeb doesn't have a "talk radio" problem, Jeb has an "America" problem.[5] At a time when citizens were screaming for someone to enforce the law and stop the influx of illegal immigrants into American communities, Jeb Bush was lecturing working-class Americans that these lawbreakers weren't committing crimes, they were committing "acts of love." That was perhaps one of the most tone-deaf comments I've ever heard a Republican utter. (Right up there with Romney's 47 percent.)

For conservatives, Jeb's candidacy was a nonstarter. He represented the past. The last time he had run for office the iPhone hadn't been invented. His policy positions were firmly anti-populist, and it wasn't clear that there was a single issue on which he deviated from the views of his brother. (Remember George W. had left office with a 22 percent approval rating.) The dynastic notion that a single American family should give us three of our presidents seemed absurd on its face. Another Bush running against another Clinton? How did that work out for Republicans last time they tried it?

But the old Bush hands were not deterred. The Bush donor network stepped up to support Jeb, contributing close to $130 million to both his campaign and the political action committees supporting him.

Think of all the good that could have been done with that money besides making consultants and pollsters and media ad buyers insanely rich.

Early on, Jeb tried to shake the downside of his last name. In February 2015, Bush took the first stab at distinguishing his political identity from that of his brother. Addressing the Chicago Council on Global Affairs in what was dubbed his "first major foreign policy speech," he said, "I love my father and my brother. I admire their service to the nation and the difficult decisions they had to make. But I am my own man."[6] Pretty amorphous stuff.

Some consultant must have told him he didn't go far enough. *The Washington Post* covered Jeb's attempt to put some more space between himself and his older brother, referring to the "slow-motion and seemingly reluctant distancing effort as he moves toward a White House bid."[7] Watching Jeb field questions at a local sports bar in Concord, New Hampshire, it was obvious it pained him to say these words: "I think that in Washington, during my brother's time, Republicans spent too much money," Jeb said. "I think he could have used the veto power—he didn't have line-item veto power, but he could have brought budget discipline to Washington, DC."[8]

This strategy was a major miscalculation. The Bushes didn't exactly have a reputation for self-reflection. It was simply inconceivable to them that Republican voters would turn on them. But they did.

The OTB (Other Than Bush) candidates would eventually number 16, which on its face seemed like great news for Jeb. The largest GOP primary field since 1916 included all shades of the ideological spectrum.[9] The field would become bifurcated into the anti-Establishment outsiders like Donald Trump, Dr. Ben Carson, Rick Santorum, Carly Fiorina, Mike Huckabee, and Sen. Ted Cruz; and the Establishment group made up of everyone else. In my judgment, this meant that conservative-populist voters would be severely divided, thus making it far easier for the dominant Establishment candidate to win. Many of the candidates appeared multiple times on my radio show throughout the primary season. I also held numerous on-and-off-the-record meetings with several of the candidates. My goal with each was always the same: when Americans hear you, they need to know that you're not only going to represent a break from the Obama agenda, but with the Bush agenda, too. Some were more receptive than others. Only a few, such as Bush and Rubio, had the ability to raise the money necessary. Only one didn't need my advice—Donald Trump.

Several weeks after CPAC I had former Hewlett Packard chief Carly Fiorina on my show to discuss her candidacy and why Jeb Bush should not be the GOP's presidential nominee. The year prior, Fiorina asked to meet me at Off the Record, the basement bar of the Hay Adams. I told her I was happy to offer counsel but politely declined endorsing anyone for the time being. I always appreciated that she wasn't afraid to come on my show and answer tough questions. She wasted no time taking aim at the Establishment front-runner.

"Jeb Bush is dead wrong on a couple of issues," Fiorina said during her April 15, 2015, appearance on my show. "He's dead wrong on comprehensive immigration reform. He's dead wrong on Common Core. He's dead wrong about government being too powerful. I think government is too powerful, I'm not sure he believes that." Fiorina added: "Jeb Bush's record suggests that he is a big government Republican." She was right. Just as devastating as Bush's position on immigration was his position on the Common Core educational standards that robbed local school districts of control over their curricula.

Fiorina made a strong case, without hesitation, speaking in full paragraphs. But as much as I liked her and loved the idea of a woman facing off against Hillary Clinton, I didn't support her because I didn't think she could win. Her impressive debate performances notwithstanding, Fiorina's record as CEO of Hewlett Packard was difficult to defend (although she tried mightily).

ENTER THE DONALD

In the annals of great political stage entrances, Donald and Melania Trump's golden escalator ride at Trump Tower on June 16, 2015, easily ranks as the most memorable. Against a blaring soundtrack of Neil Young's "Rockin' in the Free World," Donald Trump descended into Trump Tower's famous salmon-colored marble atrium wearing his trademark blue suit and red power tie with Melania, resplendent as always, wearing a flowing white dress. I, like everyone else, could think only one thing . . . WOW. The billionaire real estate mogul's grand entrance into the presidential arena was pure Trump: glitzy, eye-catching, and riddled with instant controversy. After an adoring introduction by his daughter Ivanka, Donald Trump stood against a royal blue curtain lined with a row of American flags and delivered words that hit like lightning bolts.

"The U.S. has become a dumping ground for everybody else's problems," said Trump. "When Mexico sends its people, they're not sending their best. They're not sending you. They're sending people that have lots of problems, and they're bringing those problems [to] us. They're bringing drugs. They're bringing crime. They're rapists. And some, I assume, are good people." The far-flung speech also covered unfair trade deals, jobs, Iraq, Obamacare, China, Russia, Japan, ISIS, and the troops, but none of that mattered. In the collective bubble known as the Establishment Media, Donald Trump had launched his campaign by calling Latino immigrants rapists, drug pushers, and criminals. Establishment consultant-types were sure that these were words that would doom Trump's candidacy.

But the Americans who had grown exhausted by the polite and perfectly ineffective politics as usual—"sound and fury signifying nothing"—disagreed. When I stopped by my neighbor's house later in the day, his sons were watching the replay on Fox News and loving every minute of it. "This is awesome!" said Charlie, a freshman at UNC–Chapel Hill, pointing at the television. "The Donald Rocks!"

commented Robert, 22, who had just graduated Bowdoin. "He's gonna win, I'm telling ya."

Seeing their reactions—and how much fun they were having watching Trump—struck me in the moment. The billionaire was an anti-Washington force of nature, a showman who didn't give a rip about how politics had been done before. In retrospect, maybe these college kids saw his appeal before most others (even me!) because their generation, more than any other, was forced to grow up under the tyranny of political correctness. "In a world increasingly traumatized by micro-aggressions, Donald Trump is a master of macro-aggression," wrote Judd Garrett in RealClearPolitics.[10] Even on the day of his campaign's debut, he said the kind of things that university students today would be punished for saying on campus:

- "We have losers. We have people that don't have it. We have people that are morally corrupt. We have people that are selling this country down the drain."[11]
- "[W]e won't be using a man like Secretary Kerry that has absolutely no concept of negotiation, who's making a horrible and laughable deal . . . and then goes into a bicycle race at 72 years old, and falls and breaks his leg. I won't be doing that."

You can almost hear the cries from the "safe spaces" to make Trump stop.

Media "experts" ridiculed and dismissed the prospect of a human grenade like Trump being rolled into the middle of the GOP primary. The *New York Times*'s Maggie Haberman ran a story laying out what Trump would need to do to win. Under the header "Why He Will Win," she simply wrote: "We are stumped. And we really tried."[12] Another *Times* reporter, Alexander Burns, dismissed a Trump GOP nomination as "a remote prospect."[13] "It's a big headache for the Republican Party," said Rothenberg & Gonzales Political Report editor Nathan Gonzales. "Donald Trump is not going to be the Republican nominee for president."[14] Conveniently, the nasties in the media rushed out polls and "analysis" to demonstrate that a Trump candidacy was doomed. The ABC News/*Washington Post* poll released the day before his speech claimed the real estate mogul had a fatal 70 percent unfavorable rating.[15] The New York *Daily News* ran a picture of Trump wearing clown makeup and a big red nose with the headline "Clown Runs for Prez."[16] The CNN June poll two weeks after Trump's announcement speech showed Jeb Bush in the lead with 19 percent, Trump in second with 12 percent, and Mike Huckabee and Ben Carson at 8 and 7 percent, respectively.[17]

Like the press, the "we're smarter than you" crew over at the Democratic National Committee relished the chance to humiliate the buffoon billionaire and watch him morph into a disruptive force that would embarrass the Republican Party. The DNC released a sarcastic statement intended to mock his candidacy: "He adds some much-needed seriousness that has previously been lacking from the GOP field, and we look forward to hearing more about his ideas for the nation."[18]

On radio, I was supportive of Trump's speech and awaited his next move. In early July I expressed modest doubt about whether he would last until the fall—but my skepticism didn't last long. It became apparent by mid-month that Donald Trump was in this to win it. Unlike most Republicans, Trump led with illegal immigration and job-crushing trade deals as two of his top policy issues and represented a welcome populist voice to millions of Americans. Given his previous flirtations with running, however, I was a bit doubtful he would hang in and wondered whether he might get bored with the primary slog.

The first time I met Donald Trump was in May 2002. We were introduced by a mutual friend, newspaper executive and author Conrad Black. The three of us had lunch at the old Le Cirque restaurant that used to be located at the Palace Hotel in midtown Manhattan. Its over-the-top ornate décor was very Trumpian. I was curious about what the man would be like in person after reading for so many years about his big, bold, brash life in the tabloids. To my surprise, he spent very little of the lunch talking about himself and most of it asking me about my work in television and radio. He was funny, engaging, and politically astute. We laughed a lot about the Clinton follies (although he said they were pals). When we were finished, he insisted I take his limousine to wherever I needed to go. A total germophobe, he handed me a bunch of disinfectant wipes and said something like "the city is beautiful, but dirty; and you don't want to get sick before your next TV appearance." I laughed, thanked him, and said good-bye.

Trump seemed essentially post-partisan to me. He had as much criticism for the GOP as he did for the Democrats. Frankly he was unlike anyone I had ever met before, and we became casual friends. It was years later that he would begin appearing occasionally on my radio show to comment on everything from Mexico to monetary policy.

The Establishment wasted no time intensifying their attacks on what they called Trump's "racist" presidential run. GOP squishes like presidential hopeful Senator Lindsey Graham chimed in right on cue. Graham called Trump "a wrecking ball for the future of the Republican Party," "a complete moron," and a "faux Republican." With clairvoyant-like foresight, Graham predicted on CNN that if Republicans do not "reject this demagoguery," "we will lose, and we will deserve to lose."[19] Similarly, Jeb Bush dismissed Trump as "not a constructive force" and "out of the mainstream of what Republicans think."[20]

The GOP Establishment was worried about its brand, and they had reason to be—though it had nothing to do with Trump. Ever since taking control of Congress in November, House Speaker John Boehner and Senate majority leader Mitch McConnell had done next to nothing to defund Obama's executive amnesty. To the contrary, McConnell bent over backward to assure Obama and Democrats that there would be no government shutdowns over policy. Moreover, Paul Ryan defended Trade Promotion Authority (also called "Fast Track"), a power presidents can request from Congress when negotiating trade deals that require Congress to give a deal an up-or-down vote without being able to make any amendments. (Fast Track all but guarantees passage—no deal with it has ever been defeated.)[21] The GOP brand was in such lousy shape because Republicans would suit up for one team and end up playing for the other. Donald Trump's presence in the race and his surge in popularity wasn't causing dissatisfaction with the Republican Party. It was a response to it.

Still, on numerous occasions, Trump suffered self-inflicted wounds by uttering or tweeting unnecessary statements that knocked his campaign off message. Three weeks before the first Republican presidential primary debate, pollster Frank Luntz interviewed Trump before a crowd at the Iowa Family Leadership Summit. Fresh in Trump's mind were John McCain's comments that the billionaire's run had "fired up the crazies." When the subject of McCain came up, Trump took the bait. "He's not a war hero," Trump said. "He's a war hero 'cause he was captured. I like people that weren't captured, OK? Perhaps he's a war hero, but right now he's said some very bad things about a lot of people."[22]

The condemnation was swift and widespread—a full-on dogpile. Many of the Republican presidential candidates saw their opportunity to hammer Trump and took it. Former Texas governor Rick Perry called for Trump to "apologize immediately" and said that his comments "make him unfit to be commander-in-chief of the U.S. Armed Forces." Furthermore, said Perry, Trump "should immediately withdraw from the race for president." (Trump is a forgiving soul apparently; Rick Perry is now his secretary of energy.)

New Jersey governor Chris Christie tweeted: "I know @SenJohn McCain. Senator John McCain is an American hero. Period. Stop."

"When it comes to attacking an American hero, I am going to call that out," said Wisconsin governor Scott Walker. "I denounce Donald Trump for that. He needs to apologize to Senator McCain and all the other men and women who have worn the uniform. That's just a disgrace."

McCain's wingman, Lindsey Graham, was livid. "The good people of Iowa, the good people of New Hampshire, and the good people of South Carolina are going to figure this out. And here's what I think they're going to say: Donald Trump, you're fired!"[23]

The GOP Establishment went into overdrive. Former George W. Bush White House aide Peter Wehner (who I knew long ago, when we both worked for Bill Bennett at the U.S. Department of Education) declared "Trump is toast" and said his comments marked a "tipping point for the Trump campaign" and "the moment it all blew apart for The Donald."[24] Michael Needham, the CEO of the conservative Heritage Action group, lowered the boom. "Donald Trump is a clown. . . . He needs to be out of the race."[25]

But as we know, that's not what happened. As I wrote the following week in my LifeZette column, "Once again, the Establishment GOP and mainline media outlets are out to lunch. A week after the above conventional wisdom saturated the political landscape, Donald Trump has proven he cannot only weather a media firestorm, he can use it to grow his base of supporters." The CNN/Opinion Research survey showed Trump still leading the pack by three percentage points over Jeb. "A week after the Beltway consultancy class declared Trump's campaign DOA, we see that the only thing flat-lining is their credibility," I wrote.[26]

Despite getting hit from all sides, Trump refused to melt or back down. On my show I discussed with callers why Donald Trump was seemingly immune from fallout for his missteps. "He says things that in my lifetime I've never heard a politician say," explained Evan from New York. "We just are tired of canned speeches." Another caller, Dave from Indiana, agreed. "The simple fact of the matter is that he fights. That's why he's worth supporting."[27]

Meanwhile, in their quixotic quest to breathe life into his voterless campaign, Jeb's Establishment cheerleaders in the press splashed effusive praise across readers' iPad screens. Jeb's immigration reform ideas evince "bracing, reformist rigor," waxed *Washington Post* columnist Michael Gerson, a former George W. Bush speechwriter. When pressed on why Donald Trump led the polls and not him, Jeb explained that "the left is angry" but "the right is angrier." He said that he was different, "a committed conservative, but not an angry one."[28] He was probably accurate. One would have to have a pulse to summon anger.

What Jeb and his wealthy enablers never seemed to grasp was that conservatives were tired of the buddy-buddy Republican approach to governance. They relished the idea of an outsider who fought for them more than the Super PAC donors. They wanted a gladiator—a fearless, smart, aggressive pugilist who would enter the arena and stand strong. Voters didn't want to watch a fight they felt was rigged from the start, where both boxers worked for the same management team. After running "grownup campaigns" in 2008 and 2012, GOP voters were ready to rumble. They knew Hillary Clinton and her team of political killers were ready to brawl.

FIGHT NIGHT!

Twenty-four million people. That's how many Americans tuned in on August 6, 2015, to watch the first Republican primary debate held in Governor John Kasich's backyard in Cleveland, Ohio. To say it was a ratings bonanza for debate host Fox News is an understatement. The record-smashing program generated eight times as many viewers as the first GOP primary debate four years prior.[29] Everyone tuned in to see what Donald Trump would say and do. Would he be out of his policy depth and embarrassed? Would his digs against Rosie and other women resurface and be used against him? Would the other candidates have the brass to hit back?

Early in the debate, Fox News moderator Megyn Kelly took aim at Trump. "You've called women you don't like fat pigs, dogs, slobs, and disgusting animals," said Kelly.

"Only Rosie O'Donnell," Trump interrupted to thunderous cheers.

"For the record, it was way beyond Rosie O'Donnell," Kelly fired back. "Your Twitter account has several disparaging comments about women's looks. You once told a contestant on *Celebrity Apprentice* it would be a pretty picture to see her on her knees. Does that sound to you like the temperament of a man we should elect as president? And how will you answer the charge from Hillary Clinton . . . that you are part of the war on women?"

Trump responded that political correctness was crippling the country and alluded to Kelly's past sharp-elbowed coverage of him. "What I say is what I say, and honestly, Megyn, if you don't like it, I'm sorry. I've been very nice to you, although I could probably . . . not be based on the way you've treated me. But I wouldn't do that."

Others on the stage turned in commendable performances. Mike Huckabee was his eloquent self, and Dr. Ben Carson was as soft-spoken, gracious, and thoughtful as ever, finishing with a flourish about his color-blind vision for America. But the Kelly-Trump cage match was all anyone was talking about the following day. Then, during a call-in telephone interview with Don Lemon on CNN, Trump doubled down, dismissing Kelly as an "overrated," "lightweight" journalist, and said, "You could see there was blood coming out of her eyes, blood coming out of her wherever."

Instantly, my cell phone and in-box started blowing up with the best-known political reporters all seeking quotes to include in their daily "Trump, RIP" articles (Trump's supposed obituaries could fill a library). Republican elites smugly tweeted that Trump was finished. Women would revolt. Trump had *really, really* done it this time! Adults would finally rule the GOP presidential race. Former RedState editor Erick Erickson (he's since left the website he founded for something hilariously named The Resurgent) rescinded Trump's invitation to speak at a RedState shindig. "I have tried to give a great deal of latitude to Donald Trump in his run for the Presidency," Erickson wrote imperiously. "His comment was inappropriate. It is unfortunate to have to disinvite him. But I just don't want someone on stage who gets a hostile question from a lady and his first inclination is to imply it was hormonal. It was just wrong."[30] The following week, 30,000 of Erickson's email newsletter readers unsubscribed.[31]

The conservative base saw the RedState (I dubbed it JebState) stunt for what it was: a sad ploy for 15 minutes of relevance. Erickson was even on the cover of *The New York Times Magazine* celebrating his independent spirit (remember: red-on-red violence is the surest PR tactic to win the media's instant adoration). They wanted to interview me as well and snap photos, but I knew better than to help *The New York Times* with their disinformation campaign.

The supposed JebState "rift" wasn't a big deal, and commentators pointed out that Erickson lecturing anyone on decorum and civility was a tad much (he once called former Supreme Court justice David Souter a "goat-[expletive] child molester").[32] Erickson later became a leader among pygmies in the NeverTrump humiliation (more on that later). As for Trump, he jumped seven points higher in the polls to 32 percent versus JebState's patron saint, who received just 11 percent.

Two weeks later, Trump packed the Ladd-Peebles Stadium in Mobile, Alabama, with 30,000 people (probably the same ones who unsubscribed from Erickson's newsletter). Populist Jeff Sessions, the first sitting senator to support Donald Trump, pumped up the crowd and welcomed the candidate "to my hometown, Mobile, Alabama."

(Sessions would prove to be a wise and loyal adviser to Trump throughout the campaign before later becoming his attorney general.) When Trump hit the stage with Lynyrd Skynyrd's "Sweet Home Alabama" rocking in the background, the crowd erupted.

The candidate's promise of an America First populist agenda was clearly connecting with voters. The first person to stand in line for the event was a retired marine. "This isn't about Republicans, it isn't about Democrats," he told CNN. "This is a movement of citizens across America tired of the BS."[33]

THE ESTABLISHMENT HITS THE WALL OF REALITY

As the campaign lumbered toward Labor Day 2015, a clear pattern started to emerge. The anti-Establishment candidates—led by Donald Trump, Ben Carson, and Ted Cruz—clustered toward the top of most polls. Of greater concern to the GOP Establishment was the fact that the anti-Establishment group's combined support was approaching a majority of the vote. The Establishment took solace in predictions by the "experts." "I don't think that Donald Trump is very likely to win the nomination," said famed pollster Nate Silver.[34] Then Carly Fiorina had her commanding performance in the second debate viewed by 23 million people, lending further momentum to the anti-Establishment candidates. Her riff against Planned Parenthood resonated with pro-life conservatives, and her detailed response on Syria showed she had studied the issues. Wisely, she kept her focus on attacking Hillary Clinton more than anyone else. As for Jeb, his support kept trending down, spurring whispers that perhaps Marco Rubio or Ohio governor John Kasich might emerge as the globalists' best hope.

Kasich struggled to shake his image as a moderate dullard. *Washington Monthly* called him "abrasively boring."[35] The Ohio governor tried to dismiss such characterizations as merely a function of his "positive message." But most conservatives saw his warmed-over Bush-style views differently. "If Kasich were any more boring, he'd be Jeb! Bush," Ann Coulter tweeted.[36]

In mid-September I had Kasich on my radio show. I asked him about comments he had recently made in New Hampshire lauding

the benefits of illegal immigrants and his desire for a path to legal status. "Well, we're certainly not going to ship them out of the country,"
Kasich snipped. "What I'm saying is a lot of these folks who are here,
they're law-abiding, they're God-fearing, they're family-oriented. And
what do you want to do with them?" I said that response sounded
similar to the same things Jeb Bush was saying. "Let's not pit one
American against another," Kasich shot back.

"Well, they're not Americans, Governor. That is the problem," I
replied. "They're not Americans. They violated our laws."

"Well, I have to think about some of the questions you ask," Kasich said. "So, we have these people here and some of them are working for employers and some employers don't even know they're not
here legally. Okay? I know most people who want to hire people don't
want to hire people who came here illegally. But, let's get beyond this.
Let's get this issue settled and let's expand the pie so more people can
work so we can reduce the frustration."[37]

What the pundits and the GOP Establishment could never understand was that a former Democrat and Manhattan billionaire was
more in touch with the concerns of everyday Americans than they
were. The more they hurled their insults (Trump's a "vulgarian," a
"charlatan," his campaign's a "traveling circus"), the more defiantly
his supporters dug in their heels. Until Trump emerged, the self-
righteous and self-appointed arbiters of conservativism were able to
ignore the wrath of working Americans. Trump changed that, and
people loved him for it. It was the most seismic shift in American politics since Ronald Reagan barnstormed the country in 1980. The GOP
elites weren't just politically tone-deaf, they were downright hostile to
their own voters. (Case in point: a couple weeks after the first debate,
Jeb named Eric Cantor the chairman of his Virginia campaign.)[38]

But the elites couldn't see reality. The Consultant Class spent decades convincing rich contributors and unknowing candidates that
their outrageously expensive invoices were justified. After all, they
were the "professionals" and must be paid handsomely for their vast
campaign knowledge.

For example, who could do without the penetrating insights
of Romney campaign chief Stuart Stevens who, after the first GOP

debate, penned a Daily Beast article titled "Why Trump Will Never Make the Ballot."[39] When that turned out wrong, Stevens went thermonuclear and spent the rest of the campaign machine-gunning headlines like: "A Vote for Donald Trump Is a Vote for Bigotry," "How to Beat Trump—For Real," "Stopping the GOP Apocalypse," "The GOP Myth of the Untapped White Voter," and my personal favorite, the subtly titled classic, "The Flat-Earth Set Helped Donald Trump Hijack the GOP and Crash It into the Ground," which Stevens published 24 hours before Donald Trump won the presidency.[40]

No wonder consultants were furious. With a Twitter account, some amateurish YouTube ads, and a bunch of MAKE AMERICA GREAT AGAIN red hats serving as walking billboards, Donald Trump exposed just how clueless and unnecessary high-paid consultants like Stevens truly are.

The Establishment Media had lectured and shamed the hayseeds for their "racist" and "bigoted" lack of politically correct opinions. Donald Trump told the media to go to hell and exposed them for the opposition party they truly are. He also highlighted the folly of their failed business model. "I love Twitter," he said. "It's like owning your own newspaper—without the losses."[41]

Even the so-called conservative "intelligentsia" and think-tankers felt threatened. For decades, libertarian and conservative elites had convinced rich donors that their white papers and conferences must be funded and that their money-losing publications must be subsidized so that their message could "shape the debate" and "move the needle." For a sense of how massive these think tank budgets can get, consider that in fiscal year 2016, the libertarian Cato Institute reported an unaudited operating income of $28,626,000 and net assets of $68,821,000.[42] (That's enough to make Atlas stop shrugging!) Donald Trump demonstrated that what people really wanted was less talk and more action—less theoretical navel-gazing and more focus on solving the real problems of real people.

These Establishment groups would not go down quietly or without a fight. Each would pop up throughout the campaign in a woeful attempt to reclaim and assert their dominance and put down the people's populist rebellion.

On September 25, 2015, Speaker of the House John Boehner announced he would resign from Congress and leave by the end of October. That Boehner's announcement drew more conservative cheers than lamentations was a telling reminder of just how far the GOP Establishment had strayed from the grass roots. A Fox News poll taken at the time found that 62 percent of Republicans felt "betrayed" by their own party.[43] And an NBC/*Wall Street Journal* poll found that 72 percent of GOP voters were dissatisfied with Boehner and Mitch McConnell's leadership.[44]

The grass roots was giddy. When the news broke, I was on air and told my board op to cue the song "Ding-Dong! The Witch Is Dead." Listeners were elated. The Speaker was so unpopular that attendees of the conservative Values Voters Summit being held in Washington whooped and cheered over the Boehner announcement.

The reaction of the leading Establishment presidential candidate Jeb Bush offered an interesting window into how out of touch he was with Republican voters. "I admire John Boehner greatly," said Bush wistfully. "He's a great public servant . . . I think people are going to miss him in the long run, because he's a person that is focused on solving problems."[45] (I'm sure that his sadness had zero to do with the fact that Boehner supported Jeb's candidacy.)

By October, Jeb's donors were getting nervous. The Fox News poll had Bush in fifth place at 8 percent with Donald Trump still at the top of the heap with 24 percent.[46] Indeed, the combined support of the anti-Establishment candidates (Trump, Carson, Cruz, and Fiorina) totaled 62 percent of the GOP primary vote. Jeb's campaign tried to allay donor concerns over the whereabouts of (and results from) their $130 million in donations. The campaign reminded contributors that two governors from large states—Texas governor Rick Perry and Wisconsin governor Scott Walker—had already exited the race. Bush's operatives also said they planned to erect a South Carolina "firewall" that would break Trump's momentum once and for all. The Establishment Media was still insisting that Trump could not win. As Bloomberg columnist Jonathan Bernstein put it in his October 19, 2015, column titled "Seriously, Trump Won't Win": "Everything we know about how presidential nominations work says Trump isn't going to be the nominee, or even come close."[47] Finally, there were 10 out of 12 primary debates left to go—still plenty of time to mount a comeback.

But by the time the third debate in Colorado rolled around on October 28, the television audience size had shrunk considerably. The first and second debates attracted 24 and 23 million viewers respectively. The third debate: just 14 million. Indeed, none of the remaining GOP primary debates reached audiences anywhere near the high-water marks of the initial two. And Trump had already damaged his opponents. "Low-energy Jeb," "Little Marco," and "Lyin' Ted" had already made their way into voters' consciousness. The billionaire's blunt talk and bare-knuckled tactics were working. If any of the candidates were going to take down front-runner Trump, they had just three months to do it before the February 1, 2016, Iowa caucuses.

PREELECTION WHACK-A-MOLE

By November, with 15 candidates still in the hunt, an intense game of whack-a-mole emerged as competing factions angled for ways to knock each other out of the race. During the third debate in Boulder, Donald Trump ridiculed John Kasich's work for Lehman Brothers, a symbol of populist rage against the big banks who had helped crater the nation's financial system through corporate malfeasance and irresponsibility. It was a classic example of Trump the populist renegade battling the Old GOP Guard with an attack on cronyism that offered the Republican Party much-needed distance from its long-standing perception of being owned by Wall Street.

After Kasich bragged about his record of achievements, Trump went in hard on the Ohio governor's record: "This was the man that was a managing general partner at Lehman Brothers when it went down the tubes and almost took every one of us with it, including Ben and myself, because I was there and I watched what happened," said Trump. "And Lehman Brothers started it all. He was on the board. And he was a managing general partner."[48] Trump's attack was a populist channeling of the people's fury toward the big banks, cronyism, and Washington's revolving door, which so many politicians pass through to monetize their access to power. Ronald Reagan wasn't afraid to criticize big business for cutting to the front of the line for lucrative favors through what he called the Washington "buddy system"—and neither was Trump. It was a key moment that tele-graphed that while Donald Trump may be from Manhattan, he would not be bought and paid for by the globalists on Wall Street.

That made many in high finance nervous. "A nasty—and igno-rant—anti–Wall Street climate prevails in both parties, and it's some-thing our industry has to worry about," Horizon Investments chief global strategist Greg Valliere was quoted saying in *The Wall Street Journal*. The *Journal* also noted that throughout the primary the anti-Establishment GOP candidates were "competing to bridge their populist message with the party's traditional support for lower taxes and less regulation" by opposing crony capitalism, TPP, and the Fed-eral Reserve's role in the financial crisis.[49] Among them, Trump did it most convincingly.

The Boulder debate also featured an increasingly desperate Jeb Bush making an awkward attempt to whack fellow Floridian Marco Rubio by hitting him on his woeful voting attendance record in the U.S. Senate. "What is it, like a French work week?" Jeb muttered. Marco was ready for the obvious attack line and dismantled his Florida mentor, albeit kind of nicely. "Someone has convinced you that attacking me is going to help you," said Rubio. "I will continue to have tremendous admiration and respect for Governor Bush. I'm not running against Governor Bush, I'm not running against anyone on this stage. I'm running for president because there is no way we can elect Hillary Clinton to continue the policies of Barack Obama." The post-debate aftermath for Bush was deflating. Marco the protégé had beaten Jeb the mentor. The GOP Establishment began turning its fickle gaze away from Bush and toward Rubio as the possible Trump slayer.

Four days before the November 10 debate in Milwaukee, Marco Rubio's Gang of Eight past came roaring back with a vengeance when New York senator Chuck Schumer, the Democrat cosponsor of his 2013 amnesty bill, went on CNN and took a political bat to Rubio's campaign. Democrats thought Rubio might be a stronger candi-date who could attract Latino voters, so they needed to knock him down. Just as the Florida senator began to think he had finally put the Schumer-Rubio amnesty fiasco behind him, Schumer reminded Americans of Marco's role in creating the 1,200-page monstrosity. "[Marco Rubio] was not only totally committed, he was in that room with us," Schumer said. "His fingerprints are all over that bill. It has a lot of Rubio imprints. He understood it, he molded it, he made it a tough path to citizenship. . . . He was all for it."[50] In a final kick to his cosponsor's teeth, Schumer added: "The amount of votes he's missed is very bad."

Lesson to Republicans: when you lock arms with Democrats, prepare to have them snapped in half at your most vulnerable moment.

Heading into Thanksgiving, the Fox News national poll showed Trump gaining support and in the lead with 28 percent, Carson falling five percentage points to the number two slot with 18 percent, and Cruz and Rubio tied at 14 percent. Jeb came in fifth with a low-energy five percentage points. Christie, Fiorina, Huckabee, Kasich, and Paul remained in the low single digits.[51] Nevertheless, "experts" were still promising Trump was a surefire loser.

Writing in *U.S. News & World Report,* George Washington University professor Lara M. Brown explained to us dummies that "Celebrity businessman Donald Trump is a loser. While his die-hard supporters are sure to protest this logic with an endless number of self-righteous platitudes and personal insults that are as shallow as their understanding of presidential politics, the fact remains that Trump will not win either the Republican nomination or the White House as an independent candidate."[52] (Thank goodness academia operates on the cushy principle of tenure and not real world merit or the professor might be out of a job!)

Then two weeks before Christmas, Donald Trump, sensing that Ted Cruz's 10-point lead in Iowa had climbed too high, questioned whether the Texas senator had "the right temperament" to be president because he acted like a "maniac" in the U.S. Senate. "You can't walk into the Senate, and scream, and call people liars, and not be able to cajole and get along with people," Trump said.[53] Ted played it well, tweeting out a video clip from the '80s movie classic *Flashdance* of Jennifer Beals doing her frenetic dance to the song "Maniac."[54]

Predictably, in the wake of Trump's Cruz attack, Jeb Bush test-drove a "Trump-as-bully" theme before the New Year, calling Trump a "bully" who is "not quite all in command."[55] It wasn't a new line of attack. Before dropping out of a race that many were unaware he had ever entered, former New York governor George Pataki had taken it up a notch, labeling Trump a "schoolyard bully spewing nonsense."[56] The bully attacks failed precisely because the Establishment remained clueless about what was happening in the country. The people were looking for a bully of their own. The voters supporting Trump didn't care whom he hit between the eyes, as long as he defended them. The GOP Old Guard's bully narrative was exactly backward; voters felt like *they* were the ones who had been bullied for years—until Trump arrived and began punching back at the Establishment on their behalf.

The first week of 2016, Chris Christie tried a different and better approach. In a speech delivered at St. Anselm College in Manchester, New Hampshire, Christie said:

> You, the people, have a right to be angry. . . . Showtime is over. We are not electing an entertainer-in-chief. Showmanship is fun, but it is not the kind of leadership that will truly change America. . . . If we are going to turn our frustration and anger with the D.C. insiders, the politicians of yesterday, and the carnival barkers of today into something that will actually change American lives for the better, we must elect someone who has been tested—someone with proven experience, someone who knows how to make decisions because he has been making them for years, in the middle of the firefight that's been going on the last seven years between big government liberal-ism and our brand of freedom-loving conservatism.[57]

Christie's approach recognized what the GOP Establishment ignored: you cannot lead those whose feelings you dismiss or ignore.

Despite his new populist moxie, Christie never caught fire. As Trump and Cruz began to pull into the lead, the GOP Establishment faced a Hobson's choice. They absolutely despised, with every fiber of their being, Ted Cruz. A Capitol Hill staffer told me that they nicknamed him "Green Eggs Ted," mocking his filibuster stunt during the government shutdown. As for Trump, he had spent the past several months trashing everything the Old Guard represented. He had to be stopped.

In early January, with just weeks until citizens began voting, the GOP Establishment unleashed a blitzkrieg against Trump in the hopes of razing his 15-point lead in the polls. On January 6, Bush loyalist and strategist Karl Rove issued an ominous warning. "If Mr. Trump is its standard-bearer, the GOP will lose the White House and the Senate, and its majority in the House will fall dramatically," Rove wrote in a widely cited *Wall Street Journal* op-ed. The Bush people hated Ted Cruz, too, so Rove (George W. Bush, in a burst of inspiration, had nicknamed Rove "Turd Blossom") worked in some combination punches as well. "If the nominee is Ted Cruz the situation will be dicey," Rove warned. The solution to avert mass destruction? "Any of the other candidates, if nominated, will best Mrs. Clinton in a close race and help the GOP narrowly keep the Senate."[58]

The next day, NeverTrump columnist Michael Gerson used his *Washington Post* column to warn Republican voters that if they refused to give up their infantile support for Donald Trump, the Establishment might pick up their marbles and go elsewhere—to a third-party run:

> If Trump were the nominee, the GOP would cease to be. . . . Trump would make the GOP the party of racial and religious exclusion. American political parties are durable constructions. But they have been broken before by powerful, roiling issues such as immigration and racial prejudice. Many Republicans could not vote for Trump but would have a horribly difficult time voting for Clinton. The humane values of Republicanism would need to find a temporary home, which would necessitate the creation of a third party. This might help elect Clinton, but it would preserve something of conservatism, held in trust, in the hope of better days.[59]

Is it any wonder that Gerson was W's chief scribe?

In a tag-team effort, Establishment Media also sowed seeds of doubt in the hopes of dissuading Republican voters from nominating their arch nemesis. Vox ran a piece the first week of January titled "Here's What I Think Donald Trump's Loss Will Look Like" written by their editor-in-chief Ezra Klein. His incisive analysis: "Trump could just . . . not win. He could lose the Iowa caucuses. He could fall short in New Hampshire. A loss in any early state might lead to a loss in every state."[60]

Then, days before the Iowa caucuses, *National Review* dropped its now-infamous "Against Trump" cover issue. The magazine's editor Rich Lowry rounded up 22 conservatives to write essays in an effort to take down the "menace to American conservatism," Donald Trump. The move was roundly castigated by conservatives and was a public relations disaster whose damage only grew after Donald Trump's historic victory. That some of the signatories were my friends made it all the more disappointing. The list included: Bill Kristol, Glenn Beck, Erick Erickson, Brent Bozell, Dana Loesch, Michael Medved, Katie Pavlich, John Podhoretz, Thomas Sowell, and Cal Thomas.

This wasn't the first time *National Review* tried to excommunicate conservatives. In 2003, they launched a similar effort in a cover story called "Unpatriotic Conservatives." Back then they were gunning for Pat Buchanan and the late Bob Novak. "They're Davos conservatives," Pat Buchanan said on my radio show, referencing the annual meeting of the global elite in Switzerland. The late matriarch of the conservative movement and one of my personal heroines, Phyllis Schlafly, put it to me this way: "I'm not going to tell you that Donald Trump is perfect, or right on everything . . . but immigration is the top issue today, and he's the one who made it a front-burner issue."[61] Furthermore, noted Schlafly, "*National Review* is not the authentic conservative [voice]. . . . I don't recognize *National Review* as the authority on conservatism." As evidence, she referenced *NR* founder William F. Buckley's support for giving away the Panama Canal, the axial issue Ronald Reagan ran against in his famous primary battle with President Ford. Former governor Mike Huckabee called it a "fool-hearted errand on the part of the *National Review*" and cast the stunt as yet another example of "elitists who live in their own little bubble and they think they represent rank and file."[62]

Among *National Review*'s beefs with Trump: "He is not deserving of conservative support in the caucuses and primaries. Trump is a philosophically unmoored conservative opportunist who would trash the broad conservative ideological consensus within the GOP in favor of a free-floating populism with strong-man overtones." The *National Review* editors further explained that "Donald Trump is a menace to American conservatism who would take the work of generations and trample it underfoot in behalf of a populism as heedless and crude as the Donald himself." How dramatic.

Progressive reporters and media outlets ate it up, splashing the garish "Against Trump" purple *NR* cover everywhere. Establishment Media hoped that giving the "Against Trump" cover story outsized attention and oxygen might spark a conservative mutiny before voters headed to the polls. The real tragedy from my vantage point was the fact that by maintaining a country club–like air of exclusivity toward Trump's working-class and populist supporters, *National Review* created the impression that the tenets of Bushism had become an orthodoxy conservatives weren't allowed to question. As I wrote in my column at the time, "Who really is the menace? The rough-edged Queens native or the smooth-talking GOP Establishment that has brought us open borders; massive giveaway trade deals; monstrous debt; bank bailouts; and a sprawling government that never stops expanding?"[63]

On February 1, 2016, the day of the Iowa caucuses, *National Review* tweeted out a photo of its "Against Trump" cover with the words "You're welcome." #IowaCaucus.

ALL ABOARD THE TRUMP TRAIN!

Donald Trump's neophyte political campaign spent little money and time in Iowa. The complex caucus system required an extensive and highly organized ground game that his campaign simply lacked. With Trump's Iowa operation a muddle, all eyes turned toward Ted Cruz, who held a strong lead in preelection Iowa polling. The Cruz campaign was nothing if not highly organized and efficient. They used modern micro-targeting strategies and analytics to make data-driven decisions about which voters to persuade to get out to vote. Cruz's victory in Iowa was a significant achievement and the result of a well-oiled ground game machine. Trump finished second, narrowly besting Marco Rubio, who billed his third-place finish as a triumph.

"To God be the glory," Cruz said at his victory rally. "Tonight is a victory for the grassroots. Tonight is a victory for courageous conservatives all across Iowa and our great nation."

Trump's Iowa defeat, while expected, taught him important campaign lessons. "I think we could have used a better ground game, a term I wasn't even familiar with," he said innocently. "You know, when you hear 'ground game,' you say what the hell is that? Now I'm familiar with it." Trump also said he had learned that "the caucus system is a complex system" with which he was unfamiliar. "Don't forget," said Trump, "I'm doing this for the first time. I'm like a rookie and I'm learning fast, and I do learn fast."[64]

Trump would get to apply those lessons eight days later in the first in the nation New Hampshire primary, but not before a pivotal debate moment on February 6 in Manchester. Chris Christie's masterful takedown of Marco Rubio at that debate was like watching one of those chefs at Benihana vivisect shrimp in a brilliant flash of energy.

"Let's dispel this notion that Barack Obama doesn't know what he's doing. He knows exactly what he's doing," Rubio said during the debate.

And then Marco said it again.

And again.

And again.

Rubio robotically delivered the nearly identical statement *four times* in a single debate. In a gutsy move, Chris Christie called him out for using canned sound bites instead of offering in-depth solutions. First, Christie highlighted Rubio's use of "the memorized 25-second speech that is exactly what his advisers gave him." Then, after Marco repeated the same line again, Christie busted him. "There it is. There it is. The memorized 25-second speech. There it is, everybody."[65] More than just a "gotcha" moment, the exchange underscored the perception that Rubio was too young, inexperienced, and was more style than substance when it came to policy and leadership.

Before the New Hampshire debate, Rubio had been the beneficiary of increasingly hostile exchanges between Donald Trump and Ted Cruz. Trump had raised eligibility questions over Cruz being born in Canada and claimed no one in the Senate liked Cruz—spats that distracted both campaigns and offered Rubio a path to slingshot his campaign around the others. But the New Hampshire debate changed all that. Donald Trump may have nicknamed him "Lil' Marco," but after YouTube videos of Rubio's four lines delivered back-to-back flooded social media, the internet rebranded him "MarcoBot."

Three days later, the man whom the elites said would never be a candidate or win anything notched the first primary victory of his nascent political career. Donald Trump had defied the critics in a stunning New Hampshire first-place finish, winning 35 percent of the vote compared to John Kasich, who came in second with just 15 percent. Cruz and Bush came in third and fourth respectively, with Rubio in fifth. After his disappointing sixth-place finish, Chris Christie exited the race. But the damage he inflicted on Rubio remained.

Jeb's fourth-place finish in New Hampshire spurred further calls for him to drop out of the race. After John Kasich's second-place finish, and with MarcoBot still reeling, Republican elites increasingly viewed the Ohio governor as the candidate the GOP Establishment could consolidate behind to take down the Trump-Cruz juggernaut. Jeb's campaign also believed it had erected a "firewall" in South Carolina to stop Trump and promised to roll out its biggest guns, including his brother, former president George W. Bush.

"If you are not ready to play, don't come to South Carolina," Senator Lindsey Graham told an audience during his introduction for Jeb Bush at a campaign rally before the February 20 primary.[66] At another event, Jeb brought out Bush 43, in the hopes he could sell Bushism one final time. The former president also had some score-settling of his own to do after Trump had aggressively attacked him for not keeping America safe from the 9/11 terrorist attacks and his mismanagement of the Iraq War.

"These are tough times and I know that Americans are angry, but we do not need someone in the Oval Office who mirrors and inflames our anger and our frustrations," Bush told South Carolina voters. "Strength is not empty rhetoric. It is not bluster. It is not theatrics. Real strength comes from integrity and character. And in my experience, the strongest person isn't usually the loudest person in the room."[67] The whole thing felt sort of sad—the classic tale of a big brother rushing in to protect his weaker brother from a bully. As for Jeb, he promised a South Carolina "surprise" finish. The only "surprise," however, came in the size of Donald Trump's first-place victory.

Trump beat second-place finisher Marco Rubio by 10 points in the winner-take-all state, giving him all 50 delegates. Cruz finished third with a slender 1,091 votes separating him and Rubio. Jeb finished a distant fourth, narrowly edging fifth-place finisher John Kasich. Surprise!

In the wake of his humiliating defeat, Jeb Bush announced he would drop out of a race that he was never competitive in. The Fox News poll taken days before Bush's exit showed him in fifth place at 9 percent compared to Trump's number one placement with 36 percent.[68] The Republican Old Guard's dream candidate had vaporized $130 million of Donor Class cash. When the receipts were sifted, Jeb's campaign had blown $10 million on consultants, $84 million on ads, $94,000 on fancy dinners and event tabs, and $8 million on organizational infrastructure. The *Times* hailed it "one of the least successful campaign spending binges in history."[69] Columba had a better track record at Tiffany's.

The NeverTrumpers had lost one of their heroes but remained determined; they would do everything in their power to thwart the people's support for Donald Trump.

"[Trump] will not win in November," wrote former Red State chief Erick Erickson one week after Jeb's exit. "He will not win because he turns off a large number of Republicans; he turns off women; he turns off Hispanic voters; he turns off black voters; and the blue-collar voters who support him are not a sufficient base of support to carry him over the finish line." In case readers missed it the first time, Erickson reiterated: "Donald Trump will not win in November. Period. End of story."[70]

GOP ESTABLISHMENT GOES NUCLEAR

On the eve of Super Tuesday, GOP elites were in a panic. In the past, hurling millions of dollars at campaigns altered outcomes. Bush's $130 million vanishing act, however, suggested that Donald Trump's unorthodox campaign philosophy of spending peanuts on traditional advertising may have rewritten the rules. With Jeb out of the race, the GOP Establishment poured all its dreams into Marco Rubio. Many on Fox News began touting Marco in the hope that he could somehow slow Trump's momentum coming off his wins in New Hampshire, South Carolina, and recently Nevada.

A Rubio presidency would, of course, have produced predictable outcomes. He would have urged Congress to pass any trade agreements Obama signed, worked with Democrats to pass his Gang of Eight–style amnesty bill, and followed a similar foreign policy path as the one developed by many of the same people who advised George W. Bush. To voters, that was a reason to run away from him. To the Republican globalist elites, it was a reason to run toward him. Super Tuesday would help settle the score.

The March 1 Super Tuesday contests included 11 states and would test Donald Trump's appeal with Southern voters. Trump swept the South, winning Alabama, Arkansas, Georgia, Virginia, and Tennessee. He also won in the North, including deep-blue Massachusetts and Vermont. Ted Cruz won Alaska, Oklahoma, and his home state of Texas. And as for Marco Rubio, he won the single state of Minnesota. It was a pitiful showing, but it didn't stop CNN's Jake Tapper from hailing Rubio's only win as a "big, big victory."[71]

Many people thought Rubio might drop out after Super Tuesday. I knew that would never happen.

For one, Rubio's home state of Florida didn't hold its primary for another two weeks. And second, I knew that the takeaway for the GOP Establishment—and its enablers at places like *National Review* and JebState—would be that Marco's Minnesota win, combined with Cruz's victories in Texas and Oklahoma and the relatively close Virginia race, suggested that Trump could be stopped. They just needed to go even more negative. Trump represented an existential threat to the old ways of Washington. And Washington was going to use every weapon in its arsenal to annihilate the "menace."

First up, the Establishment rolled out John McCain to lecture Republican voters to obey the wisdom of party elders. "I want Republican voters to pay close attention to what our party's most respected and knowledgeable leaders and national security experts are saying about Mr. Trump, and to think long and hard about who they want to be our next Commander-in-Chief and leader of the free world," said McCain. Presumably, he was referring to the same bunch of gurus who agreed to bring China into the WTO, invade Iraq, and allow American sovereignty to slip away through the gaping hole in our southern border. The people pondered the obvious question: if our party's "most respected and knowledgeable leaders and national security experts" were so smart, why is the world in such a mess?

Next up, presidential loser number two, Mitt Romney. In one of the most scathing and controversial speeches in modern presidential politics, Romney savaged Trump in his March 3 address delivered at the University of Utah.

Romney called Trump dumb: "Donald Trump tells us that he is very, very smart. I'm afraid that when it comes to foreign policy he is very, very not smart."[72]

Romney (a famously successful businessman) called Trump a business idiot: "His bankruptcies have crushed small businesses and the men and women who worked for them. He inherited his business, he didn't create it. And what ever happened to Trump Airlines? How about Trump University? And then there's Trump Magazine and Trump Vodka and Trump Steaks, and Trump Mortgage? A business genius he is not."

Romney called Trump a hater of women: "Think of Donald Trump's personal qualities, the bullying, the greed, the showing off, the misogyny, the absurd third grade theatrics."

Romney called Trump a liar: "Dishonesty is Donald Trump's hallmark."

Romney called Trump a flim-flam artist and worked in a KKK reference: "There's plenty of evidence that Mr. Trump is a con man, a fake. Mr. Trump has changed his positions not just over the years, but over the course of the campaign. And on the Ku Klux Klan, daily for three days in a row."

Romney claimed there were "bombshells" in Trump's taxes.

Romney called Trump a bigot: "He creates scapegoats of Muslims and Mexican immigrants. He calls for the use of torture. He calls for killing the innocent children and family members of terrorists."

After all that, Romney got to the really bad stuff.

"Here's what I know. Donald Trump is a phony, a fraud. His promises are as worthless as a degree from Trump University," said Romney. "He's playing the members of the American public for suckers. He gets a free ride to the White House and all we get is a lousy hat."[73]

Romney's broadside was unprecedented in its viciousness; never had a party's previous presidential nominee gone after his party's leading presidential contender so aggressively and personally. The moment I heard Romney's radioactive address, I took to Twitter.

"The guy who wrote off 47 percent of the country is now attacking the guy who is broadening the reach of the party," I tweeted.[74] Then another: "It's good to see Romney really fighting for something. If only he had cared this much about stopping Obama."[75]

Then I got on the radio: "I think you could call the Romney speech today one of the most glaring examples of self-projection—it's like a psychological projection—that I've ever seen. Because the people who lost this country, who couldn't beat Obama, and were part of the party Establishment that destroyed much of what we love about America, and put us in this debt, and got us in these wars, and messed up our trade policy, and couldn't stand up to President Obama—those people are now projecting their guilt and blame on Trump? Trump wasn't around when all this stuff happened. . . . But somehow this is all his fault, because the people are rising up and saying, 'No more'? It's all *his* fault?"

Ironically, Romney's attack only served to strengthen Trump's grassroots support. Two weeks after Romney's brutal anti-Trump rant, the real estate mogul stood atop the polls with a staggering 20-point lead over Ted Cruz, according to the CBS News/*New York Times* poll.[76] Most Trump haters were ecstatic over Romney's rhetorical onslaught, but across conservative media, virtually everyone was repulsed. *This is how much they despise us,* the base said to themselves. *They would rather have Hillary Clinton as president than allow the people to have their own choice. For them, it's "our way or Hillary."* But the more they messed with Trump, the more popular he grew. As the old saying goes, there are none so blind as those that will not see.

There were a handful of writers, commentators, and television personalities whose vision was 20/20 from the outset. Sean Hannity relentlessly defended Trump from unfair criticisms. Ann Coulter was with Trump from the beginning. Michael Savage wondered if Trump was too good to be true on radio. Bill O'Reilly at Fox was an old friend of Trump's and he was tough but fair covering him. Beyond that, few voices in national media consistently believed Trump could prevail.

In the two weeks leading up to the March 15 delegate-rich primaries, Trump racked up wins in Kentucky, Louisiana, Hawaii, Mississippi, and Mitt Romney's birth state of Michigan. Cruz notched victories in Kansas, Maine, and Idaho. Several of the states were not winner take all and instead allotted delegates proportionally. That meant that even though Trump had won more states, the horse race to the required 1,237 delegates was closer than it might appear. Ben Carson's decision to exit the race on March 4 meant only four candidates remained: Trump, Cruz, Rubio, and Kasich. Despite Trump's strong string of wins and standing in the polls, Establishment Media figures like the *New York Times*'s Ross Douthat maintained Donald

Trump would still lose. "Despite all the evidence that fortune favors him, Donald Trump will not be the Republican nominee," wrote Douthat.[77]

My on-air advice to Marco Rubio was that if he really wanted to stop Donald Trump, he should drop out of the race and urge his delegates to vote for Ted Cruz so he could make a real run at winning Florida. He didn't do that. Instead, Rubio stayed in until March 15 and got blown out by Trump in Florida by 18 percentage points (Trump's 45 percent to Rubio's 27 percent). Trump also scored victories in Illinois, North Carolina, and a majority of the delegates in Missouri. John Kasich received his first and only win in Ohio, the state he governs.

Two days after Trump's impressive wins, the NeverTrumpers embarrassed themselves further by announcing the launch of something called "Conservatives Against Trump." A gaggle of GOP elites had huddled at the Army Navy Club for three hours to explore the viability of a third-party run to stop Trump from winning. Radio host Erick Erickson, a capo of the group, announced on his blog that Conservatives Against Trump would "keep our options open as to other avenues to oppose Donald Trump."[78] *These people just aren't that good at politics,* I thought to myself. These folks couldn't see the writing on the wall—America had moved on, away from them and their half-baked ideas about challenging Trump. All they would accomplish was total alienation from the candidate for whom millions of Americans had rallied and voted.

Weekly Standard editor and committed NeverTrumper Bill Kristol had already pushed the idea of a convention fight, where a candidate not in the current field would become the nominee. He also argued for a third-party option, telling *The New York Times* that such a ticket "would allow voters to correct the temporary mistake (if they make it) of nominating Trump." The third-party effort would be designed to attract people like Marco Rubio's foreign policy adviser Max Boot. "I would sooner vote for Josef Stalin than I would vote for Donald Trump," Boot said. "There is no way in hell I would ever vote for him. I would far more readily support Hillary Clinton, or [Michael] Bloomberg if he ran."[79]

YES, IT'S REALLY GOING TO HAPPEN

Throughout April, a big topic of debate was whether Donald Trump could make the delegate math work to reach the required 1,237 votes needed to win the Republican nomination. The Cruz campaign's laser-targeting of delegates kept the Texas senator in the hunt. It also didn't help that the Trump campaign was highly disorganized and very late to the delegate selection game. Cruz bagged all 34 delegates through shrewd maneuvering at the Colorado GOP convention. "[I]nstead of putting together a top-notch convention team, Trump's campaign was a mess," wrote Harry Enten for the FiveThirtyEight election blog.[80] The New York Times saw "growing signs that he is not well equipped to succeed in the lower-profile skirmishes for delegates" and speculated that "he may have crippled his hopes to win a multi-ballot convention."[81]

Not only did Trump not lick his wounds, he went on a populist tear. "How is it possible that the people of the great State of Colorado never got to vote in the Republican Primary? Great anger—totally unfair!" Trump tweeted. Then another: "The people of Colorado had their vote taken away from them by the phony politicians. Biggest story in politics. This will not be allowed!"[82] And he didn't let it go. On April 19, the day after his big New York primary victory, he was back at it. "It's a rigged, crooked system that's designed so that the bosses can pick whoever they want," he boomed. "It's rigged for lobbyists. It's rigged for the donors. And it's rigged for special interests. It's dishonest."[83] The elites saw this as a blatant, weak attempt at blame-shifting. I saw it as a smart political move.

But Ted Cruz wasn't about to bow out graciously. To me it was obvious that, deep down, he believed he had earned and deserved the nomination, and that Trump was the human version of the Hindenburg—full of hot air and bound to blow up. It must have been exasperating for Cruz, who rose from modest means to become a star at Harvard Law School, a Supreme Court clerk, Solicitor General of Texas, and a U.S. senator, to be losing to a guy who just jumped into politics 10 months earlier and was a Democrat most of his life. A senior Hill aide close to the Cruz staff put it this way: "Trump's not a conservative, not particularly smart—he's an entitled billionaire brat with yellow hair."

Cruz may have lacked a realistic mathematical path to reach 1,237 delegates before the Republican National Convention, but he believed he could stop Donald Trump from getting there, too. "We are headed to a contested convention," Cruz said confidently. "At this point, nobody is getting 1,237. Donald is going to talk all the time about folks not getting to 1,237. He's not getting there, either."[84]

Then on April 25, just one day before five big GOP primaries, reports of a Cruz-Kasich alliance began hitting the wires. Ted Cruz said there was "big news" in Indiana. "John Kasich has decided to pull out of Indiana to give us a head-to-head contest with Donald Trump."

The Kasich campaign confirmed the plan with a statement: "Our goal is to have an open convention in Cleveland, where we are confident a candidate capable of uniting the party and winning in November will emerge as the nominee," said Kasich chief strategist John Weaver, who has advised a string of losing presidential candidates. The farcical plan was that Kasich would let Cruz take Indiana. "In turn," said Weaver, "we will focus our time and resources in New Mexico and Oregon, both areas that are structurally similar to the Northeast politically, where Gov. Kasich is performing well."[85] (Can you believe this guy gets paid to spout such bunk?)

Hours after the story broke, John Kasich seemed to unravel the whole thing during a campaign event in Philadelphia. Indiana voters "ought to vote for me," Kasich said. "I don't see this as any big deal."[86]

Trump's Twitter taunts soon followed. "Lyin' Ted Cruz and 1 for 38 Kasich are unable to beat me on their own so they have to team up (collusion) in a two on one. Shows weakness!"[87]

Voters apparently agreed. The next day, Donald Trump won Pennsylvania, Maryland, Connecticut, Delaware, and Rhode Island. In a last-ditch effort to reset the narrative, Ted Cruz announced the following day he had chosen Carly Fiorina as his vice presidential pick. A few days later Fiorina fell off a stage during a Cruz event. The episode went viral and served as a metaphor for what was happening to the Cruz campaign. After Trump clinched Indiana on May 3, Ted Cruz dropped out, making Carly Fiorina's the shortest vice presidential run in modern history.[88] "Well, @TedCruz ran an amazing campaign. Tough race but bright future," I tweeted. After initially head-faking that he would stay in the race, Kasich dropped out the next day.

On May 26, Trump had passed the magic 1,237 delegate mark needed to win the nomination after winning Washington State and unbound delegates in North Dakota. After 56 primaries, 12 debates, and hundreds of rallies, the last man standing was Donald J. Trump. He had never held elected office. He defied every rule, upended every assumption, spoiled every "expert" prediction. In the end, the Trump way was the winning way. The real estate mogul beat a Republican field of 16 other candidates that included nine governors and five U.S. senators. He did it without the big donors, without a bevy of consultants, and without taking on massive campaign debt from paid advertising.[89] He was his own best ad man, his own best consultant, his own best strategist.

At times he was rude and often over the top, but the voters seemed to think it was time for someone who was real and unafraid to take on the failed policies and personalities in his own party. The more conventional, go-along-to-get-along candidates in the last two election cycles lost badly. Most Republicans were willing to look past Trump's flaws because he was fighting for them. Like they did with Reagan, the people chose someone who didn't owe anything to the old GOP hacks. He was calling them out, and many voters felt "It's about time!" Let's face it, it took a a lot of guts and grit for someone at age 70, from the New York real estate world, to enter the race supremely confident that he knew best how to fix things—even better than those who had been the chief executives of large, complicated states.

Trump had already busted through many barricades on the way to sewing up the nomination, but the hard work was just beginning. Next there was the Republican National Convention in Cleveland, Ohio, where some NeverTrumpers were (still) plotting his takedown. The bad blood between Trump and Cruz bubbled up during

the outset of the proceedings with Virginia's Ken Cuccinelli (a former Cruz adviser) throwing a fit about the RNC not using a roll-call
vote but instead a simple voice vote to establish the convention rules.
(The NeverTrumpers hoped a roll-call vote would provide a chance
to embarrass Trump and therefore wanted it.) It was a harbinger of
convention-related intrigue to come. Indeed, the televised four-day
RNC spectacle would kick off what promised to be the greatest general election drama in modern U.S. history.

7.

THE PEOPLE'S VICTORY

Donald Trump's Unconventional Convention

We will no longer surrender this country, or its
people, to the false song of globalism.
—Donald Trump

The globalists might not have seen it coming, but the populists did. On June 23, 2016, the news from the United Kingdom sent shock waves through world governments. By voting to exit the European Union (EU), the British people reclaimed control of their destiny from a horde of foreign elites who had ruled them for decades. Unelected bureaucrats in Brussels were indifferent, and even hostile, to the desires of the British people. The EU imposed costly regulations and taxes on the UK that stifled economic freedom. EU indirect taxation cost the UK an average of between $11 billion and $14 billion a year. And the costliest 100 EU regulations set the UK back $49 billion, which as Forbes notes, "exceeds what the UK Treasury collects in Council tax (a tax on domestic property) on an annual basis."[1] The EU open borders immigration policies also lowered British workers' wages and opportunities while placing the UK's sovereignty and self-determination in peril. While Britain still had its Parliament and elections—the trappings of democratic governance—the real power had increasingly been ceded to an unaccountable Eurozone establishment with globalist ambitions.

It took the visionary UKIP leader Nigel Farage to build the populist Brexit movement, defying impossible odds and reshaping the contours of global politics. When I had first introduced my radio listeners to Farage years earlier, some probably wondered why his views were relevant here. Farage was a chain-smoking, joke-cracking warrior for working-class Brits. He was fearless and his views resonated with me. He properly diagnosed what ailed his country—and mine. As early as 2014, I tweeted out a photo of Nigel and me along with the words "We need a Nigel Farage!"[2]

It was only a matter of time before the British rose up against the EU globalists who had stripped them of their sovereignty through mass immigration, destroyed their wages, and disrupted communities—all while being labeled bigots by those who fancy themselves their betters in the media for grumbling about it. Defying expectations and the polls, for once, everyday working people had taken a stand against the elites and finally said, "Enough." I watched the Brexit victory live and it felt like election night here in the United States. I was ecstatic. If they could have a populist movement succeed, why can't we? I asked myself.

"Taking on the establishment and challenging consensus is certainly a rough old game," Farage said after the Brexit vote. "We heard the threats, we heard the ridiculous scare stories about world wars and apocalyptic visions, but the British people stood tall and refused to be bullied and threatened by the political class who have let so many in our country down so badly."[3] He later added, "This is a victory for ordinary people, for good people, for decent people. . . . We have done it without having to fight. We have done it without a bullet being fired. We have done it by damn hard work on the ground. . . . Let June 23 go down in history as our Independence Day!"[4]

The Establishment press in the United States and Europe went ballistic and declared the populist victory a cataclysmic event. *Time* columnist Ian Bremmer said "Brexit is the most significant political risk the world has experienced since the Cuban Missile Crisis."[5] American progressive politicians were equally hyperbolic. "It is going to have a devastating effect," warned Democratic representative John Lewis. Hillary Clinton was worried about what the British peasants had done. "Our first task has to be to make sure that the economic uncertainty created by these events does not hurt working families here in America," Hillary warned.[6]

Donald Trump, however, embraced the Brexit victory and said it foreshadowed an American populist uprising that would also shake the Old Guard in November. "They're angry over borders. They're angry over people coming into the country and taking over," said Trump. "They took back control of their country. It's a great thing." When reporters asked him whether there were similarities between Brexit and the populist movement powering his own campaign, Trump couldn't deny the resemblance. "I really do see a parallel between what's happening in the United States and what's happening [in the UK]. You just have to embrace it; it's the will of the people."[7]

That Brexit occurred just weeks before the official start of Donald Trump's general election campaign seemed providential to conservatives and worrisome to progressives. "Does Brexit Mean Donald Trump Will Win U.S. Election?" asked CNN.[8] *The New York Times* took a similar approach, asking: "Is 'Brexit' the Precursor to a Donald Trump Presidency?"[9]

The Establishment Media did its best to minimize Brexit's relevance to the U.S. presidential election, but it was clear to me the elites were feeling seriously threatened by the power and resonance of economic policies that placed the interests of ordinary workers first. As I wrote the day after Brexit:

> We Americans will soon face a similar choice. For years now, Americans have been trying to change policy at the ballot box. But the policies don't change very much, because so much power is beyond the reach of the voters. The Fed sets monetary policy without concern for what we think. The Supreme Court makes social policy without concern for what we think. The WTO makes trade policy without concern for what we think. . . . That's why Republican voters nominated Donald Trump. He was the only candidate who understood the importance of restoring American independence. And most Republicans understand that independence is essential to having real pro-American policies. Britain has chosen freedom

and independence. In November, Americans have the opportunity to make the same choice.[10]

Whether Americans would make that choice, I wasn't yet sure. But I was prepared to do everything I could to boost the odds.

AN RNC CONVENTION FOR THE AGES

In mid-June 2016, my cell phone rang and it was Don Trump Jr. He asked if I was interested in speaking at the Republican National Convention the next month in Cleveland. Considering it for about five seconds, I told him I'd love to.

Around that same time, the press was awash in stories about how few prominent Republicans were willing to take the stage at the RNC. "Hardly Anybody Wants to Speak at Trump's Convention," blared the June 27 headline in Politico.[11] The *Washington Monthly* had the same take, adding in the subtitle that it was "Trump's toxicity" that had scared potential participants away.[12]

Toxicity? The Bushes had been considered so toxic that neither George H. W. Bush nor George W. Bush were in attendance at the previous two GOP conventions. There was some dinky video tribute to Bush 41 in 2012, but other than that both McCain and Romney knew the party's base didn't fancy themselves "Bush Republicans," so both basically pretended the Bushes didn't exist.

The candidacy of a man like Donald Trump horrified the Bush Political Complex—his braggadocio, his flaunting of wealth, his refusal to play by the ground rules that always favored the Establishment. Not only were they disgusted by Trump's primary attacks against Jeb as "low-energy," they considered his entire ascendancy an affront to their internationalist, "compassionate conservatism" philosophy.

They were right. The rise of Trump represented a total break with the old Bush order, which is precisely what grassroots Republicans had wanted for years.

Nothing was going to stop me from speaking on behalf of the only candidate since Ronald Reagan who had dared to take on the old GOP Establishment and actually had a real chance of winning.

As I noted earlier, Trump wasn't the first well-known populist to run. It took time, but the pent-up yearnings of the electorate stirred by Pat Buchanan (1992, 1996, 2000), Mike Huckabee (2008), and Rick Santorum (2012), had found their champion. Trump offered a bold agenda Americans could rally around and an appealing fearlessness when dealing with his political rivals on the right and left.

Yes, there were times when Trump's "smashmouth" campaigning style pushed the bounds of civility. The media and Trump's political opponents harped endlessly on this, sure that it would drive voters away from him. But what the pundits and consultants didn't understand was that most GOP voters felt as if they had been callously ignored, lied to, and let down by Republican politicians and their policies. So Trump's rhetorical excesses were easy to forgive. Compared to the robotic, staid lifelessness of the Romney and McCain campaigns, it was refreshing.

My first GOP convention was in 1996 when the GOP nominated Bob Dole. Held in beautiful San Diego, it was meticulously organized and thoroughly dull. This one would be anything but—and I wasn't going to miss being a part of it.

I was contacted by the convention organizers and told my speaking slot would be in prime time, on Wednesday, July 20. (Okay, I had insisted on the prime-time part.)

Consistent with the primary season, the lead-up to the convention was a whirlwind of anxiety and excitement on the right. Even all the way up in Stowe, Vermont, where my family and I were visiting friends for the long Independence Day weekend, the only thing people wanted to talk about was Donald Trump. "Do you think he can win?" asked one guy from upstate New York. "I can't say it out loud here, but I kinda like him," a 50-something woman working the cash register at a mountain-side coffee shop told me.

The fireworks we watched from the balcony seemed a little brighter on that July Fourth.

Meanwhile, FBI director James Comey was setting off fireworks of his own. On July 5, Comey rendered his bizarre non-indictment-indictment of Hillary Clinton for her use of a private server and handling of classified emails. Republicans were dumbfounded and

Democrats relieved to hear Comey's conclusion. (This was the moment when liberals demanded Comey's firing. Their fervor lasted until President Trump actually fired him, at which point they demanded Trump's impeachment.) After reciting a litany of Hillary's misdeeds, the FBI director concluded:

> To be clear, this is not to suggest that in similar circumstances, a person who engaged in this activity would face no consequences. To the contrary, those individuals are often subject to security or administrative sanctions. But that is not what we are deciding now. As a result, although the Department of Justice makes final decisions on matters like this, we are expressing to Justice our view that no charges are appropriate in this case.[13]

Comey's inexplicable failure to prosecute Hillary aside, the email saga had done major damage to her credibility with voters. On July 12, NBC reported that a whopping 82 percent of those surveyed agreed that it was inappropriate for Clinton to use a personal email server while secretary of state, including 68 percent of her own supporters.[14] Interestingly, 56 percent of all voters disagreed with Comey's refusal to bring charges.

Signs of hope for Trump's "America First" general election theme were there for any honest media to notice. A July 13 Quinnipiac Poll had Trump ahead by two in Pennsylvania, by three in Florida, and tied in Ohio, despite unfailingly negative press coverage and disunity among party leaders.[15]

With the GOP convention closing in, Trump had to choose a running mate. It was widely reported that Trump seriously considered picking his longtime friend New Jersey governor Chris Christie for the slot. Christie understood Trump and vice versa. After he dropped out of the race following his disappointing finish in New Hampshire, Christie became a tireless, pugnacious Trump defender when so many of the Establishment GOP was dumping on him.

But as much as I had come to appreciate the loyalty, political skill, and brains of Christie, the selection of Mike Pence, who was still the governor of Indiana, made sense and was a great choice. I had known him for almost 20 years, and he was a reliable warrior in some of the most important political battles of the 2000s. He bucked party leaders, resisted Bush's Medicare expansion, and even opposed "No Child Left Behind." I supported Congressman Pence in his 2006 bid to become House Minority Leader after the GOP's disastrous midterm election.

A decade before he would accept the GOP nomination for vice president, then-Representative Pence was on my radio show almost presaging the rise of Trump, slamming Boehner's desire to press some grand immigration bargain. "All those debates about compromise are a thing of the past. I reject any form of amnesty, even if we've got border security," he said. "I really reject the idea that people whose first act in this country was a violation of the law ought to be able to get right with the law without leaving the country."[16]

Pence might not have succeeded in taking down the Establishment's favorite, John Boehner, but the brave effort caught my attention and we became political friends. With his background in local talk radio, he was a perfect choice to be an occasional fill-in host for me. He obliged on a few occasions, but I always thought it was more important for him to keep his day job.

To Americans who were just getting to know him, Pence came across as a sober, dependable, steady man of deep faith. At least in demeanor, he was the anti-Trump. He appealed to all three legs of the Republican stool—social conservatives, fiscal conservatives, and foreign policy conservatives. Everyone seemed reassured by the Pence pick. Again, Trump's ultimate political instinct was sharp.

I was relieved to arrive in a Cleveland so heavily fortified that protestor sightings were a welcome curiosity. One random protestor kept trying to burn the American flag, only he couldn't get the fabric to catch—somehow it made me think of Jeb Bush's campaign. No matter the malcontent's remedial arson skills, he did manage to draw a crowd: 15 cameras and a wall of police in riot gear.

I didn't pay much attention to the sideshow; prepping for my speech was all-consuming. The audience would be 20 million+, and I wanted to hit it out of the park.[17]

For nearly the entire year leading up to the convention, I had done my best to keep my listeners focused on the big picture of what

Trumpism could offer America. The lemmings in the media loved chasing his tweets, but I loved the agenda of economic nationalism, his rejection of George W. Bush's interventionist foreign policy, his anti–political correctness, his belief in real borders, and his desire to roll back Obamacare. After decades of seeing America's middle class crushed by a government that had become sickeningly corrupt through corporatism and globalism, I truly believed that this could be our last chance to turn things around.

"Remember, you're not just talking to your talk radio base," my best friend Raymond Arroyo reminded me. "You're also talking to Republicans who despise everything that Trump stands for—and the handful who haven't endorsed Trump."

An old friend from Texas, whom I tend to call when I need a pep talk, put it bluntly: "They already know you're a fighter, hon, what they need now is to see your heart."

I tweaked the speech and rehearsed it with Raymond, whose own experience in theater came in handy. He helped with pacing and inflection. "Don't rush it. Enjoy it," he advised. This wouldn't be a speech for the page, but a speech for the ear, intended to wake millions of Americans to the importance of uniting the party, supporting Trump, and finally defeating the Clinton machine.

We did a run-through in a small, cramped room with a tiny teleprompter. A handful of representatives from the RNC and the company that ran the convention were present. Somehow I managed to nail it on the first take, and it topped out at 12 minutes. "Wow. Really great," one of the staffers commented. "But it's too long—you have to cut it down."

Raymond and I looked at each other knowing the only answer I could give was "sure." We returned to the computers in the back room, proceeded to change a few words here and there, and actually made the speech longer.

By the time 8 p.m. rolled around, the butterflies had kicked in "big league." In one of the green rooms, huddled with Raymond, I ran through the speech one more time, including my exit. "Don't be in such a hurry to walk off stage," he urged me.

About 15 minutes before my intro, I was led to this upper lounge area directly backstage. Nick Ayers, who would later become Pence's vice presidential chief of staff, and whom I had met years ago when he worked for the Republican Governor's Association, was also there. We talked about how lame it was for any serious Republican to sit on the sidelines, given all that was at stake for America. Silently, in my mind, I did a quick Hail Mary, and thought about my parents and how I wished they could be in Cleveland and a part of this.

Raymond wanted to stand with the crowd on the floor, so he joined my friend Wendy Long among the New York delegation. Since they hailed from the candidates' home state they were seated up front. "Break legs," he grinned and gave me a hug.

Then the words . . . "Ladies and gentleman, Editor-in-Chief of LifeZette . . . Laura Ingraham." The walk across the expansive, empty stage to the lectern seemed to take forever. All I kept telling myself was: *enjoy the moment—and don't trip.* I began:

> You all may know me from TV and radio, but my kids know me by my most important name—mom. I am a single mother of three adopted kids. They are watching in Minnesota right now. Hi, kids! And I'm here tonight supporting Donald Trump because, like most Americans, I refuse to leave my kids a country that is worse off than the one my parents left me.

I then shared the lessons my parents had passed on to me.

> My parents, they grew up in Depression Era New England. My dad, he enlisted in the Navy in World War II. My mom, she waited tables until she was 73 years old. My dad, he worked at his car wash. My parents flew the flag at our house, and not just on the Fourth of July. And they scrimped and saved. My mother made my clothes. She wore the same winter coat for 40 years. Any extra money in our house went into the bank for our education. And we learned that there is dignity in every job. Every job. No matter what you do. . . . You see, my parents didn't believe there were jobs that Americans

wouldn't do. . . . I remember watching the news with my mom at night. And one night I asked her, I said, "Mom, why are people burning the American flag?" And she looked at me and she answered, "Honey, because their parents didn't teach them about respect."

The crowd came to its feet and cheered, a moment I hoped my mother enjoyed from above. I then talked about the decline of respect in America—for our people, for our veterans, for the police, for the Constitution, and for the life of "the infant in the womb or the elderly who languish alone."

I couldn't leave Hillary out. "Many in public office don't enforce or respect the rule of law. Isn't that right, Mrs. Clinton?" I said, pointing and looking directly into the camera. "Lock her up! Lock her up! Lock her up!" the audience chanted.

> Donald Trump knows that a nation without borders isn't a nation at all. But Hillary Clinton? She doesn't believe in borders. Donald Trump knows that a country must put its citizens first—its own people first. Hillary Clinton thinks America is just another nation in a global order. Donald Trump, he understands that America's greatness comes from her people, comes from her freedom. Hillary Clinton? Well, she believes that our greatness can only be found in the ever-growing, bloated government bureaucracy that she, her Majesty, can rule over. You can almost see the robes being placed over her shoulders. She believes that there's a government solution for every problem. No, Hillary, *you're* the problem!

MAKE AMERICA GREAT AGAIN signs waved in the air as audience members stood chanting, "Laura! Laura! Laura!" It was embarrassing.

> I want to say this very plainly. We should all—even all you boys with wounded feelings and bruised egos—and we love you, we love you—but you must honor your pledge to support Donald Trump now! Tonight! Tonight!

The crowd shot up to its feet for a 45-second standing ovation, chanting: "We want Trump! We want Trump! We want Trump!" Toward the end of their applause I said, "I hope they are listening to you. I hope they are listening."

America, we need a president who believes in the Constitution and who will fight for us, not against us. Treat us like an ally, not an enemy. Fight alongside with us. We are not the enemy. We're the people. We are not your servants. You're ours!

I then looked and pointed up at the press boxes lining the back of the arena.

To all my friends up there in the press, you all know why in your heart Donald Trump won the Republican nomination. You know it. You know why he won it? Because he dared to call out the phonies, the frauds, and the corruption that has gone unexposed and uncovered for too long. Too long. Do your job!

The crowd came to its feet for another 45-second standing ovation, something I'm sure the networks just loved.

Donald Trump respects us enough to tell us the hard truths about what has happened to our country—on issues like immigration, trade, and our diminished status around the world—even in the face of unfair criticism and sheer hatred. They had their chance. Now, it's our chance. . . . Let's defeat the Clinton machine. Let's send the consultants, the pollsters, and the lobbyists packing. Let's give the power back to the people. And let's elect Donald Trump president of the United States! God bless you and God bless the United States of America.

When I walked off, I felt grateful to have had the opportunity to speak on behalf of so many of the people I grew up with, for the America they saw slipping away. The speech went more than double the allotted time—17 minutes plus, and I only learned later that some poor guy was standing below, stage right, furiously waving his hands, trying to get me to wrap at nine minutes. Whoops.

When they handed me my cell phone backstage, it started pinging with text messages. Friends and people I hadn't heard from in years were sending their well wishes. I was relieved. "Home run!" "When are you running?" "Nice way to stick it to the press!" etc. For the previous year, anchors and pundits, pollsters and consultants had sneered at those of us who believed Trump's populist appeal was real, and now they were forced to digest a new reality. The people were mad as hell and weren't going to take it anymore.

"Ingraham Rocks the GOP," CNN reported, noting I "brought down the house with an attack on the Donald Trump holdouts."[18]

I was making my way out of the staging area when Senator Ted Cruz and his wife, Heidi, rushed by me in a flurry. His speaking slot was minutes away, and the place was buzzing with speculation about whether he was finally going to endorse Trump.

"Uh, Ted, that's no way to greet me!" I called after him. Sheepishly, he walked back and gave me a quick awkward hug. "Hello Laura, we were listening on the radio. Good job," he said. "You gotta endorse him tonight," I told him, looking him right in the eyes. "Did you hear the crowd just now?" He didn't answer and continued on his way. Heidi did say to me, "You'll hear a lot of love in his speech tonight, Laura—a lot of love."

Uh-oh, I thought to myself. *Love on the rocks, maybe.*

Soon I headed up to the skyboxes where Trump's friends and GOP donors milled around nibbling on shrimp and barbecue and drinking adult beverages. One of the first people I saw in the stairwell was South Carolina governor Nikki Haley. Months earlier I had excoriated her on radio after her "GOP response" to the State of the Union message, which she aimed more at Trump than Obama. But she was pleasant and on board with Trump, which made her far more loyal and politically savvy than Cruz, Kasich, and Bush.

"Laura!" someone called as I was dashing between events. "Good job with the speech." It was the Univision anchor Jorge Ramos, sitting on the floor with his laptop. An ardent immigration amnesty proponent and a fierce opponent of Trump's border wall, Ramos and I don't agree on much, but I thought that was magnanimous of him. Indeed, Trump's border wall proposal infuriated the globalists as much as or more than any of his policy stances. In his announcement speech he had declared America wouldn't just build any old wall, it would be a Trump wall—and the invoice would be shipped south. "I will build a great wall—and nobody builds walls better than me, believe me—and I'll build them very inexpensively," Trump declared. "I will build a great, great wall on our southern border, and I will make Mexico pay for that wall. Mark my words."[19] Had the Trump haters in the press been paying attention, they would have known he had been touting the wall for years. In his 2011 policy book, *Time to Get Tough: Making America #1 Again,* Trump offered a detailed proposal to combat illegal immigration that he called "The 5-Point Trump Plan." The number one policy item on his five-point list: building the border wall. After citing plunging-apprehension statistics from the Yuma, Arizona, sector where a serious wall had been built, Trump said the data show "properly built walls work" and that "we just need the political will to finish the job." He added that doing so "will employ a lot of construction workers."[20] The people agreed with him, but the elites—many of whom have gates and walls around their mansions—scoffed and trashed it as garish and racist.

The aftermath of my RNC speech felt like an out-of-body experience that I was watching play out from 30 feet above. Americans were looking for signs of hope—and not just from the candidate himself.

A waving Ted Cruz made his way to the lectern as the Texas delegation whirled cowboy hats in the air to greet him. But as Cruz's speech wound down, the audience realized a Trump endorsement wasn't coming:

We deserve leaders who stand for principle. Who unite us all behind shared values. Who cast aside anger for love. That is the standard we should expect, from everybody. And to those listening, please, don't stay home in November. If you love our country, and love your children as much as I know that you do, stand, and speak, and vote your conscience, vote for candidates up and down the ticket who you trust to defend our freedom and to be faithful to the Constitution.[21]

The arena reverberated with boos and chants of "Endorse Trump!" I have never heard a crowd jeer even after a speaker is finished speaking. Comments from those standing around me included such gems as: "What an ass!" "Classless." "I can't believe he's that stupid." "He's finished."

It was so bad that Virginia's former attorney general and Cruz backer Ken Cuccinelli escorted Heidi Cruz off the floor. Not "a lot of love" after all.

People were so torched by Cruz's failure to endorse Trump that talk of primarying him ignited almost the moment he walked off the stage. In fact, a tanned, good-old-boy type in his late 40s approached me and asked me if I'd consider moving to Texas to run against him. He and four or five of his friends were drinking longnecks and busy writing the Cruz obituary.

A short while after Cruz's crash and burn on stage, I stopped by the suite of GOP mega-donor Sheldon Adelson. As I entered the suite, I ran into the soon-to-be-nominee who was just leaving. "How are you feeling?" I asked Trump, knowing he just watched Cruz get booed off the stage. "I couldn't be better," Trump said. "What a great night."

About 20 minutes later, security approached Adelson to tell him that Cruz was outside. "No. Keep him out," he said flatly, and went back to his conversation with his wife as if nothing had happened.

A few moments later, a representative of another of Cruz's big backers, also from Texas, leaned over to me and said, "My boss never—and I mean never—wants to hear from that guy again. He's toast."

When my iPhone went off the next morning at the usual 6:00 a.m., I checked Twitter and Facebook. The good news: I was the number one trending topic on Facebook. The absurd news: some left-wing nutcases were claiming that my final wave to the RNC crowd was a "Nazi salute." Hillary supporters were obviously in total meltdown.

The next night, Donald Trump delivered a nomination speech that painted a stark but accurate picture of America under President Obama—and how much worse it would be under Hillary Clinton.

As Trump said in his speech, "Here, at our convention, there will be no lies. We will honor the American people with the truth, and nothing else."

What followed was a detailed, substantive description of the suffering caused by crime, illegal immigration, and poverty. The words were depressing because they were true:

In our nation's capital, killings have risen by 50 percent. They are up nearly 60 percent in nearby Baltimore. In the president's hometown of Chicago more than 2,000 people have been the victims of shootings this year alone. And almost 4,000 have been killed in the Chicago area since he took office.

The number of police officers killed in the line of duty has risen by almost 50 percent compared to this point last year. Nearly 180,000 illegal immigrants with criminal records, ordered deported from our country, are tonight roaming free to threaten peaceful citizens. The number of new illegal immigrant families who have crossed the border so far this year already exceeds the entire total from 2015. They are being released by the tens of thousands into our communities with no regard for the impact on public safety or resources.

A blizzard of economic numbers came next, including America's $800 billion annual trade deficit, $19 trillion debt, and grinding minority unemployment. "Our convention occurs at a moment of crisis for our nation. The attacks on our police, and the terrorism in our cities, threaten our very way of life," said Trump. "Nearly four in ten African-American children are living in poverty, while 58 percent of African-American youth are now not employed. Two million more Latinos are in poverty today than when President Obama took his oath of office less than eight years ago. Another 14 million people have left the workforce entirely."

The GOP presidential nominee wasn't done; there was more, particularly on national security. ISIS was on the march, Iraq was a disaster, and Syria was now engulfed in a brutal civil war with a refugee crisis that threatened to endanger Western nations. "After 15 years of wars in the Middle East," said Trump, "after trillions of dollars spent and thousands of lives lost, the situation is worse than it has ever been before." He added: "This is the legacy of Hillary Clinton: death, destruction, terrorism, and weakness."[22]

Trump then offered the nation a hopeful vision of a government that made its decisions based on what is best for the people—the individuals whom government had forgotten.

> Every day I wake up determined to deliver a better life for the people all across this nation that have been neglected, ignored, and abandoned. I have visited the laid-off factory workers, and the communities crushed by our horrible and unfair trade deals. These are the forgotten men and women of our country and they are forgotten but they're not going to be forgotten long.
>
> These are people who work hard but no longer have a voice. I am your voice. I have embraced crying mothers who have lost their children because our politicians put their personal agendas before the national good. I have no patience for injustice, no tolerance for government incompetence, no sympathy for leaders who fail their citizens.

In a moving moment, Trump attributed his connection with everyday Americans to his father, as well as his firm belief that there is dignity in every job, regardless of status or salary.

> My dad, Fred Trump, was the smartest and hardest working man I ever knew. I wonder sometimes what he'd say if he were here to see this and to see me tonight. It's because of him that I learned from my youngest age to respect the dignity of work and the dignity of working people. He was a guy most comfortable in the company of bricklayers and carpenters and electricians and I have a lot of that in me also. I love those people.

Despite the populist current running throughout his speech—or perhaps because of it—Establishment Media trashed Trump's address.

CNN's progressive Van Jones said the speech "terrified" him because Trump was "describing some Mad Max America." "He painted a dark and a frightening picture of America, talked about a people being attacked by criminals, attacked by terrorists, betrayed by their leaders, that the game is fixed," said Jones. "And he said he would be their voice, almost echoes of Richard Nixon's silent majority." (He didn't mean that last part as a compliment, but any populist would have taken it as one.) Huffington Post ran a massive bloodred headline that read "American Nightmare" with a stack of sub-headlines declaring the speech "very dark and terrifying" and full of "massive lies and distortions." The *Washington Post* editorial board weighed in with a measured piece titled "Donald Trump, the Candidate of the Apocalypse." Not to be outdone, *The New York Times* ran op-eds with titles like: "Make America Hate Again" and "Donald Trump's Campaign of Fear."[23] NBC's Willie Geist said the GOP nominee created a portrait of the nation that was "almost a dystopian" vision.[24] *Rolling Stone*'s Matt Taibbi painted with a broader brushstroke: "Trump's Appetite for Destruction: How Disastrous Convention Doomed GOP."[25]

NeverTrumpers amplified the media's anti-Trump cacophony by joining in the GOP convention bashing. Mark Antonio Wright at *National Review* went into paroxysms of outrage over the RNC convention, which he said was "slapstick," "amateur hour," and that voters "hated it." Then he intoned: "It's time to accept facts. In 2016, running against a corrupt, unlikable, career politician in Hillary Clinton, the Republican party decided to nominate the only person she could beat. Donald Trump is a historically bad candidate."[26] David Brooks of *The New York Times* called it "the most shambolically mis-run convention in memory" and said he yearned for the days when "Mitt Romney's convention was lifted by stories of his kindness and personal mentorship." (The Establishment's passion for Republicans who politely lose elections is boundless.) Brooks also lamented that Trump was changing the Republican Party's embrace of the "open movement of ideas, people, and trade."[27] You bet he was!

Not all media outlets found Trump's general election launch ineffective. Some, like even the progressive Salon, got it. "Anybody who still thought Donald Trump was a joke and a dumbass who would humiliate himself and his party or go down to Mondale-scale defeat now knows better," wrote Salon's Andrew O'Hehir. "You can pick Trump's speech apart and examine its flaws, of course, but from the point of view of performance and dynamics only one verdict is possible. He killed it. He. Killed. It."[28]

What the naysayers failed to understand was that Trump's speech contained echoes of the same populism that propelled Ronald Reagan's 1980 victory. The notion that Reagan's oratory was universally sunny is just plain wrong. In his 1980 RNC nomination speech, Reagan said: "Back in 1976, [Jimmy] Carter said, 'Trust me.' And a lot of people did. Now, many of those people are out of work. Many have seen their savings eaten away by inflation. Many others on fixed incomes, especially the elderly, have watched helplessly as the cruel tax of inflation wasted away their purchasing power. And, today, a great many who trusted Mr. Carter wonder if we can survive the Carter policies of national defense."

Reagan's populism was rooted in reality. Trump continued that tradition. As vice presidential nominee Mike Pence put it, "The most straight-talking candidate since Ronald Reagan is running against one of the most dishonest candidates ever. The American people picked a bold truth-teller in 1980 and I know they're going to elect a bold truth-teller in 2016. The spirit of 1980 that propelled Ronald Reagan into the White House is alive and kicking again."[29]

For the first time in a long time, the GOP convention reflected the energy of the people more than the party elites and megacorporations. That the left was upset over Donald Trump's nomination speech portended great things for the next three months.

READY FOR HILLARY?

If Donald Trump represented the most populist presidential candidate since Ronald Reagan, Hillary Clinton represented a bold and dangerous expansion of her husband's and Barack Obama's globalist policies. As secretary of state, Hillary had spent four years globetrotting and glad-handing foreign leaders as the chief diplomat of an administration determined to downshift America out of the fast lane of economic freedom to allow other nations to blow by us. The 5,544-page Trans-Pacific Partnership (TPP), blocking the Keystone Pipeline, Deferred Action for Childhood Arrivals (DACA), the 2012 United States–South Korea Free Trade Agreement—these policies and others like them placed foreign interests first and American workers last. Hillary wasn't just a bystander of Obama's globalist agenda. As secretary of state, she was its chief implementer and evangelist.

Hillary's globalist vision went much deeper than her public policy stances and actions. Years before she was installed as America's top diplomat, Hillary and her husband had launched their global philanthropy, the Clinton Foundation. When Obama tapped Hillary to become secretary of state, the administration made Clinton sign a "memorandum of understanding" to prevent foreign influence peddling by Clinton Foundation donors seeking favorable actions from Hillary's State Department. Government watchdogs warned that the Clinton Foundation should immediately stop taking foreign donations, since Hillary's job would give her massive foreign influence, power, and funds to disperse in the form of grants, waivers, and other lucrative concessions. Bill and Hillary ignored such calls, and the Clinton Foundation continued to bag foreign cash throughout her entire term as secretary of state.

Far from slowing down their global activities to avoid conflicts of interest, Bill Clinton accelerated his foreign fund-raising and speeches while his wife brokered deals with world governments. The arrangement was unprecedented and fraught with potential corruption. While Hillary Clinton led her disastrous "Russian Reset," Bill Clinton was in Moscow delivering a $500,000 one-hour speech paid for by a Kremlin-backed bank. As even the liberal *New Yorker* magazine wrote in 2015, "Why was Bill Clinton taking any money from a bank linked to the Kremlin while his wife was Secretary of State?"[30] Moreover, Bill Clinton's most lucrative speaking fees came during Hillary's tenure at the State Department. As Peter Schweizer revealed in *Clinton Cash*, from 2001 to 2012, Bill Clinton had been paid $500,000 or more for a total of 13 speeches. Of the 13 speeches, 11 took place while Hillary Clinton was secretary of state.[31]

There was more. The Clinton Foundation had taken in over a billion dollars from myriad donors, including "tens of millions of dollars in donations from Saudi Arabia, the United Arab Emirates, Kuwait, Oman, Qatar, Algeria, and Brunei—all of which the State Department has faulted over their records on sex discrimination and other human-rights issues," reported *The New York Times*.[32] A front-page, 4,000-word story in the *Times* by Pulitzer Prize–winning journalist Jo Becker also revealed that Hillary Clinton's State Department along with other agencies approved the transfer of 20 percent of all U.S. uranium to Russia and that nine foreign investors in the deal funneled $145 million to the Clinton Foundation.[33]

Hillary and Bill Clinton had taken globalism to new and dangerous heights. They operated the Clinton Foundation like a massive country club for foreign donors and entities seeking access and favors. A blockbuster 2016 Associated Press investigation concluded that an "extraordinary proportion" of Clinton Foundation donors met with Hillary at the State Department. "At least 85 of 154 people from private interests who met or had phone conversations scheduled with Clinton while she led the State Department donated to her family charity or pledged commitments to its international programs. . . . Combined, the 85 donors contributed as much as $156 million."[34] Trump senior policy adviser Stephen Miller summarized the Clintons' system succinctly: "Give money to Bill, get favors from Hill."[35]

Hillary's vast Clinton Foundation network of elite donors also helped fill her 2016 presidential campaign coffers. Clinton's campaign, the Democratic party, and Super PACs hauled in a combined $1.2 billion (compared to Donald Trump, who raised just $647 million).[36] Still, despite her massive war chest, Hillary struggled during the Democrat primary to put away socialist septuagenarian Bernie Sanders. Indeed, the rare places of agreement between Sanders and Trump supporters only served to create more headaches for Clinton.

For example, Trump supporters and far-left Sanders voters found themselves united in opposing the jobs-killing TPP trade deal, which Hillary Clinton praised as "the gold standard in trade agreements."[37] Sanders supporters were outraged to also learn that the Clintons' $110 million+ net worth had been amassed in part by raking in six-figure public speaking fees paid for by elite Wall Street banks. When Sanders voters pressured Hillary to release her speech transcripts, she refused. Then WikiLeaks did it for her and Americans realized why she'd kept them hidden. "My dream is a hemispheric common market, with open borders, sometime in the future," Hillary Clinton said in a 2013 speech before a Brazilian bank. She also stressed the importance of having "both a public and a private position" on controversial policy issues, giving the distinct impression that she talked one way to insiders (i.e., candidly) and another (less than candidly) to the rubes in the country at large.[38]

On the eve of the Democratic National Convention, WikiLeaks also released emails showing then-DNC chairwoman Debbie Wasserman Schultz and other top DNC officials conspiring to defeat Bernie Sanders. Other emails showed top DNC communications staffers discussing narratives against Bernie, including targeting his religion.[39] By the time Democrat activists and delegates arrived for the July 25–28 Democratic National Convention in Philadelphia, Pennsylvania, Bernie supporters were torqued and rained boos from the rafters, leaving Establishment Media to block and tackle to keep Hillary's convention from appearing more chaotic than Trump's. It was so bad, organizers decided not to allow the DNC chairwoman to even speak at the convention over fears Wasserman Schultz would get booed off the stage. (Can you imagine the media meltdown that would have occurred had the RNC chairman been banned from addressing the Republican convention?)

Nevertheless, Democrats knew how to choreograph a convention, tell a story, stay on theme, and quell opposition. For example, they successfully drowned out the voices of the Sanders' supporters with chants of "U-S-A! U-S-A!"

During their convention, Democrats couldn't talk much about the people's economic pain because their policies had caused it. Indeed, missing from Hillary Clinton's acceptance speech was any discussion of the "gold standard" of trade agreements (TPP), Benghazi, her dream of open borders, her secret email server, or her legacy project, the Clinton Foundation. Instead, the speech was larded with the kind of gauzy platitudes junior speechwriters believe are brilliant but that real people find hollow. With no accomplishments to tout whatsoever, Hillary claimed that her nomination itself was the real accomplishment:

> Tonight, we've reached a milestone in our nation's march toward a more perfect union: the first time that a major party has nominated a woman for president. Standing here as my mother's daughter, and my daughter's mother, I'm so happy this day has come. Happy for grandmothers and little girls and everyone in between. Happy for boys and men, too—because when any barrier falls in America, for anyone, it clears the way for everyone. When there are no ceilings, the sky's the limit. So let's keep going, until every one of the 161 million women and girls across America has the opportunity she deserves. Because even more important than the history we make tonight, is the history we will write together in the years ahead.[40]

Hillary's campaign lacked a central message, an argument as to why she—the living embodiment of the Washington Establishment—should be trusted more than the populist movement propelling Donald Trump's anti-Establishment revolution. Unlike "Make America Great Again," her campaign slogan "Stronger Together" was as weak as it was forgettable. That she couldn't connect in the biggest speech of her career was a telling reminder that her campaign's core thesis was, in essence, "It's my turn. Give me what I deserve."

POST-CONVENTION BLUES

The final day of the DNC convention featured a speaker who did connect with his material, Gold Star father Khizr Khan. The Pakistani American lawyer and his wife, Ghazala Khan, were the parents of U.S. Army captain Humayun Khan, who had been killed in action during the Iraq War. With his wife standing silently at his side wearing a headscarf, the Muslim Gold Star father electrified Democrats in the hall with his short and pointed speech. The key passage:

Donald Trump, you are asking Americans to trust you with our future. Let me ask you: Have you even read the U.S. Constitution? I will gladly lend you my copy. In this document, look for the words "liberty" and "equal protection of law." Have you ever been to Arlington Cemetery? Go look at the graves of the brave patriots who died defending America—you will see all faiths, genders, and ethnicities. You have sacrificed nothing and no one.[41]

The next day, Clinton strategist-turned-ABC News anchor George Stephanopoulos asked Donald Trump about Khan's speech. "He was very emotional and probably looked like a nice guy to me," said Trump. "If you look at his wife, she was standing there. She had nothing to say. Maybe she wasn't allowed to have anything to say, you tell me. But plenty of people have written that. Personally, I watched him. I wish him the best of luck, George."[42] Trump also questioned whether "Hillary's scriptwriters" had drafted Khan's remarks and said that he, too, had "made a lot of sacrifices."

I went on Lou Dobbs's program to discuss the controversy. At a time when 70 percent of the country believed America was on the wrong track, and with real U.S. median household income now lower than it was in 1999, the last thing the GOP candidate needed to do was get dragged off message into a sideshow feud with a Gold Star family.

Establishment Media raced to amplify NeverTrumpers' praise for Hillary's convention. "Why this convention is better: It's about loving America," tweeted *National Review*'s Jonah Goldberg. "GOP convention was about loving Trump."[43] CNN read comments from Erick Erickson's blog wherein he declared that "the Democratic convention was a convention of patriotism this year. Democrats were for you."[44]

After a brutal series of news cycles over Khan, and with Establishment Media extolling Hillary's convention, both the Fox News and NBC News polls showed Clinton 10 points ahead of Trump.[45] With less than 100 days left until Election Day, Hillary's double-digit lead gave the press license to further marginalize Trump as an embarrassing anomaly unworthy of being covered like a normal presidential candidate. The *New York Times*'s Jim Rutenberg wrote that all journalists who believe "Trump is a demagogue playing to the nation's worst racist and nationalistic tendencies" must "throw out the textbook American journalism has been using for the better part of the past half-century . . . and approach it in a way you've never approached anything in your career."[46]

Translation: "journalists" are justified in acting as Hillary Clinton campaign operatives and will be celebrated for Trump takedowns.

The eagerness of the GOP dinosaurs to distance themselves from Trump and their willingness to denounce him every time the press told them to wasn't helping either. Instead of fighting the Democrats and Hillary, Paul Ryan, Mitch McConnell, and John McCain were back to fighting against the will of their own base and doubling down on Trump's inevitable defeat. I wrote an urgent column on August 3 telling them to focus on the bigger picture. "Trump can win," I wrote. "Republicans can win. But they have to work together." It was the least GOP elites could do. "For years, working-class Americans have donated time, money, and effort to helping the Republicans. They have given the Republicans the House, the Senate, and many governors' mansions. Now is the time for Republicans to give something back. Stop all the whining and complaining about Trump, and stop letting the Left run all over you."[47] Instead, I said, Republicans needed to "start swinging at Hillary and her gang of radicals," and "not the man who won your party's nomination."

Whether the NeverTrumpers and GOP old guard would continue their "see-I-told-you-so'ing" about Donald Trump was unclear. One thing, however, was certain: the Trump campaign needed to do something bold.

8.

POPULISM'S LAST STAND

The Movement's Revolutionary Win

As I've said from the beginning, ours was not a campaign,
but rather an incredible and great movement. . . . It's a
movement comprised of Americans from all races, religions,
backgrounds, and beliefs who want and expect our government
to serve the people, and serve the people it will.

—DONALD TRUMP

D onald Trump's double-digit polling deficit began to shrink starting on Wednesday, August 17. That was the day he named Steve
Bannon chief executive officer of his campaign. A former naval officer, Harvard MBA, Goldman Sachs executive, Hollywood producer,
and chairman of the populist-conservative website Breitbart.com,
Bannon was known for his intellectual firepower and no-nonsense
management style.

Politically, Bannon is a true populist believer who came from a
blue-collar, Catholic, working-class Virginia family. As the chief executive of the largest populist media website in America, Bannon had
spent years thinking about how to communicate the message of economic nationalism. After achieving success in finance and filmmak-
ing, Bannon says it was watching the toll the 2008 financial collapse
took on his father, Marty Bannon, that ignited his passion for com-
bating the effects of globalism and big, unaccountable institutions on
everyday Americans. His dad had accumulated AT&T stock during
his lifelong career with the company. In October 2008, spooked by the

volatility of the market, Marty sold his AT&T shares, losing $100,000. It was seeing his father lose so much so fast due to the recklessness of the big banks that impelled Steve to embrace a philosophy of economic nationalism. "The Marty Bannons of the world were getting washed out to sea, and nobody was paying attention to them," he told *The Wall Street Journal.* "Everything since then has come from there. All of it."[1]

Joining Bannon at the helm of the campaign was Republican pollster Kellyanne Conway, whom Trump tapped to be his new campaign manager. A protégé of Ronald Reagan's strategist and pollster Dick Wirthlin, Conway had made a name for herself as a smart conservative operative with a knack for exhibiting grace and poise during political firestorms. Kellyanne was already part of Trump's campaign team but had been promoted after Corey Lewandowski's firing, which in turn followed the firing of Paul Manafort.

As soon as the leadership shake-up was announced, the Establishment went nuclear on Bannon. They rightly feared his hard-charging, take-no-prisoners style and penchant for populist policies. Despite Bannon's professional reputation for hiring and mentoring minority journalists, Establishment Media rolled out the usual lies and race-baiting smears, going so low as to label him a "racist" and a "white nationalist." Hundreds of leftists later held marches and rallies to condemn Bannon and called for his immediate ouster. (You know you've achieved conservative rock star status when Soros thugs organize demonstrations to protest your running a political campaign.)

NeverTrump and GOP old guard types also joined the bash-Bannon brigades. Marco Rubio's campaign chief Terry Sullivan trashed Bannon's appointment to Trump campaign CEO and told *The New York Times* that the GOP candidate and Bannon "both play to the lowest common denominator of people's fears. It's a match made in heaven."[2] Mitt Romney's policy director Lanhee J. Chen said Bannon's elevation was evidence that Trump was "going back to the nativism and nationalism that fueled his rise" and was "very dangerous to the future of the [Republican] party."[3]

In spite of the vitriol aimed at him, Bannon's impact was felt almost instantly. Two weeks after his and Conway's arrival, the Trump campaign made a dramatic and unexpected announcement: the candidate would travel to Mexico for a high-stakes meeting and press conference with Mexican president Enrique Peña Nieto to discuss U.S.-Mexico relations on issues like trade and the border wall. When the event went live on television, viewers saw Donald Trump and President Peña Nieto standing side by side behind two presidential lecterns placed in front of a massive green marble wall. The optics were clear: Trump looked serious, respectful, and presidential on the world stage.

Through mutual friends, I had the pleasure of getting to know one of the Mexican officials responsible for arranging the risky but bold Trump trip. Luis Videgaray, then Mexico's finance minister, had surprisingly keen insights into Trump's populist appeal. While most Mexican political players bet against the idea of a Trump presidency, not the MIT-trained economist Videgaray. Although he didn't agree with candidate Trump on the wall, and was annoyed by some of his harsher rhetoric on illegal immigration, he also understood that a president Trump could mean a new, refreshing start for his country's relationship with the United States. Smartly, he struck up a professional friendship with Jared Kushner during the early summer of 2016, which ultimately helped lead to Trump's Mexico visit.

Later that night Trump flew to Arizona and delivered a tough pro-enforcement speech that unnecessarily stepped on the powerful narrative his Mexico meeting had generated earlier that morning. Still, the surprise Mexico trip was a strategic masterstroke that boosted his credibility, heartened his supporters, and signaled a savvy and aggressive new approach to campaigning.

Critics believed Bannon's presence in the campaign would make Trump into a harder, more divisive candidate. It did the opposite. Days after his Mexico meeting, Trump traveled to Philadelphia for a September 2 meeting with black church and community leaders. He also spent time with Shalga Hightower, a black mother whose 20-year-old daughter, Iofemi, had been murdered by a group of men that included two illegal aliens. Trump consoled Ms. Hightower, who, in tears, recounted her daughter's tragic death. Iofemi's killers all received life sentences, Ms. Hightower said. "But they should have never been here," Trump interjected. "But they should have never been here, absolutely," she replied.[4]

Those in attendance expressed their gratitude for Trump's visit. A local black Republican leader named Daphne Goggins began to tear up when she met Trump. "For the first time in my life, I feel like my vote is going to count," Goggins said, crying. Similarly, Renee Amoore, a local business leader, thanked the Republican nominee for making an effort to reach out to the black community. "People say, Mr. Trump, that you have no African-American support. We want you to know that you do," said Amoore. "We appreciate you and what you've done, coming to 'the hood' as people call it. That's a big deal."[5]

Detroit native Ben Carson then accompanied Trump to the Motor City where the presidential candidate met with parishioners at the Great Faith Ministries Church, a predominantly black church. There, Trump visited privately with 100 church members with no press present before delivering simple, humble remarks inside the sanctuary. "I am here today to listen," he said. "I hope my presence here will also help your voice to reach new audiences in our country and many of these audiences desperately need your spirit and your thought."[6] The usual gaggle of anti-Trump protestors had assembled outside the sanctuary. But inside the church, for a brief instant, Trump's presence and heartfelt words revealed a candidate with a sincere desire to connect with a community unlikely to vote for him. It was a beautiful and hopeful moment.

HILLARY SPILLS HER BASKET OF DEPLORABLES

One week after Donald Trump's Philadelphia and Detroit visits, Hillary Clinton attended the LGBT gala for the Hillary Victory Fund with Barbra Streisand held at a tony New York restaurant, Cipriani on Wall Street. Despite her claims to be an "inclusive" candidate who believed we are "Stronger Together," Hillary Clinton let her mask slip and told the progressive mega-donors what she really thought about tens of millions of working-class Americans:

We are living in a volatile political environment. You know, to just be grossly generalistic, you could put half of Trump's supporters into what I call the "basket of deplorables." Right? The racist, sexist, homophobic, xenophobic, Islamaphobic—you name it. And unfortunately there are people like that. And he has lifted them up. He has given voice to their websites that used to only have 11,000 people—now 11 million. He tweets and retweets their offensive, hateful, mean-spirited rhetoric. Now, some of those folks—they are irredeemable, but thankfully they are not America.[7]

Trump supporters weren't just hateful bigots. In Hillary's eyes, the "basket of deplorables" were also "irredeemable." That last part hit with equal if not greater offense. Christians believe that even the worst of sinners are capable of redemption through God's grace and forgiveness. Yet in Hillary's worldview, Trump supporters were a wretched and irredeemable lot, devoid of human worth and dignity.

In an instant, Hillary had ignited a firestorm reminiscent of Mitt Romney's disastrous "47 percent" comment. The hashtag #Basket OfDeplorables trended across social media, as Trump supporters flooded Facebook and Twitter with memes and comments condemning her disparaging remarks. Soon, "basket of deplorables" became a badge of honor that many conservatives wore proudly and literally. "Proud Deplorable" and "Adorable Deplorable" T-shirts and hats began popping up at Trump rallies. Hillary's line was a perfect crystallization of everything the populist movement opposed—the smug and mean-spirited superiority of an out-of-touch elite.

The Trump campaign demanded that Hillary apologize. Instead, she released a statement that doubled down on the demonization, attacking Trump and Bannon:

Last night I was "grossly generalistic," and that's never a good idea. I regret saying "half"—that was wrong. But let's be clear, what's really "deplorable" is that Donald Trump hired a major advocate for the so-called "alt-right" movement to run his campaign and that David Duke and other white supremacists see him as a champion of their values. It's deplorable that Trump has built his campaign largely on prejudice and paranoia and given a national platform to hateful views and voices. . . . So I won't stop calling out bigotry and racist rhetoric in this campaign.[8]

Democrats like Obama's former deputy campaign manager Stephanie Cutter followed Hillary's defiant lead. On NBC's *Meet the Press,* Cutter said of Clinton: "I think that her only mistake is that she said half of his supporters were deplorable. . . . He is attracting a certain type of voter . . . and they tweet racist things, he retweets them, he says it from the stump. So what she said was not wrong. Her only mistake was that she described half of his supporters that way."[9] So much for being "Stronger Together"!

Democrats' bogus racism smears were nothing new. The left had dubbed every Republican presidential candidate since Barry Goldwater and Ronald Reagan a racist. What made Hillary's slander unique was that she aimed her rhetorical guns directly at 31 million voters (half of Trump's supporters). The attack left Americans asking: how can Hillary look out for the best interests of a country when she believes that so many of us are evil? How can she claim to support democracy when she believes that so many of us are not even part of America? Do these facts explain why she is so willing to give away our sovereignty? Do they explain why she has long supported granting more power to judges and unelected global institutions? Hillary's disparagement wasn't an indecorous gaffe, it was the full revelation of her belief that the people are uneducated, backward, dangerous, and therefore must be controlled by elites' superior intellect and virtue.

The fallout from Hillary's "basket of deplorables" fiasco was profound. (We know this is true because she conspicuously left it out of her extensive post-election laundry list of reasons why she lost.) The *Washington Post*–ABC News poll found that 65 percent of all voters said Hillary's statements were "unfair." When broken down by party, 84 percent of Republicans, 68 percent of Independents, and a surprising 47 percent of Democrats all agreed Hillary's comments were out of bounds.[10] Worse, she had galvanized and energized Trump supporters. Their votes were now an act of defiance and protest—a chance to defend their personal dignity and citizenship. After the election, Diane Hessan, a Clinton campaign operative hired to track the undecided vote in swing states, said Hillary's deplorables line was a decisive game-changer:

> There was one moment when I saw more undecided voters shift to Trump than any other, when it all changed, when voters began to speak differently about their choice. It wasn't FBI Director James Comey, Part One or Part Two; it wasn't Benghazi or the e-mails or Bill Clinton's visit with Attorney General Loretta Lynch on the tarmac. No, the conversation shifted the most during the weekend of Sept. 9, after Clinton said, "You can put half of Trump supporters into what I call the basket of deplorables." All hell broke loose.[11]

"Basket of deplorables" was the kind of get-out-the-voter motivator money couldn't buy.

The Clinton campaign's woes turned even worse two days later when the candidate collapsed at a September 11 memorial service at Ground Zero in Manhattan, which Trump also attended. For months, people had speculated about Hillary's poor health and whether she lacked the "stamina," as Trump put it, to be president. Bizarre coughing spells during speeches only added to lingering concerns over the 2012 news that Hillary suffered from a rare and potentially life-threatening condition. She had been diagnosed with cerebral venous thrombosis after neural scans found a blood clot near her brain.[12] Clinton's operatives and members of the Establishment Media (one and the same really) dismissed questions about Hillary's health as conspiracy theories and sexism against a female candidate. Yet on the 15th anniversary of the deadliest attack on American soil, Hillary's handlers found themselves out of excuses.

The physical evidence was stark—and it came in the form of video taken from multiple angles of her being led out of the memorial event. Hillary appeared weak, her knees buckled, and she almost fell to the ground before being lifted into a van waiting curbside. No one from the press was allowed to follow her as she was whisked away. The traveling press pool was kept in the dark for at least 30 minutes on the whereabouts of Clinton's location. Later, we were told she traveled to Chelsea Clinton's apartment before reemerging just before noon to do a show-walk for the cameras. She proclaimed, "It's a beautiful day in New York" and greeted a little girl whom she talked with for a few minutes. Asked by reporters present if she was "feeling better?" Clinton said, "Yes, thank you very much."

A few hours later, Hillary's campaign spun the press by revealing that Clinton wasn't just a seasonal allergy sufferer, she also had pneumonia! If she had pneumonia, why was she exposing voters and the little girl in front of Chelsea's apartment to her supposed illness.

CNN reporters raced to their battle stations to suffocate the blast. "Can't a girl have a sick day or two?" said CNN's Christiane Amanpour. (Can you imagine the firestorm and charges of sexism that would have exploded had a conservative referred to Clinton as a "girl"?)[13] Not to be outshone, CNN's Brian Stelter dismissed concerns about Hillary's health as rank sexism: "We're talking about the first female nominee of a major political party in American history," said Stelter. "We should be honest about the double standards that women sometimes face with regards to their health, with the idea that women are portrayed as being weaker than men."[14] CNN also rolled out the tired old liberal Watergate reporter Carl Bernstein, who said the media must "demand that Donald Trump appear with his doctor" because "we need to know if there are heart problems"—despite the fact that Trump exhibited exactly zero indications of any heart-related ailments.[15]

The whole episode offered voters further proof that Hillary Clinton and the Establishment Media were not to be trusted. With just two weeks until the all-important first presidential debate, more Americans wondered if and how Hillary's illness might affect her performance.

THE DEBATES

On September 26, 2016, the largest-ever group of Americans huddled around their screens to watch the first presidential debate held at Hofstra University in Hempstead, New York, moderated by NBC's Lester

Holt. The event smashed TV ratings records as an estimated 84 million people tuned in to watch.[16] I viewed the debate onsite in a small room with Monica Crowley and other Fox News colleagues.

The pre-debate jitters were palpable throughout the building as the nation prepared to see Donald Trump's first-ever one-on-one debate. That he was up against a seasoned debater who had lived decades of her life on the national political stage only raised the stakes.

I cringed. Even world-class rhetoricians like Ronald Reagan submitted themselves to weeks of debate prep. The Clinton team had done the same, including numerous mock debates between Hillary and one of her top advisers, Philippe Reines, who played the role of Trump. So complete was Reines's determination to simulate Trump that he had purchased a look-alike suit from Nordstrom's, ordered a Trump watch and cuff links on eBay and Amazon respectively, purchased four podiums, wore dress shoes with three-and-a-quarter-inch lifts, and even bought a backboard for his posture and knee braces to stop him from swaying while debating as Trump.[17]

But none of that mattered now. I huddled in one of the Fox News trailers with Monica and we settled in, both excited and nervous. I would appear on a few panels directly after the speech, so I had my notepad, Doritos, and iced tea. Hillary fired off her memorized, poll-tested attacks in pithy, tweet-sized talking points. She hammered Trump's economic policies: "I call it Trumped-up, trickle-down economics." Then Clinton slammed him on climate change: "Donald thinks that climate change is a hoax perpetrated by the Chinese. I think it's real." On his treatment of women, Hillary hit him mercilessly: "This is a man who has called women pigs, slobs, and dogs." She added: "And one of the worst things he said was about a woman in a beauty contest. He loves beauty contests, supporting them, and hanging around them. And he called this woman Ms. Piggy. Then he called her Ms. Housekeeping, because she was Latina." (Hillary's campaign then deftly fanned this attack line days after the debate by rolling out the woman in question, Alicia Machado, whom Trump unwisely attacked.)

Over and over, Hillary dropped lines like laser-guided munitions aimed at hitting key voter demographics.

Still, Trump held his own. Just about the time Monica and I started wondering aloud when he was going to drive home his points on jobs and trade, Trump delivered a great riff on NAFTA and TPP.

"Your husband signed NAFTA, which was one of the worst things that ever happened to the manufacturing industry," said Trump.

"Well, that's your opinion," Clinton interrupted. "That is your opinion."

"You go to New England, you go to Ohio, Pennsylvania, you go anywhere you want, Secretary Clinton, and you will see devastation where manufacturing is down 30, 40, sometimes 50 percent," Trump said. "NAFTA is the worst trade deal maybe ever signed anywhere, but certainly ever signed in this country. And now you want to approve Trans-Pacific Partnership. You were totally in favor of it. Then you heard what I was saying, how bad it is, and you said, I can't win that debate. But you know that if you did win, you would approve that, and that will be almost as bad as NAFTA. Nothing will ever top NAFTA."

"YES!" I shouted at the TV. "Really excellent stuff!" Monica chimed in. He also hit jobs being outsourced to Mexico and China— red meat to the base, a stark contrast with Clinton.

On several occasions, Trump underscored his overarching thesis of the debate: "Hillary, I'd just ask you this: you've been doing this for 30 years—why are you just thinking about these solutions right now?" said Trump. "For 30 years you've been doing it and now you're just starting to think about solutions."

The unanswerable, checkmate question, I thought to myself. *Nicely done.*

He also flipped the script on Hillary's "experience." "Hillary does have experience, but it's bad experience," he said.

When Lester Holt brought up Hillary's email scandal, she was ready with a response. "I made a mistake by using private email. If I had to do over again, I'd obviously do it differently," Clinton said.

Trump pounced. "That was more than a mistake," he interjected. "That was done purposely." And also, "Why did she delete 30,000 emails?"

Donald also used the purposeful interruption when Hillary tried to falsely saddle him with supporting the Iraq invasion. "Wrong. Wrong. Wrong," he said over her.

Nevertheless, there were plenty of Trump responses that made Republicans wince. Like when Hillary claimed Trump "rooted for the housing crisis" so he could make money and the billionaire real estate mogul interrupted with, "That's called business, by the way." Or when Trump posited that a "400-pound hacker" may have been behind the DNC hacks.

He also spent too much time defending claims better left ignored, such as when Hillary played the racism card by harkening back to questions over Barack Obama's birth certificate—a conspiracy Hillary's own supporters started way back in the spring of 2008.[18] Trump took the bait. "She failed to get the birth certificate," Trump said. "When I got involved, I didn't fail." Also missing from the debate was any discussion of the Clinton Foundation, something Lester Holt refused to ask and Donald Trump somehow failed to raise.

Still, on balance, Trump had done well. If you were scoring on Harvard debate league points, Hillary might have come out a little ahead. But that's not how real people process presidential debates. The unprecedented onslaught of attacks from Democrats, media, and NeverTrumpers had the unintended effect of lowering expectations for Trump. They claimed he was a radical with extreme views, but the people knew better—the real radicals were those who undermined the rule of law and killed off millions of American jobs by encouraging illegal immigration. By reflecting reasonable, alternative positions and committing no major gaffes, Trump defended the people with strength if not polish. A solid performance on balance, especially for someone who hadn't done much in the way of rehearsal.

By 2:00 a.m., Monica and I were done filming at Hofstra. We dragged our belongings into the car and headed back to Manhattan. I was spent. "I don't know how I'm going to make my morning hit. I'm exhausted!" I told Monica. "Laura, you're going to have no time to get ready for *Fox & Friends*," she replied. "So just sleep in your eye makeup, take off your foundation, wake up, and your eyes will already be done." A total pro, that Crowley.

The next day the Establishment Media dutifully performed their roles as the public relations arm of the Clinton campaign and eviscerated Trump's debate performance. They declared the race over. Politico's chief economic correspondent and CNBC contributor Ben White published an article titled "Donald Trump Can't Win" and said the debate was a "nightmare for the Republican nominee."[19]

A week after the first presidential debate, Mike Pence and Tim Kaine squared off in the first and only vice presidential debate held in Farmville, Virginia, at Longwood University. Pence smashed Kaine, just as I knew he would. Pence is a masterful communicator with deep rhetorical roots. In high school he was the top member of his speech team—named the Bull Tongues—had been crowned "speaker of the year," and advanced through regional and state tournaments to compete in national speech competitions.[20] His oratorical skills aside, Pence's quiet strength and humble demeanor were a stark contrast to Kaine's awkward, goofy expressions (which evoked memories of Jack Nicholson's Joker), made worse by his incessant need to interrupt the Indiana governor's every utterance. Pence persevered and managed to deliver a rhetorical round-house kick to Kaine wrapped in a compliment. He honored their sons' mutual military service and then added: "if your son or my son handled classified information the way Hillary Clinton did, they'd be court-martialed."

Then on October 7, 2016, just three days after the vice presidential debate, the campaign was set ablaze when a 2005 videotape of Donald Trump making lewd comments about women was released by *The Washington Post*. Trump was caught on a hot mic by NBC's *Access Hollywood*, chatting with host Billy Bush on his way to tape a cameo appearance on a soap opera. Condemnation and political obituaries rained down from all quarters.

Republican senator Mark Kirk reacted by calling Trump a "malignant clown" who was "unfit to serve as president of the United States."[21] It was so awful, said Kirk, that the Republican Party must appoint an "emergency replacement" to the ticket. NeverTrump U.S. senator Ben Sasse also called for the candidate to drop out of the race, saying that

Trump "is obviously not going to win" but that he can "still make an honorable move" by dropping out.[22] GOP senator Mike Lee released a Facebook video. "I respectfully ask you, with all due respect, to step aside," Lee said. "Step down. Allow someone else to carry the banner of [conservative] principles."[23] In total, three dozen Republicans had called for Trump's removal from the presidential ticket. Several more stopped just short of that, withdrawing their support.

In Los Angeles for an appearance the next day at the annual Bakersfield Business Conference, I was bombarded by telephone calls from major political figures, donors, supporters, and reporters who wanted reassurance, analysis, or advice. For several hours after the embarrassing details broke, I really did not know what to think. Top Republicans (including some in the Trump campaign) were discussing the feasibility of dumping Trump from the ticket. "That would be political suicide," I responded to one such top GOP official. "Democrats might as well start buying inaugural tickets," I added. "He's our guy." The notion that the Republican Party should jettison the man who had energized the base more than any candidate since Reagan was not just idiotic, it was election-ending. Turning against Trump would be turning against their own grass roots (something the GOP Establishment had mastered over years of practice).

The next morning, I hit the road early to drive the almost two hours to Bakersfield, one of the last conservative strongholds of California, and home of two of my musical heroes: the late Buck Owens and Merle Haggard. Every fall the Bakersfield Business Conference featured an array of speakers from business, media, sports, and politics.

Given the sordid news of the past 24 hours, my excitement about appearing before thousands of Republicans a month before the election had turned to dread. Of course there was no defending the Trump comments, which I found personally reprehensible and disgusting. When I walked into the large VIP area, I made a beeline for Ben and Candy Carson, who were also there. "Never a dull moment," he said, and I just nodded. "Oh well, I guess today will be a pretty interesting focus group for measuring the effect of the tape," I noted.

My main task during my 30-minute presentation was to keep everyone focused on the prize—keeping Hillary Clinton from the presidency and electing someone who could implement the conservative-populist reforms we needed.[24] If I revealed even a hint of my concern about the current mess, the audience would sense it and become demoralized.

The sweltering air in the long, wide, open-air tent was stifling, and attendees wearing sundresses and khakis, shorts and buttoned-downs fanned themselves for relief. It was an older crowd—small business owners and some farmers. As I was being introduced, an idea came to me. I would face the new scandal head-on, express my disgust before the crowd, but then ask them to choose between giving up on Trump and fighting the Washington political machine with everything they had.

I held up my cell phone camera after each question in my mini-poll and filmed the reaction. Hardly anyone seemed to support ditching Trump, while loud cheers erupted after I offered the "fight Hillary with everything we have" option. Once again, American voters were smarter than the Washington punditocracy and professional Consultant Class. They weren't electing a saint; they were electing someone who could help get our economy going and keep the home front safe.

My event escort and I drove around the fairgrounds after my speech to find a cold beer. I was stunned by the number of people who called out to thank me, urging me to keep battling. Although obviously not happy with Trump's comments, most chose to look past them. I hopped into the car to return to Los Angeles, firm in my belief that Trump could, in fact, win this thing. The "Bakersfield Sound" that I heard that hot fall day wasn't the twangy tunes Buck and Merle had made famous 50+ years earlier. But in the voices and reactions of regular working people at a particularly ugly period in our political history, I heard the comforting sounds of patriotism, pragmatism, and optimism.

Forty-eight hours after the tape heard around the world, Donald Trump scored an incredible surprise victory at the second presidential debate in St. Louis, Missouri, moderated by CNN's Anderson Cooper and ABC News's Martha Raddatz. When I arrived at the Washington University venue, I was escorted into a Fox News holding room where Monica Crowley and I could once again view the debate via monitor before our post-debate analysis segment with Sean Hannity and populist Brexit architect Nigel Farage (a providential guest booking, to be sure). Watching with us were the nearly one out of five Americans who tuned in (66.5 million people).[25]

The Trump campaign knew the *Access Hollywood* tape would take center stage at the debate; the moderators would do everything in their power to help Hillary put Trump away once and for all. To prepare, Steve Bannon arranged for three of Bill Clinton's sexual assault accusers—Juanita Broaddrick, Paula Jones, and Kathleen Wiley—to all be seated in the front row, along with Kathy Shelton, a woman who as a child had been raped and whose accused rapist Hillary Clinton had defended. An hour prior to the debate, Trump hosted an impromptu press conference with all four women and broadcast it live over his powerful Facebook page. As networks began their pre-debate coverage, some reluctantly flashed images of the press conference and Bill Clinton's alleged victims—women whom Establishment Media had done their best to ignore and keep in the shadows. When the debate began and the former president entered the hall, cameras caught him making furtive glances toward his accusers. Were the women there simply as psychological warfare? Or would they become reference points in Trump's debate remarks? Bill looked mortified.

In the opening minutes, Anderson Cooper hit Trump with a brutally worded question that everyone knew was coming. "We received a lot of questions online, Mr. Trump, about the tape that was released on Friday, as you can imagine," said Cooper. "You called what you said 'locker room banter.' You described kissing women without consent, grabbing their genitals. That is sexual assault. You bragged that you have sexually assaulted women. Do you understand that?"

"This was locker room talk. I am not proud of it," replied Trump. "I apologize to my family, I apologize to the American people. Certainly I am not proud of it." Trump tried to pivot to national security, but Cooper persisted with follow-ups on the tape before Hillary delivered a long soliloquy on Trump's dangerous words and attitudes about women. Then Martha Raddatz explained that due to social media interest, the debate would continue to stay "on this topic" before reading a question from a voter about whether Trump had changed since the decade-old tape. And that's when Trump said this:

> I am a person who has great respect for people, for my family, for the people of this country and certainly I am not proud of it, but that was something that happened. If you look at Bill Clinton, far worse. Mine are words and his was action. His words, what he has done to women. There's never been anybody in the history of politics in this nation that has been so abusive to women. So you can say it any way you want to say it, but Bill Clinton is abusive to women. Hillary Clinton attacked those same women, and attacked them viciously, four of them here tonight. One of the women, who is a wonderful woman, at 12 years old was raped. At 12. Her client, she represented, got him off and she is seen laughing on two occasions laughing at the girl who was raped. Kathy Shelton, that young woman, is here with us tonight. So don't tell me about words. I am, absolutely—I apologize for those words, but it is things that people say. But what President Clinton did, he was impeached, he lost his license to practice law, he had to pay an $850,000 fine to one of the women—Paula Jones, who is also here tonight. And I will tell you that when Hillary brings up a point like that and she talks about words that I said 11 years ago, I think it's disgraceful and I think she should be ashamed of herself, if you want to know the truth.

By referencing the Clinton sexual assault accusers, Trump made them part of the permanent debate transcript, sent cameras swiveling toward the women and Bill Clinton, and contrasted words versus deeds. He drew a direct line to Hillary's role in demonizing Bill's accusers through her brutal treatment of the child rape victim whose accused perpetrator she defended. The Trump campaign's strategy paid off. The political wound that many believed would prove fatal to Trump's candidacy had effectively been cauterized.

Better still, Trump's policy answers throughout the rest of the debate exhibited specificity and granularity. He landed sharp, crisp policy punches on trade, taxes, Syria, Mosul, minority poverty, Benghazi,

ISIS, and the Supreme Court. After the debate I went on air with Sean, Monica, and Nigel to declare Trump the hands-down debate winner:

> For anyone to go on television tonight and say that this was not a decisive, and frankly, masterful performance by Donald Trump should just drop the pretense of being a Republican "strategist"— they never strategize, by the way—or a Republican quote "pundit" or analyst. He came in with the entire GOP Establishment really against him. He came in with the media against him. He came in with Hollywood against him. And the entire Bush apparatus. All of them against him. And he came in and said, we're going down the tubes, you're an architect of this, and we need a new path forward . . . and he hit her in a way that not a single Republican in the last 30 years has been able to lay a glove on the Clintons. And he did it. We've been waiting for this moment for someone, face-to-face, to take down the Clintons.

With Trump's performance an overwhelming victory, Establishment Media rushed in to protect Hillary and rewrite the script. They seized on two of Trump's throwaway lines and tried to amplify them into yet another "game over" moment. First, after Hillary said "it's awfully good that someone with the temperament of Donald Trump is not in charge of the law in our country," Trump replied with the major applause line, "Because you would be in jail." Second, when discussing national disunity, Trump said his opponent had "tremendous hate in her heart" while referencing her irredeemable deplorables line.

Establishment Media pounced. Vox declared that "Donald Trump's Threat to Imprison Hillary Clinton Is a Threat to Democracy."[26] CNN's Dana Bash played the Stalin and Hitler cards: "What makes this country different from countries with dictators in Africa or Stalin or Hitler or any of those countries with dictators and totalitarian leaders, is that when they took over, they put their opponents in jail. To hear one presidential candidate say, even if it was a flip comment, which it was, 'you're going to be in jail' to another presidential candidate in the debate stage in the United States of America?

Stunning. Just stunning."[27] Speaking in his most dramatic cadence, CNN's Van Jones said it was "a new low in American democracy."[28] *The New York Times* warned that "Trump's Threat to Jail Clinton Also Targets Democracy's Institutions."[29] Never has a throw-away applause line generated so much breathless coverage.

The *Access Hollywood* tape and the media's unending anti-Trump drumbeat appeared to take a toll on Trump's standing in the polls. A CNN survey taken after the video's release found Clinton held an 11-point lead.[30] Indeed, throughout the entire campaign, only one poll—the *Los Angeles Times*/USC tracking poll—regularly showed Donald Trump leading the race.[31] We now know, of course, that all the polls save this one had it wrong. But during the election, these outrageously inaccurate polls were used as a cudgel to bash Trump's candidacy in the hopes of demoralizing his supporters and driving down Republican turnout.

Meanwhile in NeverTrump Land, the GOP elites were busy hyping an absurd gambit to sabotage Trump in the reliably Republican state of Utah. Their plan: help NeverTrump candidate Evan McMullin pick off Utah, thereby denying Trump six otherwise guaranteed electoral votes. Their hope was that Trump would win 263 electoral votes to hold Hillary below the magic 270 votes required to clinch the election. If no candidate received 270 electoral votes, the race would get kicked to the House of Representatives for members of Congress to choose the next president. It was the kind of nutty nonsense that underscored just how unhinged the GOP apparatchik had become. Naturally, the press flocked to McMullin to grant him ample oxygen in the hopes of hurting Trump weeks before the election. While McMullin's chances were virtually nonexistent, the NeverTrump ruse this late in the game clearly irked Trump and Pence. "Nobody ever heard of him," Mike Pence said dismissively about McMullin. "The guy takes votes away from me," said Trump. "He's a puppet of a loser," he said, referring to Bill Kristol, a NeverTrump leader.[32] Still, with the third debate representing Trump's final chance to make his closing argument, the campaign had bigger things to focus on.

The last debate was held on October 19 in Las Vegas, moderated by Fox News anchor Chris Wallace. With 71.6 million people tuning in to watch, each candidate did their best to persuade undecided voters and motivate their base.[33] Many of the familiar arguments and lines of attack played out in the last debate, but there were at least three flash points that stood out. First, when asked whether he would accept the election results, Trump refused to confirm that he would and said, "I'll keep you in suspense." I felt that was a mistake. He should have simply said he would accept the outcome of the election. Unless we were in a recount, there was no other option. Second, Trump referred to Clinton as a "nasty woman"—a phrase too enticing for social media not to meme and mock. Whether the line was one of Trump's psychological jujitsu tricks designed to get media to repeat a negative phrase about Hillary was unclear. If so, it worked. "Nasty woman" T-shirts and memorabilia materialized instantly. Third, and I thought most importantly, Trump articulated the pro-life cause using powerful words that exposed Hillary's radicalism on late-term abortion and her refusal to place any restrictions on abortion, even up until the final week of pregnancy.

"I think it's terrible. If you go with what Hillary is saying, in the ninth month you can take the baby and rip the baby out of the womb of the mother just prior to the birth of the baby," said Trump. "Now, you can say that that's okay, and Hillary can say that that's okay, but it's not okay with me." In graphic yet simple language, Trump had captured the moral outrageousness and extremism of Hillary's abortion on-demand regime. "That was amazing!" I said, turning to Monica with tears welling up in my eyes. We were both overjoyed that Trump had put Hillary back on the heels of her sensible shoes.

GOP elites and NeverTrumpers groused that Trump was a latecomer to the pro-life cause and would cave under pressure. Yet on that debate stage, with the election less than three weeks away and over 70 million people watching, a tough man who had previously been pro-choice chose to courageously defend life and to be a voice for the voiceless.

After the debate, Mike Huckabee and I appeared together on *Hannity*. The former Arkansas governor was as moved as I was about Trump's passionate advocacy for the unborn. "I hope that every Catholic and every Evangelical in this country paid careful attention to the stark contrast between Donald Trump and Hillary Clinton when it came to the issue of protecting innocent human life," said Huckabee. "Donald Trump boldly took a stand for life tonight. For all these NeverTrumpers out there, they need to get off their keister, if you will, just stand up and recognize, there is a clear choice here." Sean and I chided the Baptist preacher over his polite use of the word "keister," but as usual, Huckabee nailed it. Killing babies, especially those in the latter stages of pregnancy—no matter how Clinton tried to justify it—was pure evil. Hillary's fanatical embrace of infanticide had to be exposed. At a time when many other "conservatives" fell silent on abortion, Trump stood in the gap when it mattered most and defended life. Populists are pro-life because babies are people, too—individuals deserving of life and protection. For any NeverTrumper to claim to be "pro-life" and still refuse to support him now was illogical and self-defeating. Whether he won or lost the election, Donald Trump had placed himself and his supporters on the right side of history.

"WHERE I COME FROM, PEOPLE DON'T CUT IN LINE"

With his poll numbers looking grim just a few days before Election Day, Trump's campaign staff, in the 11th hour, decided to add one more stop to the four states already on his schedule.

After Sioux City, Minneapolis, Sterling Heights (Michigan), and Moon Township (Pennsylvania), he would end the day in Leesburg, Virginia. No one expected the Republican nominee to come back to the Old Dominion given Hillary Clinton's big lead there, but Trump was unconventional right until the end. At about six p.m. that night, senior campaign adviser Dave Bossie asked if I wanted to speak at the event. "You mean in, like, three hours?" I asked incredulously.

Strange as it sounds, it would be my first Trump rally. Every other chance I had to go to one, either kids or work intervened. With so little notice and virtually zero promotion of the event, it was hard to believe that the crowd would be that big, especially so late on a Sunday evening. Although it was a school night, I thought it was important to bring my eleven-year-old daughter, Maria, so she could witness a significant moment in political history. A few other friends also came along for the hour drive out of town.

Approaching the exit for the fairgrounds, we saw that the traffic was backed up for miles. A wild ruby necklace of taillights twinkled as it wrapped around the landscape. People with lawn chairs and signs, women with babies, elderly with canes and walkers were walking three and four abreast on the side of the narrow road, leaving only one lane for driving. The campaign volunteer who guided our SUV through a police perimeter told us that the crowd started forming in the early morning hours. "It's crazy," he said, "because the pavilion only holds about 1,500 people—and apparently 15,000 people are here."

The one-lane country road we turned onto was teeming with Trump supporters who parted to each side as we bumped along in the pitch black. They wore MAKE AMERICA GREAT AGAIN sweatshirts, hats, and even had dogs dressed up in Trump T-shirts. One 20-something decorated his mountain bike in Christmas lights and red-white-and-blue streamers. Music blared over personal speakers—one woman was playing Elvis singing "America the Beautiful." A Baby Boomer with a beard and cowboy boots played the Trump anthem, the Rolling Stones' "You Can't Always Get What You Want."

When we finally arrived at the opening where a "Women for Trump" tour bus had parked for "VIPs" (I hate that term), I met up with Raymond Arroyo and his family who had just arrived. The kids chatted up the guys in the Fox News satellite truck, and I began walking back along the line of what security told me was as many as 10,000 people who hoped to catch a glimpse of Trump.

By 10:30 you could see your breath in the cold night air and it was obvious the GOP nominee was way behind schedule. But I didn't hear a single person gripe or moan. They didn't mind if they couldn't get through the gate and into the covered area to see Trump. "We'll listen over the loudspeakers," one young woman said. "He *has* to win!" shouted another. There were fathers carrying toddlers on their shoulders and people helping the elderly up the hillside.

Walking back toward the bus, I came upon a man in a mechanized wheelchair, wearing a Korean War baseball cap, bundled up in an old down jacket, with a red U.S. Marine blanket over his legs. "Nothing was going to stop me from being here," he said when I asked him how he navigated all the way from the "satellite" parking lot. Accompanied by his son and grandson, he told me about his home in rural Virginia and how life had changed there (not for the better), how he lost his beloved wife months earlier—and how hard she had prayed that Trump would win.

I offered to bring them to the front of the impossibly long line.

"Appreciate it, ma'am," he said, without breaking his gaze toward the pavilion ahead. "But where I come from, people don't cut in line."

After midnight I took to the stage to rev up the crowd before Jerry Falwell Jr. would step out to introduce Donald Trump. We had another 30 minutes to fill, but if the audience was tired, they did a good job hiding it. Chants of "U.S.A.!" and "Go Trump, Go!" erupted in the back. The placards read "FARMERS FOR TRUMP," "WOMEN FOR TRUMP" and yes, "HILLARY FOR PRISON." When the motorcade carrying the future president of the United States pulled up in back, we were fortunate enough to greet him. "You're late!" I said to him jokingly, when he stepped out of the Suburban. "What a day!" he said, wearing a black overcoat and his signature red tie. "This is my . . . uh . . . how many states have we been to today again?" he asked one of this staffers. A voice shouted "Five!" "Unbelievable crowds, unbelievable energy," he told me. I've never seen my daughter happier than she was that night, when Donald Trump put his arm around her for a picture, thanked her for coming out on a school night, and said, "Now Maria, promise me you'll work hard in school!"

A few moments later, Trump bounded up on stage and the place went crazy. When he referenced me a few times, I was honored, although I didn't expect it. A bleary-eyed Steve Bannon and exhausted Jared Kushner stood off to the side, both looking like they had been through all the levels of Dante's *Inferno*. In a sense, they had. The 2016 campaign, with its fits and starts, scandals and surprises, had been the wildest, nastiest, and most unpredictable in our lifetime.

Taking in the moment, the blur and roar of the crowd, I stood back to see my daughter transfixed, clapping and cheering for him as he punched out every line.

"We are one day away from the change you've been waiting for your entire life," Trump said. "This is going to be Brexit times 50. . . . When we win on Nov. 8, we are going to drain the swamp."

When I explain to people why Trump won, I think of that proud Virginia veteran in the wheelchair whose name I'll never know. There were millions of people just like him, who live their lives in quiet dignity, according to the moral code of their ancestors, with an abiding love for America. Where I live, in Washington, people cut in line all the time. The well-connected and well-heeled always find a way around the rules that apply to everyone else. Lobbyists help the powerful interests they represent "jump the line" all the time and usually do so at the expense of the working poor and the middle class.

Voters in "middle America" concluded many years ago that our political system had been committed to policies that don't work for most Americans. We had a trade policy that helps China to the detriment of American workers. We had an immigration system that helped people who employ illegal immigrants, but hurt anyone who had to compete with those immigrants for jobs. We had a foreign policy that delighted global elites, while American citizens paid the tab. We had a regulatory apparatus that pleased environmental radicals that choked growth and innovation. Bad policies in areas too numerous to recount weighed down the free market and hurt ordinary citizens.

After decades of exasperation—from Buchanan Brigades to Tea Parties—the frustration of the American people had finally reached a critical mass. The elites be damned, on November 8 America was going to be heard loud and clear.

THE GREATEST DAY

In the run-up to Election Day, the dominant media, NeverTrumpers, and Democrats were busy reminding Trump supporters that there was no need to vote. The election was over. President Hillary Rodham Clinton was the inevitable and guaranteed victor. "Tomorrow night, I think, when Hillary Clinton wins, Donald Trump will have lost this election from the first day he announced," said CNN contributor and

Clinton supporter Hilary Rosen.[34] University of Virginia professor Larry Sabato's "Crystal Ball" must have been cloudy when he predicted a Clinton victory with 322 electoral votes.[35] Other "experts," like Richmond University professor James Boys, received prominent airtime the day before the election. In a CNBC piece titled, "Donald Trump Will Lose After Failing to Follow Mitt Romney," Boys said "it is impossible to see how [Trump] can win this."[36] The Princeton Election Consortium predicted a 99 percent probability of a Hillary victory. "Whether the Presidential win probability is 91% or 99%, it is basically settled," wrote the organization's Sam Wang.[37] Weeks prior, Wang declared confidently, "It is totally over. If Trump wins more than 240 electoral votes, I will eat a bug."[38] Let's hope Ebola wasn't on the menu.

During an election eve appearance on *Hannity*, Sean asked me whether I believed Trump would win tomorrow. I said I thought he had a really good chance of winning and retiring the Clintons—permanently. "If Donald Trump wins, we actually have a chance to begin turning this around," I said. "That's exciting." And even if he didn't prevail, the populist movement that had cropped up around his candidacy would survive regardless.

On the morning of the election I went to St. Patrick's Cathedral to pray for the country before heading over to Fox for my usual Tuesday appearance on *Fox & Friends*. I recapped the race and offered a prediction. "Trump has had much of the GOP Establishment and the money class against him. He had, of course, the Clintons, the Obamas, Hollywood, academia, media . . . he's had *all* of that against him. And he is standing. He's fighting. And . . . I think this [election] is going to show that the people of this country are defiant—and they are on to this game that the elites are playing."

An hour later, on my radio show, I rallied the troops. "Don't believe the naysayers. Believe in yourself and your desire to change this country for the better," I said. "Ignore the polls. Focus on the country you want to save, the country you think has been so poorly served by the bipartisan Establishment cabal for decades now." Listeners were describing the massive lines at the polls in Ohio, Pennsylvania,

Florida, and beyond. "I have never seen anything like this," one caller from Indianapolis noted, calling from his car directly after voting. "Line out the door, around the block." These good Americans, who had been ridiculed, disappointed, and dismissed by so many politicians for so long were giving me more hope—and I was already cautiously optimistic.

Later in the afternoon I ran into Joe Trippi, the affable Democrat pollster, in the green room at Fox News. "So what do you think?" I asked, knowing full well it wasn't going to make me happy. "Oh, a pretty big blowout for Hillary. A huge electoral win," he said, according to his final number crunching. *Ugh, if he's right,* I thought to myself, *this is going to be a long night.*

Then–Fox host Megyn Kelly and *Special Report* anchor Bret Baier were poring over exit polls on set, and I joined a large panel of contributors. It was too early to say much except to go through the exit poll question results—and at the time, those didn't look so hot for Trump.

The Trump voters were maligned, sneered at, ridiculed, called "deplorable," and in some cases physically assaulted. None of that stopped them. These same people were now heading to the polls to vote in an election experts and elites guaranteed would be a landslide victory for Hillary Clinton.

Before 7:00 p.m. on the East Coast, and with citizens still voting, pollster Frank Luntz analyzed the exit poll data and fired off the following tweet: "In case I wasn't clear enough from my previous tweets: Hillary Clinton will be the next President of the United States."[39]

Luntz may have believed the exit polls, but I wasn't convinced. It brought back memories of 2004 when the exits were proven wildly inaccurate. Then there was Bill O'Reilly on Fox, when Trump had 67 electoral votes to Hillary's 68, who said, "It doesn't look like there's going to be any shocking upsets."[40] Poring over county-by-county results in Florida, with 91 percent of the vote in, Karl Rove noted that Trump wasn't doing as well as Romney in 2012 in key areas.

After appearing on Fox early in the evening, I decided it was important to be with the people who fought for America and supported

Trump against all odds, regardless of the outcome. I went over to the Trump headquarters at the Hilton Hotel in Manhattan. The place was packed and buzzing, with MAKE AMERICA GREAT AGAIN hats dotting the room, a few open bars, and large TV screens broadcasting the latest state-by-state results. I made it a point to walk over to the TV cameras and reporters standing on risers in the back of the room, behind a plastic barrier. "I'd forgo the premature giddiness," I shouted over the crowd. Who knows if anyone heard me—I didn't care. Most of the journalists up above thought they'd be covering a wake that night. I was pretty confident that they would be covering an awakening.

The faces told the story. The expressions of the hosts on MSNBC went from glowing to glum. "America is crying tonight," said Lawrence O'Donnell. "And I mean literally crying." Rachel Maddow was a slack-jawed mess: "I don't know what happens next for Democratic politics." Former John McCain strategist–turned–MSNBC contributor Steve Schmidt seemed stunned but stumbled into an accurate analysis. "I couldn't have been more wrong about this . . . I thought it's been over for weeks," said Schmidt. "What you're seeing here is just such a backlash in the country against the Establishment of the country—a business Establishment, a political Establishment, a media Establishment across the board. . . . Steve Bannon was right when he talked about the similarities between Brexit, about a rising populism."

The Trump campaign strategy was brilliant. Even with the must-win states, Trump would still need to pick off a big blue state. The gutsy Rust Belt strategy to go after states like Michigan, Wisconsin, and Pennsylvania was a big gamble. The Hillary team considered these states a lock. But as the Trump campaign understood, workers in the Rust Belt had felt the brunt of globalism's effects personally.

The early evening scenes from the Hillary Clinton headquarters at the Javits Center in New York were jubilant. An elaborate victory stage had been erected under a massive glass ceiling, a metaphorical reminder that Hillary was about to make history as America's first female president. For the first couple of hours, the state maps were filling in as expected. When Virginia was called for Clinton, Hillary supporters cheered. But then North Carolina went for Trump, and

Ohio, and Florida. What began as an upbeat Clinton victory party soon morphed into a somber political burial.

"Globalization and the elites who sold the snake oil were put on trial tonight and convicted by the American people," I tweeted.[41] Others, like Fox News contributor Charles Krauthammer—a harsh and consistent Trump critic—were coming around to a similar conclusion. "If it continues and Trump wins, this is an ideological and electoral revolution of the kind we haven't seen since Reagan. What this means ideologically is that the Republican Party has become a populist party," said Krauthammer. At one point in the Fox broadcast, Trump's media nemesis Megyn Kelly, who went after him so aggressively in the first GOP primary debate, sat in stunned silence with wide eyes. She seemed to be mugging for the camera. Only she wasn't. It may have been her most authentic TV moment ever.

Reality had also begun setting in with the Clinton camp. "It's like Brexit," Bill Clinton said, watching the returns come in. "I guess it's real."[42]

The Associated Press called Pennsylvania for Trump at 1:35 a.m. ET. Hillary Clinton refused to concede. Instead, Clinton campaign chief John Podesta appeared before the tear-soaked crowd at the Javits Center and said there would be no more from the Hillary camp that night and that everyone should go home. Less than a half hour later, the Associated Press called Wisconsin for Trump. The race was over.

At exactly 2:29 a.m. ET, the Associated Press officially declared Donald J. Trump president-elect of the United States. The Trump crowd erupted. Smiles, high-fives, and hugs across the Hilton ballroom. The man who had dared to defy the Establishment had rallied the people and scored the greatest presidential upset in American history. Just before 3:00 a.m. ET, the president-elect appeared on stage and delivered a magnanimous victory speech.

"I've just received a call from Secretary Clinton. She congratulated us—it's about us—on our victory. And I congratulated her and her family on a very, very hard-fought campaign," said Trump. "We owe her a major debt of gratitude for her service to our country. I mean that very sincerely." He then pledged to unify the nation and be a president for all the people. "I'm reaching out to you for your guidance and your help so we can work together and unify our great country."

The president-elect explained that the victory belonged to the people, not him. Restoring power to the people was a cause far greater than one man; it was a movement that sought above all else to place America and her citizens first. "As I've said from the beginning, ours was not a campaign but rather an incredible and great movement, made up of millions of hardworking men and women who love their country and want a better, brighter future for themselves and their family. It is a movement comprised of Americans from all races, religions, backgrounds, and beliefs, who want and expect our government to serve the people—and serve the people it will."

I smiled and just took it all in. The people had united and taught everyone in Washington who's really in charge.

9.

WHERE DOES IT GO FROM HERE?

President Trump & the Populist Movement

What truly matters is not which party controls our government,
but whether our government is controlled by the people.
January 20, 2017, will be remembered as the day the people
became the rulers of this nation again. The forgotten men
and women of our country will be forgotten no longer.

—DONALD TRUMP

The red-white-and-blue regalia hanging from the columns in front of the Capitol Rotunda provided a bright pop of color against the otherwise gray Washington sky. From my seat on the inaugural dais, I peered out over the West Front of the U.S. Capitol at the hundreds of thousands of Americans gathered on the National Mall. The people—the foot soldiers who powered the populist revolution—had come to witness the history they helped make. Like a time-lapse video of a puzzle being assembled at warp speed, the political events of the previous decades flashed through my mind and snapped into place to form the scene unfolding before me. On January 20, 2017, millions of Americans tuned in to watch the peaceful transfer of power—from the committed globalist Barack Obama to the defiant conservative-populist Donald Trump.

"Today we are not merely transferring power from one administration to another, or from one party to another—but we are transferring power from Washington, DC, and giving it back to you, the

American People," said President Donald J. Trump moments after being sworn in by Chief Justice John Roberts. He couldn't resist taking another swipe at those who opposed him every step of the way. "The Establishment protected itself, but not the citizens of our country. Their victories have not been your victories; their triumphs have not been your triumphs. . . . That all changes—starting right here, and right now, because this moment is your moment: it belongs to you."

Trump's inaugural address may have lacked the grandiloquence and rhapsodic sweep of the greatest inaugural addresses, like Lincoln's second or Reagan's first. But it made one thing abundantly clear: Donald Trump had come to Washington to lay waste to the globalist legacies of the elites seated behind him on the platform:

> For many decades, we've enriched foreign industry at the expense of American industry; Subsidized the armies of other countries while allowing for the very sad depletion of our military; We've defended other nations' borders while refusing to defend our own; And spent trillions of dollars overseas while America's infrastructure has fallen into disrepair and decay. We've made other countries rich while the wealth, strength, and confidence of our country has disappeared over the horizon. One by one, the factories shuttered and left our shores, with not even a thought about the millions upon millions of American workers left behind. The wealth of our middle class has been ripped from their homes and then redistributed across the entire world. But that is the past. And now we are looking only to the future.[1]

The speech was widely decried for being overly dark, pessimistic, and "dystopian" (big word for cable news!). MSNBC's Chris Matthews called Trump's address "Hitlerian."[2] And, right on cue, NeverTrumpers sneered from the sidelines. "I'll be unembarrassedly old-fashioned here: It is profoundly depressing and vulgar to hear an American president proclaim: 'America First,'" tweeted Bill Kristol.[3] Then another, written in French: "*Je ne regrette rien*" ("I do not regret anything").[4] Few have been more pompous and wrong about Trump. What is truly vulgar is a government that no longer cares about the people paying its bills. That robs them of their God-given liberty, leeching power from them only to give it to the state.

But Trump's inaugural wasn't aimed at wooing his critics. It was about telling the citizens how he intended to govern—as a conservative-populist, as an economic nationalist.

"From this day forward, a new vision will govern our land. From this moment on, it's going to be America First," Trump said. "Every decision on trade, on taxes, on immigration, on foreign affairs, will be made to benefit American workers and American families."

The contrast between the reactions of the Old Guard seated on the temporary stage and the crowds gathered on the National Mall was stark. From my vantage point, it was surreal watching these old political combatants sitting so close to witness the swearing in of a man they loathed. George W. Bush was so unnerved by Trump's remarks, when the light rain began, he temporarily forgot how to put a poncho over his head. Michelle Obama scowled and eye-rolled her way through the entire speech. When the jumbotrons set up on the Capitol Lawn showed tight shots of her pained expressions, there were audible yowls and groans from the crowd. Hillary looked like she had eaten a bad clam. All in all, a great day.

The departure of the Obamas' helicopter from the Capitol grounds after the ceremony brought me little comfort. I knew they weren't really going away. They were going on vacation (Barack even managed a solo getaway to Bali—"me time" to work on his memoirs—for a month). Soon they'd be back to lead the resistance from the city they had occupied for eight years. Their headquarters: an eight-million-dollar mansion in the tony Kalorama neighborhood.

As I walked off the platform that day, questions turned in my mind: would the new administration and the Republicans in Congress deliver on Trump's America First agenda? Will Donald Trump fulfill the promises he made that propelled him to power? Or will endless investigations, hostile Democrats, incompetent (and hostile) Republicans, and a rabid media together form an impenetrable barricade to progress? And then there are the internal barricades: will the damaging leaks, a lack of message discipline, and certain ill-advised tweets prove his populist agenda's undoing?

The viewing stands had yet to be removed from the inaugural parade route when the White House found itself in a pointless debate over whether the crowd size of Trump's inaugural was larger than Obama's. (But who cares? Trump supporters voted and then went back to work.) What we remember most of former Press Secretary Sean Spicer's first interaction with the press was not about the Trump agenda. Instead he focused on the media's "deliberately false" reporting of inaugural attendance figures. (Earlier in the day, the president had referred to reporters as "among the most dishonest human beings on earth"—which I didn't think went far enough.) But seriously, it was a rocky start.

Beginning on a more gracious note would have been the best way to reset the narrative. After such a long and rancorous campaign, we all needed it.

Still, it didn't take long for Trump to put some populist points on the board. In his first week in office, the new president signed an executive order reinstating President Reagan's "Mexico City" policy to stop taxpayer funding of abortion overseas; sent Vice President Mike Pence to appear at the March for Life, the highest-ranking government official ever to appear there; approved the Keystone XL pipeline after years of delay by the Obama administration; signed an executive order to start withholding funds from "sanctuary cities"; froze the madness known as Obama's Syrian refugee program; and killed Obama's signature trade deal, the disaster known as the Trans-Pacific Partnership. Not a bad first week on the job.

Republicans control the House, Senate, and White House for only the third time since 1928. Trump must move quickly to leverage the GOP's unified government advantage while they still have it (midterm elections generally yield big gains for the party not in the White House). Indeed, the Trump administration's first several months in office revealed important wins and warning signs for the populist movement in the years ahead.

JOBS, JOBS, JOBS

Even before being sworn in as president, Donald Trump sent a strong and important signal during his presidential transition that American job creation would be a top priority. On the day he announced his candidacy in 2015, Donald Trump promised: "I will be the greatest jobs president that God has ever created." Among the president-elect's first acts was helping save 1,000 Carrier air-conditioning jobs from going to Mexico. Trump then held a flurry of meetings with top business leaders who vowed to hire more American workers. SoftBank Group Corp. founder and CEO Masayoshi Son traveled to Trump Tower and announced plans to invest $50 billion in America and create up to 50,000 new U.S. telecom jobs.[5] Exxon Mobil announced a $20 billion investment and over 45,000 new U.S. construction and manufacturing jobs. President Trump hailed it as "exactly the kind of investment, economic development and job creation that will help put Americans back to work" and a "true American success story."[6] After a meeting with Trump, Delta Air Lines CEO Ed Bastian said the company planned to hire 25,000 more workers over five years.[7] And at a White House ceremony in late July, President Trump announced that Taiwan-based Foxconn Technology Group will invest over $10 billion to build a state-of-the-art LCD panel-manufacturing facility in Wisconsin that will create up to 13,000 jobs. Governor Scott Walker hailed it as "the single largest economic development project in the history of Wisconsin."[8]

A new tone is being set. "What a difference a day makes," said Juanita Duggan, president and CEO of the National Federation of Independent Business (NFIB). "Before Election Day small business owners' optimism was flat, and after Election Day it soared."[9]

By the end of July, the Consumer Confidence Index hit a 16-year high, with more people saying jobs were "plentiful" than at any time since 2001. After Trump signed several executive orders slashing federal red tape, the Dow Jones industrial average broke 22,000 in August for the first time ever.[10] In total, Trump's regulatory reforms have already saved taxpayers over $86 billion.[11] Best of all, U.S. unemployment fell to 4.3 percent in May, the lowest level in 16 years.[12]

This is Trump at his populist best—using his business acumen to restore a jobs-friendly economic environment that welcomes, not punishes, American job creation. Voters elected Trump to apply his "Art of the Deal" talents to create and save American jobs. The president's detractors will try to drag him off his winning jobs focus. Trump mustn't let that happen.

Economic nationalism—pursuing fiscal policies that benefit American workers more than elites—remains our country's greatest chance to beat back years of globalist gains. Not everyone agrees, however. George W. Bush speechwriter and NeverTrumper David Frum (a friend of mine) recently tweeted a quote from the Austrian economist and libertarian icon Ludwig von Mises that captures much of the Establishment's angst over Trump's America First economic agenda. "Economic nationalism," von Mises wrote, "is incompatible with durable peace."[13] To that I would ask: What about allowing China to become the richest and most powerful country on earth? Is that compatible with peace?

Indeed, Trump's critics would do well to examine the election data on working-class rural Americans—a group who overwhelmingly went for Trump's message of economic nationalism. Rural voters accounted for nearly one out of five votes in 2016 and were a pivotal part of Trump's successful Rust Belt strategy. NBC News exit polls revealed that Trump beat Clinton 57 to 38 percent among Michigan's rural voters (Romney carried the same group but by only seven percentage points). Among Pennsylvania rural voters, Trump destroyed Clinton 71 percent to 26 percent (Romney only scored 59 percent). The same was true for rural voters in Wisconsin: Trump captured 63 percent to Hillary's anemic 34 percent.[14] The forgotten man and woman's jobs matter, too—something Trump made crystal clear.

The president and his economic team should keep slashing the byzantine regulations and taxes that hold job creators back. Trump should also broaden his consultations beyond the Fortune 500 crowd to include CEOs of small- and medium-sized companies who are more immediately impacted by the slightest changes in the economy and harmful government actions. These are the major job creators and he could learn a lot from them.

TRADE AND CLIMATE CHANGE

President Trump wasted no time fulfilling his promise to kill the behemoth 5,544-page Trans-Pacific Partnership. On January 23, the president announced the United States would formally withdraw from TPP. He then rattled progressives by meeting with union leaders at the White House who cheered the decision and welcomed the administration's jobs-friendly trade agenda. "We're going to stop the ridiculous trade deals that have taken everybody out of our country and taken companies out of our country, and it's going to be reversed," Trump told them. Teamsters president James P. Hoffa said the president had just "taken the first step toward fixing 30 years of bad trade policies." Other union leaders, like North America's Building Trades Unions president Sean McGarvey, were equally elated. "We just had probably the most incredible meeting of our careers," he said. "We will work with him and his administration to help him implement his plans on infrastructure, trade and energy policy, so we really do put America back to work."[15]

President Trump deserves enormous credit for honoring his campaign promise to end TPP as part of his pledge to put U.S. workers first. And despite what you may have heard from the usual suspects in the media, Trump remains committed to renegotiating NAFTA to produce even more wins for American workers and businesses. As I mentioned, Trump has assembled a trade "dream team" with Commerce Secretary Wilbur Ross, U.S. Trade Representative Robert Lighthizer, and my close friend Stephen Vaughn as general counsel. These are brilliant men with an unshakeable commitment to carry out the populist trade agenda Trump ran on.

As for Trump's overtures to China on trade, there have been mixed signals. On the one hand, Trump successfully struck a major deal with China to allow American exports for beef and liquefied natural gas in exchange for the United States allowing Chinese cooked poultry and banking into America. Secretary Ross called the deal a "herculean accomplishment" and an important step to begin to "bring down" our $310 billion trade deficit with China.[16] So far so good.

On the other hand, the deal included an agreement that the United States would send representatives to an international forum on Chinese president Xi Jinping's major globalization project, the "One Belt, One Road" infrastructure plan to build high-speed trains and highways in other countries. (The acronym OBOR is inspired by the ancient Asian "Silk Road" trading routes.) OBOR "looms on a scope and scale with little precedent in modern history, promising more than $1 trillion in infrastructure and spanning more than 60 countries," reported the *Times*.[17] Business Insider dubbed it "a love song for globalization" and one that "flies in the face of the 'Buy American, Hire American' ideology Trump has touted. . . . Cue [Steve] Bannon grabbing his smelling salts."[18]

Is sending a couple of U.S. representatives to a Chinese globalization meeting a mistake? Or is it merely one of Trump's savvy negotiating tactics? We don't know yet. But one thing we do know is that the president ranks North Korea as the major nuclear threat against the United States. His gambit is to use trade as an enticement to get China to help contain the North Korean threat. During President Xi Jinping's visit to Mar-a-Lago, Trump told him, "a trade deal with the U.S. will be far better for them if they solve the North Korea problem." Whether the Chinese got the message remains to be seen. After North Korea tested a ballistic missile in late July that it claimed could reach the United States, Trump tweeted that he was "disappointed in China" which could "easily solve this problem" but did "NOTHING for us with North Korea." Japanese Prime Minister Shinzo Abe agreed with Trump's criticism and signaled increased assistance in containing North Korea.[19] After China's inaction, the Trump administration wisely moved forward with trade policies to crack down on Chinese intellectual property theft.[20] Unlike the previous administration, this one is unafraid to use carrots *and* sticks to notch wins for America.

Trump killing TPP on his third day in office was a strong start. Renegotiating NAFTA with an America First strategy will be a major step toward righting the wrongs that have wrecked the livelihoods of hundreds of thousands of Americans. It took decades to build the globalization rules that Trump accurately describes as putting

Americans at an unfair disadvantage. Those rules cannot be dismantled overnight—the new administration will have to move in a manner that will encourage businesses to locate here without scaring markets trained to fear "protectionism." But the president and his team are clearly committed to making trade policy work for the average American.

To the horror and disgust of world leaders and global elites here at home, on June 1, 2017, the president kept his campaign promise and withdrew the United States from the Paris Agreement. His reasoning was pure economic populism. According to the president, compliance with the agreement would have cost America 2.7 million jobs by 2025. "The agreement is a massive redistribution of wealth to other countries. . . . As President, I have one obligation, and that obligation is to the American people. The Paris climate accord would undermine our economy, hamstring our workers, weaken our sovereignty, impose unacceptable legal risks, and put us at a permanent disadvantage."

Opposition to the Paris accord unified the libertarians, the neoconservatives, and the populists. Only the globalists supported this new world welfare program. Predictably, Richard Branson, Elon Musk, Mitt Romney, and Pope Francis broadcast their disdain over Trump's decision. The Greeniacs went wild predicting doomsday scenarios: lung maladies, flooding, superstorms, and mass starvation. Vacationing Barack Obama called the Trump pullout "the absence of American leadership."

In fact, for the first time in decades, a president is showing real American leadership. In U.S. trade and foreign policy Trump is putting the American people above the New World Order. What a concept!

THE BORDER WALL & IMMIGRATION

If Trump said it once he said it a hundred times: "We will build the wall. And Mexico will pay for that wall." It remains one of his biggest campaign promises. It's also one of the most visual; there either will be a physical barrier on the border or there won't be. Democrats remain united in opposing the wall. Way too many Republicans on

Capitol Hill are against it as well. During a private meeting of the most senior GOP senators, a source who was there in the room told me that Republican leaders laughed out loud at the idea that Trump's border wall would ever be built.[21] This is disheartening and frustrating. It's also a reminder that the populist movement that delivered Trump into office must remain vigilant and keep the heat on the GOP Establishment.

In late April, Republicans once again ran from their own shadow over fears of a possible government shutdown and agreed to Democrat demands to pass a $1.07 trillion continuing budget resolution to fund the government through the rest of the fiscal year. While the measure contained $15 billion in increased military spending, it did not include a down payment for building the wall. Democrats could hardly believe their luck and celebrated their enormous victory. "The omnibus does not fund President Trump's immoral and unwise border wall or create a cruel new deportation force," Nancy Pelosi declared in a gleeful statement.[22]

Congressional Republicans' entire approach to budget negotiations was antithetical to what Donald Trump is about and has stood for. You don't give up your number one bargaining chip right off the bat by removing the threat of a government shutdown. Trump won on the message of a border wall and he won big. The GOP leadership should have defied recalcitrant lawmakers and shut the government down if necessary until they appropriated the funds to start building the wall. That might be the cost of doing the people's will.

Republicans claim the bad continuing budget resolution will be rectified in the fall and that the next budget will pay for the wall. We'll see. The idea that vulnerable lawmakers are going to grow a backbone before a midterm election is doubtful at best. Mark these words: If a wall—a physical wall—is not erected along our southern border, the president and his party will pay a severe political price. Like George Bush's promise to "Read [his] lips: no new taxes," the promise of a border wall was a searing pledge to the American people. To renege on it, or in any way get around it, will be considered a breach of faith in the minds of voters, and they will not forget at election time. Neither will the president's opponents.

Democrats and NeverTrumpers know that defeating Trump's border wall would deliver a crushing and demoralizing blow to his base. Conservatives should expect a dogfight. Citizens must be prepared to melt Capitol Hill phone lines and flood in-boxes like they did during the 2007 and 2013 amnesty wars against the Establishment. They must also be armed with the facts.

The notion that Congress can't find $25 billion—the higher end estimated cost of building the wall—in our nearly $4 trillion annual budget is absurd.[23] Democrats have never met a spending or building project they didn't like. But now all of a sudden they're fiscal hawks? Get real. And the Establishment Republicans who cowered in the corner for eight years while Obama nearly *doubled* the national debt to $19 *trillion* dollars now expect us to believe they're courageous pennypinchers? Spare us.

The entire cost of the wall won't be paid in one lump sum; rather, it will be divided over several years. But just to put its total cost in perspective, consider this: under George W. Bush, the federal government spent $25 billion in a single year maintaining vacant and unused buildings. (Great news: by Obama's second term, we only blew $8 billion a year on dormant properties!)[24] If our government can spend $25 billion dusting empty buildings, surely it can find the funds to protect our people. And here's the reality: the wall pays for itself in the long run. Each year California taxpayers spend $25 billion on illegal immigrants in the form of law enforcement, medical, educational, and public assistance costs.[25] The wall will yield substantial savings to state budgets.

There are also creative ways to cover most of its costs. Shortly after Trump's inauguration I said on radio and TV that the federal government should freeze and seize Mexican drug cartel funds to pay for the wall. Months later Senator Ted Cruz rolled out a nearly identical idea. His "El Chapo" bill would seize Mexican drug kingpin Joaquín "El Chapo" Guzmán's $14 billion in estimated assets and use them for wall construction.[26] I also said we could tax the $20 billion in remittances to Mexico.

Bottom line: the political fight over the wall is not about money, it is about denying Trump and his voters a major victory. That's why

Democrats and Trump's GOP Establishment detractors are going to do everything in their power to stop it. It's also why citizens must be ready for a major political battle. Republicans should welcome this fight. A 2017 analysis by Democrat pollster Stanley Greenberg determined that Democrats turned off working-class voters during the presidential election because "the Democrats have moved from seeking to manage and champion the nation's growing immigrant diversity to seeming to champion immigrant rights over American citizens." Moreover, 41 percent of Democrats believe immigrants "take jobs from U.S. citizens" and half believe granting legal status "would be a drain on government services."[27] Voters agree with conservative populists on illegal immigration. The key will be holding spineless Republicans accountable to enact the immigration policies the people want. In late July, the House approved $1.6 billion in border wall spending, and the administration plans to have prototypes built by winter.[28] Even Speaker Paul Ryan may be coming around. In August, his office released a statement titled "The Wall: Let's Get It Done" that included a video of Ryan touring the border and the words, "It's time for the wall."[29]

Another bright note: the Trump administration's strong commitment to enforce the nation's immigration laws has already begun producing impressive results. Illegal immigration has fallen 73 percent to its lowest levels in 17 years.[30] More than 30,000 criminal aliens have been apprehended since Inauguration Day. (Contrast that with a year earlier, when Obama *released* almost 20,000 criminal aliens.) "When you are caught, you will be detained, adjudicated, and deported," Attorney General Jeff Sessions said in a message aimed at would-be illegal aliens. "Do not come unlawfully. Wait your turn."[31] Border Patrol agents say the administration's approach is working. "We're at a trickle," says Chris Cabrera of the National Border Patrol Council. "It hasn't stopped but it's slowed considerably that we're at a point where we have empty cells now."[32] Oh, the horror!

The administration must also enact smart immigration policies. The first executive order barring entry to individuals from hot spots in the Middle East was stymied by the courts. It's clearly constitutional for the president to set restrictions on entry into the

United States. No foreigner has a constitutional right to come into our country. But you don't get do-overs on executive orders. Remember, the first order was rewritten (exempting Iraqis and green card holders and dropping language giving preference to religious minorities). And it still didn't pass muster. Federal appeals courts ruled that Trump's intent remained discriminatory—based on his campaign statements favoring a "Muslim ban." Talk about judicial overreach. This tied up the agenda for weeks while the media breathlessly reported on every immigrant turned away at a U.S. Customs checkpoint, including tearjerker-tales of Iranian grandmothers who couldn't visit their American grandkids. In July, the Trump administration won a partial victory when the Supreme Court ruled to temporarily uphold most of the president's restrictions on refugees. This bodes well for the Court's determination on the constitutionality of the executive order itself. Regardless of how the Court rules when it hears arguments beginning in October, the administration must maintain a razor-sharp legal strategy that protects national security.

In the wake of the repeated terror attacks in the UK and throughout Europe, the president's travel restriction executive order looks not only wise, but prescient. We resist these commonsense policies at our own peril. If you doubt me, just ask Theresa May.

OBAMACARE FUMBLE RECOVERY?

Health care has long been a third rail in American politics. In 1993, Hillary Clinton's blatant attempt at single-payer health care went down in spectacular flames. Small businesses quickly pressured Congress at the time to quash "Hillarycare." Various legislative attempts to address rising health care costs did nothing of the kind. Instead they increased "covered lives" but never addressed cost. Legislation like Medicare Part D made costs worse and effectively transferred the wealth of the American Middle Class to the insurance and pharmaceutical industries. Once just 4 percent of GDP, today Medicare and Medicaid consume nearly 20 percent. U.S. health care had become too big to fail. With the huge diversion of monies into this segment of the economy, America has experienced the same loss of competitiveness, wage stagnation, and fiscal insolvency seen in Europe.

For decades the costs of medical goods and services were never addressed. Inflation in health care far exceeded that of the overall economy. In 2009, the states couldn't bear the budgetary stress any longer and the Affordable Care Act (aka Obamacare) was passed. The incentive to adopt Medicaid expansion was that for the first six years, the federal government would cover the costs. But the citizens would lose their personal choice in choosing doctors, insurance, and health care—or ever having the freedom to not be involved in Obamacare. The Republicans recognized that there was nothing "conservative" about Obamacare. It was the federal government mandating to insurance companies, pharmaceutical companies, device makers, and doctors what the costs would be, what they would be paid, and ultimately deciding who would be treated.

The middle-class taxpayers who have been footing the cost for these entitlements saw promises broken and out-of-pocket expenses rise. What good is guaranteed access to health care insurance if your premiums and deductibles quadruple and—of course—you can't keep your doctor? And to top it off, you are forced to buy it?

The people's righteous anger led them to turn out in record numbers and propel Trump to the presidency.

Regrettably, Trump outsourced health care to the Congressional Republicans like the developer he was. They had claimed that they would "Repeal and Replace" if only one of their own was president. He has discovered that the Congress will fight any change in the status quo. In the summer of 2016, the cronyism and rent-seeking that had become an integral part of Washington, DC stymied any legislative attempt by Trump.

Trump's election was a direct populist attack by the silent majority on Washington corruption. On health care, Trump can still snatch victory from the jaws of seeming defeat for himself and the American people. He needs to pick three or four proposals that, if implemented, would immediately lower out-of-pocket costs to his middle-class base. Candidate Trump was well-aware that lowering drug prices to match other developed countries would be popular and result in a legitimate reduction in consumer costs. Americans pay four to 10 times more for prescription drugs than citizens of other developed countries. It's true that drug prices must be high enough to pay for research and development, but there is no reason that only American consumers should bear the costs as they do now. We effectively subsidize the generous national health care systems of Canada and other western countries by allowing them to get away with paying much lower prices that don't reflect the much greater R&D costs of drugs they use. The Pentagon demands and gets "most favored" nation status on their purchases—so should the American people. The time for "negotiating" prices has long past—it hasn't worked anyway as the system is too corrupt.

Viscerally, Trump knows that the only humane and sensible alternative to the current system is to go back to a free market for health care goods and services—bypassing both the government and the insurance companies. He knows that doesn't mean there could not also be insurance against unplanned or catastrophic health emergencies or negotiated packages of prepaid services, such as getting a discount for agreeing to a two-year phone contract. It also doesn't mean that there can be no government subsidies or private charities to help those who cannot easily afford market-priced health care.

President Trump abandoned his convictions to the Republicans in Congress and look where that has gotten him. Ultimately only by restoring a true free market to U.S. health care can costs to American consumers and businesses drop. Only when Trump truly re-embraces this free-market ethos will the cost of health care to the federal government and the middle class drop. Freeing up that money for the rest of the economy is what it will take to make America truly great again.

Entitlements are hard things to pull back from people once they get used to them. Nevertheless, the (almost) free ride for some will crash and burn because Obamacare's numbers never added up. Its exchanges are imploding as more insurance companies flee them, and the entire bureaucratic mess is going to crater. In any future effort to revisit Obamacare, the president must fully engage in the district of every vulnerable congressman and senator. The salesmanship lacking in the first few runs at health care must then be employed. An Oval Office address and campaign-style events highlighting the plight of those crushed by Obamacare will help the president control the narrative next time. Ceding health care reform to Congress was a monumental mistake. Democrats smartly turned defeating Obamacare repeal and defeating the "skinny" repeal bill into a rallying cry for the resistance. Every single Democrat voted against every serious Republican effort to repeal Obamacare. Unlike Republicans, Democrats stick together. There's no way around it. Going forward, the president must put pressure on GOP lawmakers to put a bill on the president's desk that he can sign. All of this will take negotiating and finesse. But hey, if the Artisan of the Deal can't pull it off, who can?

It's also important that the president bolsters his popularity during the process. Senate leadership has begun shrugging him off. After the president argued for changing Senate rules to a simple majority vote and urged the GOP to remain focused on health care, Mitch McConnell told Trump that senators don't support a rules change and brushed aside his legislative request to focus on taxes instead. Even though Trump's approval rating is nearly double that of Congress, Trump must continue building goodwill with the American public. Doing so will force lawmakers to enact his America First agenda—the one the people want.[33]

As we saw in late July during the Senate's Obamacare repeal vote, six feckless Republican turncoats voted against a straight repeal in 2017 when it counted, despite having voted for a full repeal in 2015 when it had no chance of becoming law. Their names are: Senators Dean Heller (R-NV), Shelley Moore Capito (R-WV), John McCain (R-AZ), Lamar Alexander (R-TN), Lisa Murkowski (R-AK), and Rob Portman (R-OH).[34] Then the so-called "skinny" Obamacare repeal failed when Senators John McCain (R-AZ), Susan Collins (R-ME), and Lisa Murkowski (R-AK) voted against it. This is a shameful and outrageous display from Establishment Republicans who, for years, used anti-Obamacare ire to fire up voters, but then refused to follow through when it mattered most.

Obamacare must end. It will take strong leadership to make it happen.

MIDDLE EAST ENTANGLEMENTS
& FIGHTING ISIS

On April 6, as President Trump and Chinese president Xi Jinping ate chocolate cake at Mar-a-Lago, 59 U.S. Tomahawk missiles struck Syria's Shayrat Airbase. Their target: Syrian chemical weapons used to bomb the town of Khan Shaykun three days prior. Globalists cheered. Everyone was left wondering why had President Trump's Syria policy seemingly changed overnight?

"I think a lot of Trump voters will be waking up this morning and scratching their heads," said Nigel Farage. Pat Buchanan was even more forceful. "I think [President Trump] reacted emotionally, ineffectively, and also unconstitutionally," said Buchanan. "You don't change your entire foreign policy, or your Middle East policy, based on emotion."[35]

Throughout the campaign Donald Trump pounded the populist message of avoiding Bush-style Middle East quagmires and meddling in other nations' civil wars. "What we should do is focus on ISIS. We should not be focusing on Syria," Trump said weeks before the election. "You're going to end up in World War III over Syria. . . ."[36] What happened?

The answer: President Trump was shown gruesome images of dead Syrian children. He said they were "horrible," "awful," and affected him emotionally. In particular, two scenes hit Trump the hardest: "young, listless children being splashed with water in a frantic attempt to cleanse them of the nerve agent; and an anguished father holding his twin babies, swathed in soft white fabric, poisoned to death," reported *The Washington Post*.[37]

I have no doubt that the images the president viewed were morally reprehensible and emotionally gut-wrenching. And to state the obvious, Syrian president Bashar al-Assad is one of the world's many morally abhorrent despots. Tragically, we live in a world where evil remains ever-present. But if haunting images of atrocities are going to direct America's foreign policy, there will be no end to the wars and tribal conflicts we enter. Just days after the Syrian airstrikes someone sent me 15 images of the brutal carnage from the Palm Sunday attacks targeting Coptic Christians in Egypt. Why weren't missiles fired there? Also, what about the gory scenes from Central African Republic, where children were locked in huts and burned to death with flamethrowers? No missiles sent there either. And hadn't the president just hosted and toasted China—a nation that puts people in reeducation camps and cuts babies out of the wombs of women who have more than one child? The painful reality is that the planet is pocked with atrocities, yet we don't send cruise missiles into all of them. Nor should we.

After the Syrian airstrikes I went on television and was asked for my reaction. I called Syria a "complete cauldron of disaster" (an understatement) and said that full-scale U.S. involvement would devolve into another Iraq. "I'm not sure getting rid of Bashar al-Assad was at the top of the list of those people in Pennsylvania that showed up at his rallies," I said. "There's a lot of selective moral indignation going on out there about atrocities. I hope the Trump team is true to what he campaigned on, which is pragmatic foreign policy that is a break from the Bush path. Because that has been an electoral, political, and humanitarian disaster for the Middle East."

The Trump administration must not succumb to the same kind of fantastical thinking and nation-building that afflicted (and doomed) the Bush administration. We cannot be the world's policeman. President Trump knows this.

Interventionists like to toss out the "isolationism" canard any time a populist warns against inserting ourselves militarily into global conflicts. No person I know who considers themselves a populist advocates a total retreat from foreign affairs; allowing the country to get conquered would weaken the people's power and our national sovereignty. At the same time, citizens are ill-served when our government throws trillions of our hard-earned dollars away on foreign entanglements that kill thousands of our people. Ronald Reagan proved there's a better way.

The Reagan Doctrine of "peace through strength" allowed America to win the Cold War without firing a single shot and with an awareness that military might is not enough. There are indications that the Trump team has been studying the lessons of the Reagan era.

President Trump's first foreign trip in late May 2017 was significant in that he reasserted American interests on the world stage while using the Reagan model of engaging religion to do battle with the evil of our day. As Reagan turned to Pope John Paul II for assistance in the battle against atheistic communism, so Trump reached out to the three major religions on the planet to do battle with Islamic terrorism. Trump boldly addressed a meeting of 55 Muslim heads of state in Saudi Arabia and defined the challenge before them: "This is not a battle between different faiths, different sects or different civilizations," Trump said. "This is a battle between good and evil." Then the president urged the Sunni world to band together and do its part: "Drive them out. Drive out the terrorists," he said. "Drive out the extremists. Drive them out of your places of worship. Drive them out of your communities. Drive them out of your holy land and drive them out of this Earth. . . . We can only overcome this evil if the forces of good are united and strong and if everyone in this room does their fair share and fulfills their part of the burden. Muslim majority countries must take the lead in stamping out radicalization."

Without committing more U.S. lives to the region, Trump used the economic and cultural force of America to encourage leaders in the Middle East to restore order in their own countries. And he got the Saudis to agree to invest $110 billion in American military equipment before Air Force One left Riyadh. From there the president visited shrines holy to Jews and Christians in Israel, concluding with an audience with Pope Francis at the Vatican. Awakening the religious world to the major threat of our time—Islamic Jihad and its wicked ideology—while calling on them to engage it in their own way makes spiritual and foreign policy sense.

These creative efforts put American interests first and provide needed leadership on the world stage. And best of all, it does so without putting our fighting men and women in harm's way.

SUPREME ACHIEVEMENT

Perhaps no issue motivated voters more during the election than the control of the Supreme Court. After the sad passing of conservative icon Justice Antonin Scalia, the Court's four-to-four split between liberal and conservative judges elevated the issue to an even higher level of importance. As someone who clerked for Supreme Court justice Clarence Thomas, I stressed the importance of judicial nominations throughout the campaign. NeverTrumpers' decision to let their ill feelings toward Trump risk giving progressives control of the Supreme Court seemed illogical and foolish to me. Thankfully, most conservatives felt the same way and showed up on Election Day.

Donald Trump's selection of Judge Neil Gorsuch for the Supreme Court proved conservatives made the right choice. Trump nominated a serious legal mind with a strong and impressive record. Best of all, Gorsuch's judicial philosophy of "textualism"—following the Constitution as it is written—mirrors that of the late great Antonin Scalia.

Democrats' decision to filibuster the Gorsuch nomination was further evidence they feared his appointment. After decades of judicial activism from the courts, progressives recoiled at the notion of a Supreme Court justice unwilling to usurp the people's power by rewriting laws to align with their leftist views. Conservatives believe in judicial restraint because we believe that "We the People" are in charge, not unelected judges with political axes to grind. In the opening statement of his Senate confirmation, Judge Gorsuch cited Justice Scalia as an inspiration and said he shared a similar judicial outlook:

> Justice Scalia was a mentor, too. He reminded us that words matter. That the judge's job is to follow the words that are in the law, not replace them with those that aren't. . . .
>
> If judges were just secret legislatures declaring not what the law is but what they would like it to be, the very idea of a government by the people and for the people would be at risk. And those who came before the court would live in fear, never sure exactly what the law requires of them except for the judge's will.
>
> As Alexander Hamilton said, "Liberty can have nothing to fear from judges who apply the law. But liberty has everything to fear if judges try to legislate, too."[38]

On April 7, Senate Republicans exercised the so-called "nuclear option" ("constitutional option" is more accurate) and confirmed

Gorsuch as the 113th justice of the Supreme Court. Conservatives have been disappointed by Republican High Court picks before; only time will tell what kind of legacy Justice Gorsuch leaves behind. For now, conservatives can take solace in knowing that the president of the United States undertook a serious search to identify a judicial nominee of the highest quality and track record, one committed to following, not rewriting, the Constitution.

President Trump is likely to have at least one more future Supreme Court pick. He must, at all costs, resist the temptation to select a milquetoast candidate in the hopes of avoiding a messy Senate confirmation fight. In fact, if I were Trump, I would do the opposite. A battle over first judicial principles is exactly what we need. Judicial activism has been one of the major forces to rob the American people of their God-given rights to self-determination. Having an open debate about the role of the courts in American life is bound to be a winner with an electorate fed up with the imperial judiciary.

4 KEY LESSONS FOR TRUMP MOVING FORWARD

Smart presidential administrations know their strengths and fix their weaknesses. The Trump administration's first several months in office have produced important victories and revealed critical vulnerabilities. As a strong and early supporter of the "America First" agenda, I offer President Trump and his team four key lessons to keep their populist efforts on track.

MESSAGE DISCIPLINE

Advancing a robust conservative agenda requires strong message discipline. Shepherding populist policies through Congress also means forging strategic alliances, including with Democrats.

Every presidential talking point, speech, TV appearance, Facebook post, and tweet must drive the same core message. The White House communications team plays a vital supporting role, but presidents must deliver the message as planned. If the quarterback is constantly changing plays without telling his teammates, balls are dropped, fumbles occur, and momentum gets stopped. The same is true for presidents and their communications staff.

Contrary to the conventional wisdom spouted on cable television by strategists and consultants—most of whom predicted a Clinton victory in 2016—I do not lose sleep over President Trump's tweets. They are his only instantaneous, direct line to the American people. Of course the content of the tweets matter. Bombshell tweets like warning James Comey there may be "tapes" of his conversations with the president or hurling critiques at "weak" Attorney General Jeff Sessions during a critical health care vote on the Hill squander precious political capital. Candidates are already jockeying for position in the 2018 midterm elections. Trump must use his GOP House and Senate advantage while he still has it.

The Comey firing offers an instructive case study. Presidents are free to fire an FBI director any time they please. But a decision of that magnitude requires precise communication planning. Sometimes you don't have the luxury of time, but in this case the White House controlled the timing. Unfortunately, Trump's communications staff were reportedly given one hour's notice before Comey was removed.[39] That meant they had exactly one hour to: coordinate a clear and cogent explanation for the decision; assemble a team of surrogates to hit the airwaves to defend the move; book those surrogates on all the right shows; prepare press statements and place them with key reporters; and amplify a unified message across social media and elsewhere.

Moreover, the brusque manner in which Comey was fired—no advance notice, a tersely worded letter—unnecessarily antagonized him and his supporters within the agency. According to reports, Comey only learned of his firing from the press while on the west coast. Worse, every digital screen in America was glued to the dramatic O. J. Simpson–style aerial footage of Comey immediately being sped down the highway to a waiting government jet. Why escalate an already controversial decision into a national spectacle?

Instead, the president could have met with Comey privately, thanked him for his service, explained that the election had created a growing chorus of bipartisan critics, and said that, for the good of the nation, it was time to turn the page and give the FBI a fresh start. It wouldn't have been perfect, but it would have been less radioactive.

In Washington, you either control the message or the message controls you. One theme a day communicated clearly and consistently—that should be Trump's messaging goal.

TRUST YOUR POPULIST INSTINCTS

Donald Trump has the best policy and political instincts of any politician I've ever seen. The "experts" said voters would yawn at a policy platform built around something as boring as trade. Trump knew otherwise. There's nothing "boring" about losing your job and struggling to feed your family. The Gucci loafer–wearing consultants claimed a tough message on illegal immigration would be too extreme, too toxic, and would alienate voters. Trump understood the reverse was true. The real "extremists" were the elites who cared only about preserving the comfortable status quo, not everyday Americans who wanted laws enforced fairly and consistently.

Throughout the election, Trump refused to bow to the critics of his America First populist agenda. This was very brave and smart. Yet since entering the White House, he has at times seen staff conflicts stymie his bold efforts. While strong, sharp differences among Trump's advisors are inevitable, populist conservative goals must be defended and advanced.

The base will view any undermining of the populists' roles as a signal that the president has lost sight of the mandate he was elected to fulfill. Many reporters (including Joe Scarborough) have tried to drive a wedge between Trump and populist Steve Bannon by portraying the strategist as a Machiavellian figure who "controls" the president. That's *Saturday Night Live* nonsense. Anyone who knows Trump knows he's in charge. And anyone who knows Bannon knows he's intensely loyal and talented. For example, Bannon possesses a unique understanding of how to perform what he calls the "deconstruction of the administrative state." As Bannon explained at the 2017 CPAC:

If you look at these cabinet appointments, they were selected for a reason and that is the deconstruction. The way the progressive left runs, is if they can't get it passed, they're just going to put in some sort of regulation in an agency. That's all going to be deconstructed and I think that that's why this regulatory thing is so important. . . . The center core of what we believe, that we're a nation with an economy. Not an economy just in some global marketplace with open borders, but we are a nation with a culture and a reason for being . . . I think one of the most pivotal moments in modern American history was [President Trump's] immediate withdrawal from TPP. That got us out of a trade deal and let our sovereignty come back to ourselves, the people.

As has been reported, behind Bannon's desk is a big whiteboard with all the president's populist campaign promises. As Trump fulfills each one, Bannon places a checkmark beside it.[40] In other words, Bannon cares about whether the Trump administration keeps its promises. Wouldn't it be nice if everyone in Washington cared about doing what they promise?

There's value in partnering with Democrats to pass Trump's legislative agenda and he should reach out to them when possible. But the president must also remember that dozens of congressional Republicans opposed his nomination and continue to slow-walk his agenda. That means his base must remain rock solid in its support.

Trump raised eyebrows when he said he was "both" a globalist and a nationalist. I think he means that a stronger U.S. economy—benefiting from fairer rules on global trade—will be good for the world. And I think he's right. But he's got to stay on the nationalist course. If Trump's conservative base senses a globalist shift, his core constituency will crack. The president must stick with what works and wins.

America First. Period.

STOP THE LEAKS

The number of high-level leaks coming out of the Trump White House in its first several months is astounding and alarming. I can't think of any other administration that has been hit by so many leaks so early. Beyond the political havoc they inflict on the administration, the leaking of sensitive and classified material endangers our national security.

Even former Democrat congressman Dennis Kucinich agrees. "Look, I disagree with President Trump on a number of issues, but on this one, there can only be one president and somebody in the intelligence community is trying to upend this president in order to pursue a policy direction that puts us in conflict with Russia," said Kucinich. "The question is why? And who? And we need to find out."[41]

Trump's "Deep State" problem is real. Allowing Obama holdovers like Sally Yates to serve as acting attorney general—even for a matter of days—was a mistake and an unforced error. Obama bureaucrats are not there to help—they are there to sabotage the administration.

Rooting out moles is difficult. One thing the administration must do is get a handle on all the Obama holdovers still burrowed in the system. One White House source estimated that over 60 percent of National Security Council employees "are not Trump administration appointees, but career officials who were appointed to the White House from other agencies under the Obama administration." Worse, the NSC has "whole departments" that have only a single Trump appointee.[42] Obviously not all Obama-appointed bureaucrats are willing to commit federal crimes to undermine the Trump administration. But the fact that so many Obama officials are working in sensitive NSC capacities with almost no Trump appointees around is disturbing.

A big part of the problem rests with the Trump administration. They have been slow to nominate and fill key posts. As of August 2017, a *Washington Post* analysis found that no nominees had yet been named for 354 of the 577 positions that require Senate confirmation. More Trump loyalists in mid-level and executive bureaucratic roles means more eyeballs and ears monitoring and managing information security to minimize leaks.[43] The Trump team needs to get it in gear and fill slots with competent and trustworthy professionals.

It starts with jettisoning Obama holdovers and pushing through confirmation votes for key national security appointments, judges, and ambassadors who share, not undermine, the president's principles.

The problem, of course, is that Republicans don't have an actual working majority—but a majority in name only. While it's fine for the president to tweet about changing Senate rules, he shouldn't stop there. He must put slow-walking Democrats on defense by making a sustained argument to the American people about the need to jack-hammer through the congressional barricades blocking the change voters demand.

Trump has moved swiftly to appoint and confirm conservative federal judges, despite Democrat delays. By August, the president had already confirmed more judges than Barack Obama had at the same point in his term.[44] It's critical that Trump's team apply that same focus and urgency to ousting Obama bureaucrats and installing national security professionals committed to protecting the nation's secrets.

The GOP leadership can help, too. We need a full investigation of the Obama administration's "unmasking" scandal that revealed Americans' names in intel documents. Former Obama officials like National Security Adviser Susan Rice, CIA Director John Brennan, UN Ambassador Samantha Power, and speechwriter and adviser Ben Rhodes should all be investigated and held to account. The launch of a House Intelligence Committee probe and Attorney General Jeff Sessions's leak investigations are a good start.[45] But so far, a 25-year-old outside contractor named Reality Winner (you can't make this stuff up; that's her actual name) is the only person who has been arrested and charged with leaking classified information. Much work remains.

One way *not* to stop leaks is to conduct ham-fisted, profane late-night on-the-record interviews with liberal publications. Just ask former White House director of communications Anthony Scaramucci. Ranting that he wanted to "kill all the leakers," as "The Mooch" reportedly did during his ever-so-brief 10-day tenure, may have provided him with momentary emotional relief.[46] But it dragged the White House off-message, birthed a million mocking memes, and did little to root out the leakers placing our national security in peril. Dangerous threats demand seriousness and professionalism. When it comes to protecting America's secrets, there's no margin for error.

The dangerous national security leaks must stop. Revealing top-secret and classified material to score political points is an act of treason and betrayal. The administration must find the perpetrators and prosecute them to the fullest extent of the law before it's too late.

A NEW MEDIA STRATEGY

Trump's very presence in the Oval Office reminds the media of Election Night. His winning embarrassed and infuriated them to their core.

The president is unafraid to confront the press on its bias and "fake news" reporting. Now for the media, it is payback time. Anytime the president gains traction on his agenda, the media will work overtime to divert attention to the Russia investigations, invariably through anonymous sources.

As Trump adviser Steve Bannon put it, media are the "opposition party":

> They're corporatist, globalist media that are adamantly opposed— adamantly opposed to an economic nationalist agenda like Donald Trump has. . . . Here's why it's going to get worse: Because he's going to continue to press his agenda. And as economic conditions get better, as more jobs get better, they're going to continue to fight. If you think they're going to give you your country back without a fight, you are sadly mistaken. Every day—every day, it is going to be a fight.[47]

During the campaign, the Trump team dominated social media and energized voters with its populist message. They must now continue to develop new methods to reach all Americans with their agenda while avoiding message fatigue.

Sometimes less is more. Reserve the president's access for the big moments and policy initiatives. The president's first address to a joint session of Congress was a smashing success because he delivered an articulate and well-crafted populist message in a prime-time venue. Wisely, the White House canceled the next day's press briefing to let the public's positive response linger in the news cycle. Giving good stories time to breathe brings a sense of stability and steadiness voters find reassuring.

The president should spend at least two days a week outside of Washington and the White House bubble, to be with the people. Doing more rallies to sell his agenda and visiting Americans where they live and work will not only invigorate the president's spirits, but will create needed pressure to pass key legislation. And he should not just visit red state America. He is president of all the people and must spend time in California, New York, Illinois, and even my home region of New England. There are millions of Trump voters in all of those states, and they—and their moderate neighbors—deserve to hear from their president. "The resistance" must not be allowed to restrict his travel out of fear of mass protests. This is where good advance work and political strategy come in—both must be engaged and coordinated.

There is one bit of media advice that Trump could learn from the Obama team: go local. The Obama administration invited local anchors into the White House to interview the president to get around the Washington press corps. This is a smart strategy. Not only does it give the president a chance to target his message to key markets, but those reporters are thankful for the opportunity and more likely to give him a fair shake.

Opening the White House pressroom to new voices was a masterstroke. Bloggers, regional reporters (asking questions via Skype), religious and conservative press were suddenly invading the elite's most exclusive club. It's the only time I supported open borders! When the site I cofounded, LifeZette, got the first question at Sean Spicer's first full White House briefing, sneers of condescension reverberated in fancy media circles. Too bad. Our gifted political editor Jon Conradi leads a team of talented journalists with a diversity of thought and experience. Conservative media should be welcome, even in the West Wing.

A FINAL WORD

No one can predict what will become of the Trump presidency. It's up to the conservative-populist movement to hold the administration accountable to ensure it remains on track. Winning an election is never enough. Politicians stray from their promises, and poorly implemented policies produce unintended consequences. Conservatives must remain active and engaged throughout Trump's presidency. Successful and enduring political movements are built on principles, not a single leader—even ones as dynamic as Reagan or Trump. Populists and pure conservatives each have the same basic goal—a great country where the average person has a chance at a better life. The Establishment has the system it wants and will attempt to steamroll anything and anyone that seeks to change it. As I said earlier, Reagan resisted and defeated the Establishment on the people's behalf. We must do the same. If we do, we will continue to see major wins for our country.

America First populism works when words are backed up by action. As previously noted, an ironclad commitment to enforcing the nation's laws has sent illegal immigration rates plunging. Illegal aliens realize the U.S. government is serious about cracking down and are less likely to make border-crossing attempts as a result. Likewise, illegals' violent criminal gangs, like the notorious MS-13, are being hunted down and deported. Under Trump, ICE performed the largest gang crackdown in history, resulting in over 1,378 arrests and the deportation of nearly 400 gang members to El Salvador.[48]

The same pattern of populist success extends to economic trends as well. There are, of course, the record highs in the Dow Jones industrial average. But beyond that, U.S. manufacturing activity has hit a three-year high—a strong achievement and further proof that Trump's "Buy American, Hire American" agenda is breaking through.[49] Other countries are cheating less on trade, too. In a report that must have pained them to publish, CNN was forced to admit that "America's biggest trade partners have taken far fewer protectionist measures against U.S. business so far this year, possibly because they're worried about retaliation."[50] (Having one of the nation's preeminent trade lawyers, Bob Lighthizer, as America's U.S. trade representative was a Trump masterstroke.) Even at the G20 summit in Hamburg, Germany, amid international whining about the U.S. withdrawal from the Paris climate accord, President Trump still managed to score key concessions on climate change and trade policy.[51] These early and significant wins demonstrate what happens when America has a president with the resolve and determination to advance an America First populist platform.

The more victories the president racks up for working-class Americans, the more elites will rise up in opposition. Barricades to the success of populism under Trump come in many forms: special prosecutors, side probes of Russia's involvement in the election, and a media exaggerating even the most tangential Trump family business interest in foreign countries. But for America's sake, these must be overcome. Reagan's transformative presidency inspired a new generation of young conservatives (like myself)—and Trump's, if successful, can do the same. But, it won't be easy.

We know what doesn't work: global trade deals that enrich other countries at the expense of our own workers; lax immigration policies that compromise the nation's security, health care system, schools, and jobs; a tax and regulatory regime that stifles economic growth and competitiveness, and strangles innovation; and an imprudent interventionist foreign policy that costs us trillions of dollars and thousands of American lives. For decades a bipartisan Establishment blindly embraced these ruinous policies. The resulting economic and personal pain, felt across the vast American landscape, has fueled the rise of populism and its stalwarts—from Goldwater to Reagan, Buchanan to Trump. But it bears repeating that the conservative-populist movement that President Trump inherited and consolidated is not restricted to one man or one era. It will go on and it must be sustained by the members of the movement—one that will at times need to form alliances with disparate political factions in order to advance their common interests. This is especially important now since the populists are outnumbered. Remember, the president lost the popular vote by three million people.

Throughout the improbable 2016 presidential election, I personally witnessed the fighting spirit and sacrificial devotion of the American people. Though the media sought to depict Trump voters as "haters," they embodied just the opposite: love of family, love of home, and love of country (and utter disdain for the media and political hacks who ignored them from day one). Sure, many of the Trump voters were angry—they had a right to be. The things they held most dear were under attack and no politician from either party was willing to even listen to their concerns. Then came Trump . . .

While some, even in his own party, continue to throw rocks, other pols—particularly left-wing Democrats—are smart enough to see the political handwriting on the wall. Socialist Bernie Sanders has smartly continued to play to the workingman through a series of regular prime-time debates on CNN. Crossing swords with everyone from John Kasich to Ted Cruz, (virtual CNN Contributor) Bernie is good at pointing out the problems Americans face. It's his solutions that fall apart. (Note to CNN: the presidential campaign is really over and so is the Bern.) Joe Biden has also caught the populist bug since Trump's election. The Amtrak addict opened a new PAC in June of 2017, teasing voters that he might mount a challenge against Trump in 2020. The man has been running for president since I was in college. Nothing would cement the Democrat Party's "dinosaur" status quite like a Biden bid.

Liberal darling Senator Elizabeth Warren is also making a populist pitch to voters. She is extolling her version of populism: "the power of the people to make change in this country." Shortly after the presidential election (November 19) in a speech to the Center for American Progress, Warren suggested that the problem facing America was not the size of government, but "Rather, it's a deep down concern over who government works for." (Actually, the bloated government and its distance from the people are *exactly* the problems.) She claimed the economic "game is rigged" and urged action to "level the playing field." Her diagnosis of middle-class angst is partially on the mark. It's her prescriptions that are poisonous: "invest in education" (tax and spend), "invest in infrastructure" (see previous), "Wall Street needs stronger rules and tougher enforcement" (that Warren gets to write).

This idiocy, peddled by the left, must be monitored and countered. Sanders's and Warren's polluted populism defaults to familiar socialist answers: an ever-expanding (and expensive) big government with layers of regulation written by career bureaucrats and enforced by elites. This will not cure what ails the American people. To shut down these populist pretenders, it will be up to President Trump and his allies to offer their own robust market-driven solutions. They'll have to explain to the American people how their policies will benefit the voters prior to rolling out any legislation. Before the midterm elections, substantive legislative victories must be delivered or the president and his party will face a potentially detrimental populist assault from the left.

As Pat Buchanan recently reminded me, the principle of protecting liberty and freedom at all costs was at the heart of the American founding. "The ideal of Hamilton—everybody that built this country—was to make America economically independent to sustain and support our political independence," Buchanan said. This is liberation from the New World Order. At the founding of the Republic, patriots made their own goods and defended their market. The Hamiltonian idea that we wouldn't rely on British ships fueled economic and political independence that allowed the United States the freedom to engage in foreign affairs and conflicts only when it served our national interest. Massive international agreements tie a nation to the world's problems (in 1914, European countries were tied together). Populist and nationalist movements in Europe have produced a mixed bag of successes and defeats. Emmanuel Jean-Michel Frédéric Macron trounced populist Marine Le Pen in the French presidential election, and the globalists have fiercely opposed Brexit's implementation. Still, there are populist bright spots in Europe. Leaders in Poland, Hungary, and the Czech Republic, for example, have refused to accept more refugees in order to protect working people and national culture. Whether the EU will override those decisions and crush populist uprisings throughout Europe remains to be seen. Regardless, the historical connection between trade and security, economic strength and influence are lessons the world would do well to remember.

That same spirit of liberty and independence is what drives the populist movement today. The throngs I witnessed at that Leesburg rally that cold Sunday night and the voices I hear on the radio each day aren't going away. They love this country, and they love their families too much to stop fighting. We all realize that the core problems we face in domestic and foreign affairs aren't going to be solved in four years. Trump gave us the promise of a reprieve and a renewal. But victory is not yet assured. Bold steps must be taken by the administration to show its loyalty to the people and a willingness to do battle for them despite the pressures to do Washington's bidding.

Things are now coming to a head. We are on the knife's edge in this country. The left's blind hatred for President Trump and Republicans has produced a disturbing new wave of dangerous rhetoric and violence by far-left radicals willing to settle political differences using the most extreme means possible. After Trump's inauguration, Madonna said she "thought an awful lot about blowing up the White House." Comedian Kathy Griffin took an ISIS-style photo of herself holding a blood-drenched severed head made to look like the president of the United States. A "Shakespeare in the Park" New York City play featured the stabbing of a Donald Trump look-alike in the role of Julius Caesar. And of course, in June 2017, a Bernie Sanders supporter named James Hodgkinson targeted Republicans before gunning down Republican House majority whip Steve Scalise and three others who were practicing for the annual Congressional Baseball Game. Until Democratic leaders denounce the corrosive, vile anti-Trump rhetoric and conspiracy theories peddled on cable TV, I'm afraid the left's unhinged rage will continue. "[A] more civil and honest public discourse can help us face up to the challenges of our nation," President Obama said in 2011.[52] Members of his party would do well to heed those words and get their political house in order before the nation suffers the loss of innocent lives.

Beyond right and left, there are goals we must achieve for all Americans. This includes encouraging patriotism among all our people, ensuring their safety, balancing the federal budget, liberating the potential of our innovators, and restoring local control over our schools. All of these objectives—and many others—are well within our reach. To achieve them, however, we need new laws—and those laws must be well-crafted and expertly promoted.

Nearly two and a half years after his campaign began, President Trump still has barricades to overcome. There's the barricade of a press corps that would rather see the country fail than see him succeed. There's the barricade of a left dominated by radicalism and anti-Americanism. There's the barricade of the bipartisan Establishment in Congress that is hostile to his America First priorities. There's the barricade of China—an enormous economy dominated by a single tyrannical party determined to dominate Asia, if not the world.

These barricades—and others—may seem too imposing to clear, but they're not. We must go forward undaunted, determined, and have confidence in the prudence, patriotism, and decency of the American people. We must reject those who would tell us that this country is too wicked, too corrupt, too unsophisticated, too stupid, or too decadent to govern itself—and that we have no choice but to submit to the dominion of elites at home and abroad. President Trump has won great victories already—and may win many more. But the promise of populism rests on its trust in the people, not in one person. We must fight for the power that is our birthright. We must fight for America—we must keep reminding the president and his political opponents in government that they work for us. In the end, the greatness of America lies not in its wealth, its armies, its beauty, or even its rich history. The greatness of America is that here, we are trying to build a country where the people—all the people—are the rulers, not the servants. If President Trump and his supporters can restore this simple truth to its proper place in American life, then this administration will have been a great success.

ACKNOWLEDGMENTS

This book would not have been possible without the support and encouragement of my family and friends. Giving on-air support and off-air guidance, Raymond Arroyo was critical to getting this done. Craig Shirley's insights kept me thinking and refining my work. Chris Edwards kept me laughing and sane when I most needed it. Pete Anthony led our media company, LifeZette, which reached new key milestones as I was writing.

My biggest cheerleaders were Chuck and Ina Carlsen, whom I miss every day. The Cipollones always made my family feel at home during deadline pressure. Pat's counsel was, as usual, spot-on. Dear friends Gay and Stanley Gaines, Conrad and Barbara Black, Jon and Sarah Talcott, and George and Sarah Vassiliou have helped me keep my perspective during these tumultuous times. As always my "big bro" Jimmy was there any time I needed to talk. Thanks also to Ramin Oskoui, MD, who helped me with his discerning eye and free market approach. Going back to 1994, Stephen Vaughn has provided key insights into the key issues that fueled the populist wave.

My hard-working radio team of James Coluccio and Drew Carmichael and assistants Karolina Wilson and Alexis Papa were instrumental in steadying the ship during this hectic time.

The team at Fox News—especially Sean Hannity and Bret Baier—were most generous in showcasing my analysis during the exciting 2016 campaign.

My talented researcher and collaborator, Wynton Hall, never doubted this book's importance as part of the historical record of the

2016 campaign and populism. I am grateful to my editor, Adam Bellow, at St. Martins—it's been a long road since we both appeared on the cover of *The New York Times Magazine*.

Finally, my children, Maria, Dmitri & Nikolai, kept me grounded and smiling. I love you.

NOTES

Introduction

1. https://www.nytimes.com/2014/06/11/us/politics/eric-cantor-loses-gop-primary.html?_r=0
2. http://www.nbcnews.com/politics/congress/dramatic-defeat-cantor-v-brat-numbers-n128761
3. https://www.washingtonpost.com/local/virginia-politics/eric-cantor-faces-tea-party-challenge-tuesday/2014/06/10/17da5d20-f092-11e3-bf76-447a5df6411f_story.html?utm_term=.fd9abdf5f92c
4. http://www.politico.com/story/2014/06/eric-cantor-primary-election-results-virginia-107683
5. https://www.washingtonpost.com/politics/what-went-wrong-for-eric-cantor/2014/06/11/0be7c02c-f180-11e3-914c-1fbd0614e2d4_story.html?utm_term=.2ed256b15c23
6. http://www.nbcnews.com/meet-the-press/meet-press-transcript-june-15-2014-n131601

1

1. https://reaganlibrary.archives.gov/archives/reference/8.19.76.html
2. http://www.pbs.org/wgbh/americanexperience/features/transcript/reagan-transcript/
3. http://www.nytimes.com/1980/11/05/politics/05REAG.html?_r=0
4. Dick Wirthlin, *The Greatest Communicator: What Ronald Reagan Taught Me About Politics, Leadership, and Life* (Hoboken: Wiley, 2004), p. 161.
5. http://www.presidency.ucsb.edu/ws/index.php?pid=38699
6. https://www.craigshirley.com/archive/remembering-ronald-reagan/
7. https://object.cato.org/sites/cato.org/files/pubs/pdf/pa107.pdf
8. Craig Shirley, *Rendezvous with Destiny: Ronald Reagan and the Campaign That Changed America* (Wilmington: ISI Books, 2009), p. 181.
9. University of Virginia Miller Center, Richard M. Nixon Presidential Recordings, Nixon Conversation 620-008. Audio and transcript: http://millercenter.org/presidential recordings/rmn-620-008
10. http://www.nytimes.com/1998/10/11/us/clark-clifford-a-major-adviser-to-four-presidents-is-dead-at-91.html
11. Peggy Noonan, *What I Saw at the Revolution: A Political Life in the Reagan Era* (New York: Random House, 2010), p. 167.
12. Lou Cannon, *President Reagan: The Role of a Lifetime* (New York: Public Affairs, 2000), p. 67.
13. Lou Cannon, *Governor Reagan: His Rise to Power* (New York: Public Affairs, 2005), p. 108.
14. Caspar Weinberger, *In the Arena: A Memoir of the 20th Century* (Washington, DC: Regnery, 2001), p. 155.
15. Ibid., p. 163.
16. Michael Kazin, *The Populist Persuasion: An American History* (Ithaca: Cornell University Press, 1998), p. 249.
17. http://www.presidency.ucsb.edu/ws/?pid=25968
18. Kazin, *The Populist Persuasion*, p. 252.

19. http://prop1.org/protest/1987/870108wp.buchanan.html
20. Craig Shirley, *Reagan's Revolution: The Untold Story of the Campaign That Started It All* (Nashville: Nelson Current, 2005), p. xix.
21. Gerald Ford, *A Time to Heal* (New York: Harper & Row, 1979), p. 333.
22. http://articles.baltimoresun.com/2004-06-06/news/0406060322_1_ronald-reagan-president-ronald-president-reagan
23. As quoted in Shirley, *Reagan's Revolution*, p. 95.
24. https://reaganlibrary.archives.gov/archives/reference/11.20.75.html
25. https://reaganlibrary.archives.gov/archives/reference/3.31.76.html
26. Wirthlin, *The Greatest Communicator*, p. 23.
27. https://news.google.com/newspapers?nid=2209&dat=19830727&id=8qYrAAAAIBAJ&sjid=6fwFAAAAIBAJ&pg=7079,4522705&hl=en
28. http://www.presidency.ucsb.edu/ws/?pid=114982
29. Shirley, *Reagan's Revolution*, 197.
30. http://www.latimes.com/politics/la-pol-sac-skelton-political-conventions-20160718-snap-story.html
31. Shirley, *Reagan's Revolution*, p. xxvii.
32. Noonan, *What I Saw at the Revolution*, p. 149.
33. https://www.fordlibrarymuseum.gov/library/document/0204/1512162.pdf
34. http://www.presidency.ucsb.edu/ws/?pid=32596
35. Shirley, *Rendezvous with Destiny*, p. 6.
36. As quoted in Shirley, *Rendezvous with Destiny*, p. 6; Douglas Hallett, "John Connally's Slick Image," *Wall Street Journal*, May 17, 1979, p. 26.
37. As quoted in Shirley, *Rendezvous with Destiny*, p. 6; James R. Dickenson, "Reagan, Already the Front Runner, Formally Enters GOP Race Tuesday," *Washington Star*, November 11, 1979, A4.
38. http://www.cnn.com/ALLPOLITICS/1996/analysis/back.time/9603/06/index.shtml
39. https://www.washingtonpost.com/archive/politics/1980/06/01/reagan-iowa-loss-allowed-him-to-campaign-his-way/8175e913-1252-4c19-98ad-e6ff64ed1750/?utm_term=.59508f746b5a
40. http://www.presidency.ucsb.edu/ws/?pid=25970
41. http://federal-tax-rates.insidegov.com/l/65/1980
42. http://www.heritage.org/taxes/commentary/reagans-tax-cutting-legacy
43. http://www.nytimes.com/1981/07/30/politics/30REAG.html
44. http://www.nationalreview.com/article/440127/tax-cuts-king-dollar-and-growth-jfk-reagan-trump-economic-club-new-york
45. http://time.com/4511870/john-f-kennedy-and-ronald-reagan-tax-policy/
46. http://www.nationalreview.com/article/420153/what-would-reagan-make-current-gops-tax-debate-edwin-j-feulner-stephen-moore
47. Arthur Laffer and Stephen Moore, *The End of Prosperity: How Higher Taxes Will Doom the Economy—If We Let It Happen* (New York: Threshold Editions, 2009), p. 3.
48. http://fortune.com/2016/11/10/donald-trump-arthur-laffer-prediction/
49. https://www.ft.com/content/8cb63288-bc85-11e6-8b45-b8b81dd5d080
50. https://www.whitehouse.gov/blog/2017/04/26/president-trump-proposed-massive-tax-cut-heres-what-you-need-know
51. http://www.nationalreview.com/article/221231/wall-paul-kengor
52. http://www.foxnews.com/story/2004/06/06/quotes-nation-reacts.html
53. Peter Schweizer, *Reagan's War: The Epic Story of His Forty-Year Struggle and Final Triumph Over Communism* (New York: Doubleday, 2002), pp. 11–12.
54. http://www.heritage.org/report/the-crusader-ronald-reagan-and-the-fall-communism
55. http://www.nytimes.com/2004/06/07/opinion/ronald-reagan.html
56. http://www.presidency.ucsb.edu/ws/?pid=37990
57. Ibid.
58. As quoted in Craig Shirley, *Last Act: The Final Years and Emerging Legacy of Ronald Reagan* (Nashville: Thomas Nelson, 2015), p. 321.

59. http://www.heritage.org/defense/commentary/33-years-and-33-minutes-why-missile-defense-more-necessary-ever

60. http://www.washingtonpost.com/wp-dyn/content/article/2004/06/07/AR2005033002003.html

61. http://www.margaretthatcher.org/document/110356

62. http://money.cnn.com/2016/10/07/news/economy/obama-15-million-jobs/index.html

63. http://www.nytimes.com/1976/03/25/archives/campaigns-against-washington-termed-racism-by-humphrey.html?_r=0

64. Shirley, *Last Act,* p. xix.

2

1. https://www.nytimes.com/2014/03/01/arts/music/long-lost-video-of-rb-stars-at-1989-inaugural-is-to-air.html

2. Richard Viguerie, *Takeover: The 100-Year War for the Soul of the GOP and How Conservatives Can Finally Win It* (Washington, DC: WND Books, 2014), p. 100.

3. Ed Rollins, *Bare Knuckles and Back Rooms: My Life in American Politics* (New York: Broadway Books, 1996), p. 196.

4. Tom Wicker, *George Herbert Walker Bush* (New York: Viking, 2004), p. 106.

5. http://www.presidency.ucsb.edu/ws/?pid=25955

6. Noonan, *What I Saw at the Revolution,* p. 308.

7. Dick Darman, *Who's In Control?: Polar Politics and the Sensible Center* (New York: Simon & Schuster, 1996), p. 191.

8. http://www.presidency.ucsb.edu/ws/?pid=25955

9. In fact, a 2008 Associated Press obituary for Dick Darman was headlined: "Richard Darman, Who Convinced Bush 41 to Break 'No New Taxes' Pledge, Dies at 64." http://www.foxnews.com/story/2008/01/25/richard-darman-who-convinced-bush-41-to-break-no-new-taxes-pledge-dies-at-64.html

10. http://www.nationalreview.com/article/271217/budget-danger-ahead-james-c-capretta

11. Darman, *Who's In Control?,* p. 84.

12. Ibid., pp. 293, 361.

13. http://www.nytimes.com/1990/06/27/us/bush-now-concedes-a-need-for-tax-revenue-increases-to-reduce-deficit-in-budget.html?pagewanted=all&src=pm

14. Mary Matalin and James Carville, *All's Fair: Love, War, and Running for President* (New York: Random House, 1994), p. 221.

15. http://time.com/2854306/the-curse-of-friendly-fire/

16. Matalin and Carville, *All's Fair,* p. 69.

17. Peter Goldman, Thomas M. DeFrank, Mark Miller, et al., *Quest for the Presidency: 1992* (College Station: Texas A&M University Press, 1994), p. 335.

18. Ibid., pp. 335, 345.

19. Ibid.

20. Ibid., p. 325.

21. http://www.thedailybeast.com/articles/2016/06/01/pat-buchanan-donald-trump-is-running-as-me

22. http://voicesofdemocracy.umd.edu/buchanan-culture-war-speech-speech-text/

23. http://www.americanrhetoric.com/speeches/patrickbuchanan1992rnc.htm

24. http://www.presidency.ucsb.edu/ws/?pid=21617

25. http://www.nytimes.com/1992/10/16/us/the-1992-campaign-transcript-of-2d-tv-debate-between-bush-clinton-and-perot.html?pagewanted=all

26. Matalin and Carville, *All's Fair,* pp. 129–30.

27. Rollins, *Bare Knuckles and Back Rooms,* 260.

28. John B. Judis, *The Populist Explosion: How the Great Recession Transformed American and European Politics* (New York: Columbia Global Reports, 2016), p. 50.

29. Goldman et al., *Quest for the Presidency,* pp. 361–62.

30. https://www.c-span.org/video/?25063-1/american-political-system

31. Ibid.

32. http://www.presidency.ucsb.edu/ws/?pid=46216
33. http://www.presidency.ucsb.edu/ws/?pid=47070
34. https://www.washingtonpost.com/archive/opinions/1993/11/07/america-first-nafta-never
    /c8450c08-b14b-4a25-abe8-0b7cfc992e11/?utm_term=.5ce6c5a71129
35. http://www.nytimes.com/1992/10/16/us/the-1992-campaign-transcript-of-2d-tv-debate
    -between-bush-clinton-and-perot.html?pagewanted=all
36. http://www.nytimes.com/1992/03/04/us/1992-campaign-white-house-bush-says-raising
    -taxes-was-biggest-blunder-his.html?pagewanted=all
37. http://www.reuters.com/article/us-usa-kennedy-bush-idUSBREA4308G20140505
38. https://www.youtube.com/watch?v=zKeSAI8uS8g
39. Rollins, *Bare Knuckles and Back Rooms*, p. 264.
40. http://c-pol.com/syndrome.html
41. Rollins, *Bare Knuckles and Back Rooms*, p. 240.

3

1. https://www.lauraingraham.com/images/pdf/NewYorkTimesArticle.pdf
2. http://articles.latimes.com/1997-04-06/opinion/op-45900_1_clinton-administration
3. Bill Clinton, *My Life* (New York: Knopf, 2004), p. 330.
4. Ibid., p. 330.
5. https://www.washingtonpost.com/archive/politics/1992/10/05/governors-camp-feels
   -his-record-on-crime-can-stand-the-heat/184f3659-154d-41f3-9ee2-4d34bf2acfd5/?utm
   _term=.e13befde0b1b
6. https://www.washingtonpost.com/video/politics/bill-clinton-in-1992-ad-a-plan-to-end
   -welfare-as-we-know-it/2016/08/30/9e6350f8-6ee0-11e6-993f-73c693a89820_video.html
7. http://www.nytimes.com/1992/07/24/us/1992-campaign-democrats-clinton-houston
   -speech-assails-bush-crime-issue.html
8. https://ropercenter.cornell.edu/polls/us-elections/how-groups-voted/how-groups-voted
   -1992/
9. http://www.nytimes.com/1993/01/26/us/hillary-clinton-to-head-panel-on-health-care
   .html
10. http://www.reuters.com/article/us-usa-election-hillarycare-idUSKCN0YS0WZ
11. http://www.economist.com/blogs/democracyinamerica/2009/09/can_he_top_clinton
12. http://www.heritage.org/health-care-reform/report/guide-the-clinton-health-plan
    #pgfId-929615
13. http://www.salon.com/2016/10/02/own-up-to-nafta-democrats-trump-is-right-that-the
    -terrible-trade-pact-was-bill-clintons-baby/
14. Michael Waldman, *POTUS Speaks: Finding the Words That Defined the Clinton Presidency*
    (New York: Simon & Schuster, 2000), p. 57.
15. Clinton, *My Life*, p. 540.
16. Ibid., p. 557.
17. Bob Woodward, *The Agenda: Inside the Clinton White House* (New York: Simon & Schuster,
    1994), p. 318.
18. http://www.presidency.ucsb.edu/ws/?pid=47070
19. http://articles.baltimoresun.com/1993-07-12/business/1993193135_1_pact-american-free
    -trade-cbs-news-poll
20. https://www.washingtonpost.com/archive/opinions/1993/11/07/america-first-nafta-never
    /c8450c08-b14b-4a25-abe8-0b7cfc992e11/?utm_term=.48d809048c27
21. https://www.washingtonpost.com/archive/politics/1993/09/19/in-anti-nafta-push-perot
    -builds-support-among-clinton-backers/505cdc7d-c3a0-4f3b-8640-719771ecf2f9/?utm
    _term=.573d773fd102
22. http://www.cnn.com/TRANSCRIPTS/0011/09/mn.09.html
23. https://news.google.com/newspapers?nid=2245&dat=19931025&id=EWczAAAAIBAJ&sjid
    =IzIHAAAAIBAJ&pg=5696,7925486&hl=en
24. https://www.buzzfeed.com/andrewkaczynski/trump-spoke-against-nafta-at-1993-con
    vention?utm_term=.hoO2BRoMr#.buOWy2nEw
25. https://www.govtrack.us/congress/votes/103-1993/h575

26. http://www.presidency.ucsb.edu/ws/?pid=46216
27. https://ideas.repec.org/a/elg/rokejn/v2y2014i4p429-441.html
28. https://en.wikipedia.org/wiki/List_of_United_States_cities_by_population
29. https://ideas.repec.org/a/elg/rokejn/v2y2014i4p429-441.html
30. https://newrepublic.com/article/134983/newt-gingrich-laid-groundwork-donald-trump
    -rise
31. http://www.breitbart.com/big-government/2016/02/24/newt-gingrich-2012-the-overture
    -to-donald-trump-2016/
32. Lou Cannon, *Ronald Reagan: The Presidential Portfolio: History as Told Through the Collec-
    tion of the Ronald Reagan Library and Museum* (New York: Public Affairs, 2001), p. 379.
33. Ibid., p. 379.
34. http://www.heritage.org/political-process/report/the-contract-america-implementing
    -new-ideas-the-us
35. Ibid.
36. George Stephanopoulos, *All Too Human: A Political Education* (New York: Little, Brown,
    1999), p. 322.
37. http://www.washingtonpost.com/wp-srv/politics/special/welfare/stories/wf080196.htm
38. http://www.nytimes.com/1995/09/09/us/new-senate-push-on-welfare-revives-tensions-in
    -both-parties.html
39. http://www.nationalreview.com/article/439075/welfare-reform-successful-statistics-show
40. Clinton, *My Life*, p. 922.
41. https://partners.nytimes.com/library/world/asia/052500clinton-trade-text.html
42. https://www.gpo.gov/fdsys/pkg/WCPD-2000-03-13/html/WCPD-2000-03-13-Pg487-2
    .htm
43. http://www.presidency.ucsb.edu/ws/?pid=58305
44. http://articles.latimes.com/2000/mar/29/news/mn-13769
45. https://partners.nytimes.com/library/world/asia/052500clinton-trade-text.html
46. https://www.cato.org/publications/commentary/trade-china-business-profits-or-human
    -rights
47. http://articles.baltimoresun.com/2000-05-10/news/0005100024_1_china-trade-bill-white
    -house-clinton
48. https://partners.nytimes.com/library/world/asia/052500clinton-trade-text.html
49. David H. Autor, David Dorn, and Gordon H. Hanson, "The China Shock: Learning from
    Labor-Market Adjustment to Large Changes in Trade," *Annual Review of Economics* 8
    (2016): pp. 205–40. Available online at: http://www.ddorn.net/papers/Autor-Dorn-Hanson
    -ChinaShock.pdf
50. http://www.epi.org/press/growing-trade-deficit-with-china-has-cost-3-2-million-u-s-jobs
    -since-2001/
51. http://www.slate.com/articles/business/the_next_20/2016/09/when_china_joined_the
    _wto_it_kick_started_the_chinese_economy_and_roused.html
52. https://en.wikipedia.org/wiki/List_of_U.S._states_and_territories_by_population
53. http://www.lifezette.com/polizette/flashback-bill-clintons-false-promise-trade-china/
54. http://www.lifezette.com/polizette/elites-blew-world/
55. https://www.foreignaffairs.com/articles/united-states/2016-02-15/age-secular-stagnation

4

1. http://www.indyweek.com/indyweek/a-kerry-landslide/Content?oid=1192172
2. http://www.washingtonpost.com/wp-dyn/articles/A22188-2005Jan19.html?nav=rss_poli
   tics/elections/2004
3. http://www.foxnews.com/story/2004/11/03/egg-on-face-exit-pollsters.html
4. Ibid.
5. https://www.wsj.com/news/articles/SB122460651917154585?mod=googlewsj
6. https://georgewbush-whitehouse.archives.gov/news/releases/2004/08/20040818-13.html
7. http://edition.cnn.com/2001/ALLPOLITICS/06/07/bush.taxes/
8. http://www.presidency.ucsb.edu/ws/?pid=45820

9. https://georgewbush-whitehouse.archives.gov/news/releases/2001/08/print/20010809-2.html
10. http://www.pbs.org/newshour/bb/politics-july-dec00-for-policy_10-12/
11. Ibid.
12. Ibid.
13. http://www.presidency.ucsb.edu/ws/?pid=29419
14. Ibid.
15. Ibid.
16. http://avalon.law.yale.edu/21st_century/gbush2.asp
17. http://www.cnn.com/2003/US/03/06/bush.speech.transcript/
18. http://avalon.law.yale.edu/21st_century/gbush2.asp
19. http://www.un.org/webcast/ga/57/statements/020912usaE.htm
20. http://www.cnn.com/2003/WORLD/meast/03/17/sprj.irq.bush.transcript/
21. George W. Bush, *Decision Points* (New York: Crown, 2010), p. 205.
22. http://www.gallup.com/poll/102655/opinions-iraq-war-show-little-movement.aspx
23. http://www.politifact.com/truth-o-meter/statements/2016/oct/27/donald-trump/did-us-spend-6-trillion-middle-east-wars/ and https://www.dmdc.osd.mil/dcas/pages/report_oif_all.xhtml
24. https://www.youtube.com/watch?v=fjmh2k5W-6Q
25. https://www.washingtonpost.com/archive/lifestyle/2003/03/25/hollywood-partyers-soldiering-on/06327347-83d3-44c4-ab7b-dcd6fbda5437/?utm_term=.8e652bbe6dc7
26. http://www.factcheck.org/2016/02/donald-trump-and-the-iraq-war/
27. http://www.esquire.com/news-politics/a37230/donald-trump-esquire-cover-story-august-2004/
28. http://www.nytimes.com/2000/10/04/us/2000-campaign-transcript-debate-between-vice-president-gore-governor-bush.html
29. http://www.lauraingraham.com/agnosticchart?charttype=minichart&chartID=21&formatID=1&useMiniChartID=true&position=68&destinationpage=/pg/jsp/general/eblasttext.jsp
30. https://web.archive.org/web/20061227235207/http://reid.senate.gov/newsroom/record.cfm?id=246777&&year=2005&
31. http://www.nbcnews.com/id/9623345/#.WN1lVGNtEks
32. http://www.washingtonpost.com/wp-dyn/content/article/2005/10/06/AR2005100601468.html
33. http://www.washingtonpost.com/wp-srv/nation/documents/miers/EWDSpeech.pdf
34. Bush, *Decision Points*, p. 101.
35. Ibid.
36. http://www.snopes.com/photos/politics/mexicoflag.asp
37. George W. Bush, *Decision Points*, p. 305.
38. http://www.nytimes.com/2006/05/15/washington/15text-bush.html
39. https://www.bop.gov/about/statistics/statistics_inmate_citizenship.jsp
40. https://www.dps.texas.gov/administration/crime_records/pages/txCriminalAlienStatistics.htm
41. http://www.presidency.ucsb.edu/ws/?pid=82455
42. Bush, *Decision Points*, p. 304.
43. http://www.gallup.com/poll/24616/iraq-war-positioned-potent-election-issue.aspx
44. http://www.cbsnews.com/news/why-the-democrats-won/
45. http://www.presidency.ucsb.edu/ws/index.php?pid=24269
46. http://www.nbcnews.com/id/15750949/ns/politics-national_journal/t/seven-lessons-midterm-elections/#.WSufHGVtFDc
47. http://www.presidency.ucsb.edu/ws/index.php?pid=24269
48. http://thehill.com/blogs/pundits-blog/immigration/295776-who-really-benefits-from-immigration-reform
49. http://www.heritage.org/immigration/report/the-fiscal-cost-unlawful-immigrants-and-amnesty-the-us-taxpayer
50. Bush, *Decision Points*, p. 302.

51. Dinesh D'Souza, *Ronald Reagan: How an Ordinary Man Became an Extraordinary Leader* (New York: Touchstone, 1997), p. 93.
52. Bush, *Decision Points,* p. 305.
53. http://www.nytimes.com/2008/09/24/business/economy/24text-bush.html?mcubz=0
54. https://www.washingtonpost.com/news/the-fix/wp/2016/02/13/in-2008-donald-trump-said-george-w-bush-shouldve-been-impeached/?utm_term=.e43f5dad5fff

5

1. http://www.nytimes.com/2008/02/07/us/politics/08romney-transcript.html
2. http://www.presidency.ucsb.edu/ws/index.php?pid=96066
3. http://www.newsweek.com/why-right-hates-mccain-93575
4. http://www.nytimes.com/2008/10/04/us/politics/04ayers.html
5. http://politicalticker.blogs.cnn.com/2008/10/11/mccain-to-crowd-dont-be-scared-of-obama-presidency/
6. David Axelrod, *The Believer: My Forty Years in Politics* (New York: Penguin, 2016), p. 315.
7. http://abcnews.go.com/Blotter/DemocraticDebate/story?id=4443788&page=1
8. Mark Halperin and John Heilemann, *Double Down: Game Change 2012* (New York: Penguin, 2014), p. 305.
9. http://www.realclearpolitics.com/video/2013/07/26/sarah_palin_i_was_not_allowed_to_tell_the_truth_about_obama_in_2008.html
10. David Plouffe, *The Audacity to Win: How Obama Won and How We Can Beat the Party of Limbaugh, Beck and Palin* (New York: Penguin, 2010), pp. 354–55.
11. http://www.cbsnews.com/news/bush-agrees-to-obama-bailout-request/
12. https://newrepublic.com/article/61721/conservatism-dead
13. http://michellemalkin.com/2009/04/15/a-tax-day-tea-party-cheat-sheet-how-it-all-started/
14. http://www.cbo.gov/sites/default/files/cbofiles/attachments/45122-ARRA.pdf
15. https://thinkprogress.org/pelosi-tea-parties-are-part-of-an-astroturf-campaign-by-some-of-the-wealthiest-people-in-america-ad5d6c86cd95
16. http://nymag.com/news/features/67285/
17. http://www.pearceyreport.com/blog/2009/12/code_red_rally_dec_15_us_capit.php
18. http://www.politico.com/story/2009/07/town-halls-gone-wild-025646
19. https://www.usatoday.com/story/money/cars/2014/12/30/auto-bailout-tarp-gm-chrysler/21061251/
20. http://www.politico.com/news/stories/0711/60202_Page2.html
21. http://www.nytimes.com/2011/08/02/opinion/the-tea-partys-war-on-america.html?_r=0&mtrref=undefined&gwh=99325652428C112B81B43D0791C5DEB7&gwt=pay&assetType=opinion
22. http://www.nbcnews.com/id/35990654/ns/msnbc-countdown_with_keith_olbermann/t/olbermann-gop-self-destruction-imminent/#.WO5lNGNtEks
23. http://www.huffingtonpost.com/2009/04/15/anderson-cooper-its-hard_n_187318.html
24. https://www.washingtonpost.com/opinions/colbert-king-the-tea-party-resurrects-the-spirit-of-the-old-confederacy/2013/10/04/95b37f6e-2c7b-11e3-97a3-ff2758228523_story.html?utm_term=.bfc5c72ccdef
25. http://www.foxnews.com/politics/2010/04/15/tea-party-protesters-descend-dc-new-contract-america.html
26. http://www.nytimes.com/2010/02/16/us/politics/16teaparty.html?pagewanted=all&_r=0
27. http://www.salon.com/2010/05/03/tea_party_populism_history/
28. http://www.nytimes.com/2010/05/08/opinion/08blow.html
29. http://www.washingtonpost.com/wp-dyn/content/article/2010/09/12/AR2010091201425.html
30. Halperin and Heilemann, *Double Down,* p. 14.
31. http://www.politico.com/blogs/ben-smith/2008/04/obama-on-small-town-pa-clinging-to-religion-guns-xenophobia-007737
32. http://www.washingtonexaminer.com/populist-convert-santorum-takes-on-mitts-elites/article/1042716

33. http://hotair.com/archives/2012/01/04/gingrich-why-yes-id-team-up-with-santorum-to
    -take-down-romney/
34. https://thehill.com/blogs/blog-briefing-room/news/202755-santorum-not-planning-a
    -team-up-with-gingrich-anytime-soon
35. http://abcnews.go.com/blogs/politics/2012/11/romney-campaign-acknowledges-high-tech
    -election-day-monitoring-system-had-its-challenges/
36. http://www.businessinsider.com/romney-project-orca-disaster-2012-11
37. http://www.breitbart.com/big-government/2012/11/08/orca-how-the-romney-campaign
    -suppressed-its-own-vote/
38. http://www.politico.com/blogs/burns-haberman/2012/11/romneys-fail-whale-orca-the
    -vote-tracker-left-team-flying-blind-updated-149098
39. http://www.businessinsider.com/romney-project-orca-disaster-2012-11
40. http://www.breitbart.com/big-government/2012/11/08/orca-how-the-romney-campaign
    -suppressed-its-own-vote/
41. http://www.cnbc.com/id/48737475?view=story&$DEVICE$=native-android-mobile
42. http://abcnews.go.com/Politics/OTUS/richard-mourdock-rape-comment-puts-romney
    -defense/story?id=17552263
43. https://www.theatlantic.com/politics/archive/2012/10/richard-mourdock-mitt-romney
    -and-the-gop-defense-of-coerced-mating/264035/
44. https://www.theatlantic.com/sexes/archive/2012/11/women-are-not-a-unified-voting
    -bloc/265007/
45. http://www.nytimes.com/2012/03/22/us/politics/etch-a-sketch-remark-a-rare-misstep-for
    -romney-adviser.html
46. http://www.politico.com/story/2012/09/inside-the-campaign-how-mitt-stumbled
    -081280?o=4
47. https://www.wsj.com/articles/SB10000872396390443524904577649932701725706
48. Halperin and Heilemann, *Double Down*, p. 311.
49. http://www.motherjones.com/politics/2013/03/scott-prouty-47-percent-video
50. http://www.gibson.com/News-Lifestyle/News/en-us/gibson-0825-2011.aspx
51. http://humanevents.com/2014/05/30/the-true-villains-behind-the-gibson-guitar-raid
    -are-revealed/
52. http://www.cnn.com/2014/07/18/politics/irs-scandal-fast-facts/
53. http://www.mediaite.com/online/ann-coulter-laments-to-ingraham-if-romney-cant-win
    -in-this-economy-its-over-there-is-no-hope/
54. http://www.corestandards.org/about-the-standards/
55. http://www.independent.co.uk/news/uk/politics/eu-referendum-bill-gates-says-brexit
    -would-make-britain-significantly-less-attractive-a7086906.html
56. https://www.washingtonpost.com/politics/how-bill-gates-pulled-off-the-swift-common
    -core-revolution/2014/06/07/a830e32e-ec34-11e3-9f5c-9075d5508f0a_story.html?utm
    _term=.5a3880943bf4
57. http://www.ajc.com/news/opinion/common-core-caught-elite-populist-crossfire
    /jDnpJXTi5bss5DNbHuRdPI/
58. http://www.freedomworks.org/content/battle-against-common-core-standards
59. https://www.washingtonpost.com/politics/tea-party-groups-rallying-against-common
    -core-education-overhaul/2013/05/30/64faab62-c917-11e2-9245-773c0123c027_story
    .html?utm_term=.7d6524937c91
60. https://www.washingtonpost.com/politics/tea-party-groups-rallying-against-common
    -core-education-overhaul/2013/05/30/64faab62-c917-11e2-9245-773c0123c027_story
    .html?utm_term=.23ef42812087
61. https://www.washingtonpost.com/local/education/common-core-educational-standards
    -are-losing-support-nationwide-poll-shows/2014/08/19/67b1f20c-27cb-11e4-8593-da634
    b334390_story.html?utm_term=.10647c66bed5
62. https://www.washingtonpost.com/news/answer-sheet/wp/2013/11/16/arne-duncan-white
    -surburban-moms-upset-that-common-core-shows-their-kids-arent-brilliant/?utm_term
    =.359090c6f922

63. https://www.washingtonpost.com/politics/tea-party-groups-rallying-against-common
-core-education-overhaul/2013/05/30/64faab62-c917-11e2-9245-773c0123c027_story
.html?utm_term=.90cf12827f6a
64. https://www.washingtonpost.com/news/answer-sheet/wp/2013/11/08/common-core
-implementation-called-worse-than-healthcare-gov-launch/?utm_term=.464f69854244
65. https://www.washingtonpost.com/local/education/common-core-educational-standards
-are-losing-support-nationwide-poll-shows/2014/08/19/67b1f20c-27cb-11e4-8593-da634b
334390_story.html?utm_term=.10647c66bed5
66. https://www.washingtonpost.com/politics/tea-party-groups-rallying-against-common
-core-education-overhaul/2013/05/30/64faab62-c917-11e2-9245-773c0123c027_story
.html?utm_term=.7d6524937c91
67. http://www.nationalreview.com/corner/351649/tea-party-vs-immigration-reform-betsy
-woodruff
68. http://www.breitbart.com/big-government/2013/06/12/rubio-apologizes-for-telling
-different-things-to-spanish-english-audiences/
69. http://www.foxnews.com/transcript/2013/06/28/senates-immigration-reform-bill-passes
.html
70. http://www.nationalreview.com/corner/351649/tea-party-vs-immigration-reform-betsy
-woodruff
71. http://www.foxnews.com/transcript/2013/06/25/laura-ingraham-how-moderate
-republicans-are-killing-party.html
72. http://www.huffingtonpost.com/2014/04/24/john-boehner-immigration_n_5207854
.html
73. http://www.businessinsider.com/eric-cantor-aei-speech-full-text-2013-2
74. http://www.breitbart.com/big-government/2013/07/08/rove-bush-gop-special-interest
-allies-make-new-push-on-house-republicans-to-cave-into-senate-immigration-bill/ and
https://www.opensecrets.org/lobby/clientbills.php?id=D000067575&year=2013
75. http://www.nytimes.com/2013/07/02/us/politics/gop-groups-offering-cover-for-lawmakers
-on-immigration.html
76. http://www.politico.com/story/2014/06/eric-cantor-primary-election-results-virginia
-107683
77. http://www.realclearpolitics.com/articles/2014/07/28/laura_ingraham_tea_party_giant
_killer_eyes_her_next_scalp_123477.html
78. https://takingnote.blogs.nytimes.com/2014/09/02/eric-cantor-cashes-in-goes-to-wall
-street/
79. http://www.breitbart.com/big-government/2014/12/11/laura-ingraham-blasts-republican
-leadership-over-cr-omnibus-budget-bill/
80. http://www.breitbart.com/video/2014/09/05/farage-on-ukips-success-voters-dont-want
-perfect-politicians/

6

1. https://www.washingtonpost.com/politics/documents-show-the-expensive-tastes-of-jeb
-bushs-low-key-wife/2015/02/22/5bb480da-b9f4-11e4-9423-f3d0a1ec335c_story.html?utm
_campaign=pubexchange_article&utm_medium=referral&utm_source=huffingtonpost
.com&utm_term=.0b50e82b8016
2. https://twitter.com/ananavarro/status/571307568938815490
3. https://twitter.com/JRubinBlogger/status/571301870544805888
4. https://twitter.com/JRubinBlogger/status/571302582242553856
5. http://www.politico.com/story/2015/03/gop-talk-show-primary-116479
6. https://www.washingtonpost.com/news/post-politics/wp/2015/02/18/jeb-bush-considers
-himself-lucky-to-have-family-that-shaped-americas-foreign-policy-from-the-oval-office
/?utm_term=.a7c029bb1684
7. https://www.washingtonpost.com/politics/jeb-bush-puts-more-space-between-himself
-and-george-w-bush/2015/05/21/b8f29cf4-ffd7-11e4-833c-a2de05b6b2a4_story.html?utm
_term=.8af69b4b6cb2

8. http://thehill.com/blogs/ballot-box/presidential-races/242801-bush-critical-of-spending-during-brothers-administration

9. https://www.usnews.com/news/blogs/run-2016/2015/07/02/the-biggest-republican-primary-in-100-years

10. http://www.realclearpolitics.com/articles/2016/06/09/donald_trump_a_master_of_macro-aggression_130821.html

11. https://blogs.wsj.com/washwire/2015/06/16/donald-trump-transcript-our-country-needs-a-truly-great-leader/

12. https://www.nytimes.com/interactive/2015/06/16/us/elections/donald-trump.html?mcubz=0

13. https://www.nytimes.com/2015/06/17/us/politics/donald-trump-runs-for-president-this-time-for-real-he-says.html

14. https://www.usatoday.com/story/news/politics/elections/2015/06/16/donald-trump-announcement-president/28782433/

15. http://abcnews.go.com/Politics/trumps-unfavorables-spike-clintons-challenged-poll/story?id=39856303

16. http://www.businessinsider.com/newspapers-donald-trump-president-2015-6

17. http://i2.cdn.turner.com/cnn/2015/images/06/30/trumpbushclinton.pdf

18. https://www.usatoday.com/story/news/politics/elections/2015/06/16/donald-trump-announcement-president/28782433/

19. http://www.businessinsider.com/sen-lindsey-graham-trump-is-a-wrecking-ball-for-the-future-of-the-republican-party-2015-7

20. https://thehill.com/homenews/campaign/247588-gop-strategists-to-jeb-treat-trump-with-kid-gloves

21. http://www.lauraingraham.com/b/Expert:-TPA-Guarantees-Passage-Of-Secret,-Scandalous,-Sovereignty-Crushing-Trade-In-Services-Agreement/-334084243804048283.html?dest=/mobile/blogdetail.jsp

22. http://www.cbsnews.com/news/donald-trump-john-mccain-war-hero-captured/

23. Ibid.

24. https://www.commentarymagazine.com/politics-ideas/campaigns-elections/donald-trump-2016-is-over/

25. http://insider.foxnews.com/2015/07/19/donald-trumps-clown-fox-news-sunday-panel-reacts-trump-mccain-fallout

26. http://www.lifezette.com/polizette/the-apprentices/

27. https://www.nytimes.com/2015/07/23/us/politics/conservative-airwaves-grapple-with-donald-trump-aiding-his-rise.html

28. https://www.lifezette.com/polizette/hillary-hits-jeb-ducks/

29. http://money.cnn.com/2015/08/07/media/gop-debate-fox-news-ratings/

30. http://www.redstate.com/erick/2015/08/07/i-have-disinvited-donald-trump-to-the-red-state-gathering/

31. https://www.nytimes.com/2016/10/02/magazine/how-donald-trump-set-off-a-civil-war-within-the-right-wing-media.html?mcubz=0

32. https://www.nytimes.com/2016/10/02/magazine/how-donald-trump-set-off-a-civil-war-within-the-right-wing-media.html?_r=0

33. http://www.cnn.com/2015/08/21/politics/donald-trump-rally-mobile-alabama/

34. https://www.businessinsider.com.au/nate-silver-donald-trump-wont-win-2015-9

35. http://washingtonmonthly.com/2015/06/19/the-abrasively-boring-kasich-making-his-move/

36. https://twitter.com/anncoulter/status/721403321643192320

37. http://www.lauraingraham.com/b/Kasich:-Illegals-are-Law-Abiding,-Provide-Valuable-Services/466378084479528984.html

38. http://www.politico.com/story/2015/08/eric-cantor-endorse-jeb-bush-virginia-co-chair-campaign-2016-121815

39. http://www.thedailybeast.com/articles/2015/08/20/why-trump-will-never-make-the-ballot.html

40. http://www.thedailybeast.com/articles/2016/11/07/the-flat-earth-set-helped-donald-trump-hijack-the-gop-and-crash-it-into-the-ground.html and http://www.thedailybeast.com

/articles/2016/03/17/the-republican-myth-of-the-untapped-white-voter.html and http://
www.thedailybeast.com/articles/2016/03/08/it-s-too-late-to-stop-the-gop-apocalypse.html
and http://www.thedailybeast.com/articles/2016/02/29/a-vote-for-donald-trump-is-a-vote
-for-bigotry.html and http://www.thedailybeast.com/articles/2016/02/17/hey-republicans
-this-is-how-you-beat-trump-for-real.html

41. https://twitter.com/realdonaldtrump/status/267286284182118400?lang=en

42. https://object.cato.org/sites/cato.org/files/pubs/pdf/cato-annual-report-2015-update-ii
.pdf

43. http://www.foxnews.com/politics/2015/09/24/fox-news-poll-outsiders-rule-2016-gop-field
-support-for-biden-nearly-doubles.html

44. http://www.nbcnews.com/politics/congress/poll-72-gop-voters-dissatisfied-boehner
-mcconnell-n433731

45. http://thehill.com/blogs/ballot-box/presidential-races/255080-jeb-were-going-to-miss
-boehner

46. http://www.foxnews.com/politics/interactive/2015/10/13/fox-news-poll-carson-giving
-trump-run-for-his-money.html

47. https://www.bloomberg.com/view/articles/2015-10-19/trump-candidacy-will-fade-as-other
-republicans-rise

48. https://www.washingtonpost.com/news/the-fix/wp/2015/10/28/the-third-republican
-debate-annotating-the-transcript/?utm_term=.f444977280cd

49. https://www.wsj.com/articles/populism-on-the-rise-in-gop-race-for-president-1447262303

50. http://thehill.com/blogs/ballot-box/presidential-races/259374-schumer-rubio-all-over
-senate-immigration-reform-bill

51. http://www.foxnews.com/politics/2015/11/22/fox-news-poll-trump-gains-carson-slips
-cruz-and-rubio-climb-in-gop-race.html

52. https://www.usnews.com/opinion/blogs/lara-brown/2015/12/11/donald-trump-wont-win
-as-a-republican-or-an-independent

53. http://www.politico.com/story/2015/12/ted-cruz-donald-trump-216724

54. http://www.cnbc.com/2015/12/14/as-cruz-rises-in-us-presidential-polls-trump-calls-him
-maniac.html

55. http://www.breitbart.com/video/2015/12/16/jeb-trump-is-a-bully-hes-not-quite-all-in
-command/

56. https://twitter.com/GovernorPataki/status/656171623423332352

57. http://www.app.com/story/news/politics/new-jersey/chris-christie/2016/01/04/christie
-kneecaps-trump-new-hampshire-speech/78256098/

58. https://www.wsj.com/articles/my-crystal-ball-scoreplus-2016-predictions-1452124623

59. https://www.washingtonpost.com/opinions/trumps-nomination-would-rip-the-heart
-out-of-the-republican-party/2016/01/07/c9cb3f08-b49b-11e5-a842-0feb51d1d124_story
.html?utm_term=.f4ace36908b5

60. http://www.vox.com/2016/1/5/10717690/donald-trump-loss

61. http://www.lifezette.com/polizette/national-reviews-unwise-pig-pile-on-donald-trump/

62. http://www.lauraingraham.com/b/Huckabee,-Buchanan,-Schlafly-Pummel-NR/254329
413551385022.html

63. http://www.lifezette.com/polizette/national-reviews-unwise-pig-pile-on-donald-trump/

64. http://www.vanityfair.com/news/2016/02/donald-trump-explains-iowa-loss

65. https://www.washingtonpost.com/news/the-fix/wp/2016/02/06/transcript-of-the-feb-6-gop
-debate-annotated/?utm_term=.667fb7f43aa0

66. http://www.politico.com/magazine/story/2016/02/south-carolina-gop-primary-firewall
-lee-atwater-213648

67. http://www.reuters.com/article/us-usa-election-idUSMTZSAPEC2FLJFZSL

68. http://www.foxnews.com/politics/interactive/2016/02/18/fox-news-poll-national-presiden
tial-race-february-18-2016.html

69. https://www.nytimes.com/2016/02/23/us/politics/jeb-bush-campaign.html

70. http://theresurgent.com/the-importance-of-disclosing-this-immediately/

71. http://edition.cnn.com/TRANSCRIPTS/1603/01/se.06.html

72. https://www.nytimes.com/2016/03/04/us/politics/mitt-romney-speech.html

73. Ibid.
74. https://twitter.com/IngrahamAngle/status/705369650935296001
75. https://twitter.com/ingrahamangle/status/705442800981164032
76. http://www.cbsnews.com/news/cbsnyt-poll-who-do-gop-voters-blame-for-violence-at-donald-trump-rallies/
77. https://douthat.blogs.nytimes.com/2016/03/08/how-trump-loses-revisited/?_r=1
78. http://theresurgent.com/statement-from-conservatives-against-trump/
79. https://www.nytimes.com/2016/03/03/us/politics/anti-donald-trump-republicans-call-for-a-third-party-option.html?_r=0
80. https://fivethirtyeight.com/features/trump-made-a-mistake-by-overlooking-colorado/
81. https://www.nytimes.com/2016/04/13/us/politics/donald-trump-losing-ground-tries-to-blame-the-system.html?_r=0
82. http://www.denverpost.com/2016/04/10/angry-donald-trump-blasts-colorado-gop-results-as-totally-unfair/
83. http://www.cnn.com/2016/04/20/politics/donald-trump-ted-cruz-1237-delegates/
84. http://www.cbsnews.com/news/ted-cruz-nobody-is-getting-1237-delegates/
85. http://abcnews.go.com/Politics/ted-cruz-john-kasich-alliance-trump/story?id=38652514
86. https://www.nytimes.com/2016/04/26/us/politics/ted-cruz-john-kasich-donald-trump.html
87. https://twitter.com/realDonaldTrump/status/724567219062059008
88. https://www.washingtonpost.com/news/the-fix/wp/2016/05/03/carly-fiorina-and-the-shortest-vice-presidential-candidacy-in-modern-history/?utm_term=.f0c354f75432
89. http://www.cnn.com/2017/03/15/politics/donald-trump-campaign-rallies/

7

1. https://www.forbes.com/sites/greatspeculations/2016/06/20/brexit-push-is-all-about-taxation-and-regulation-without-representation/2/#bb56b5f48ad3
2. https://twitter.com/ingrahamangle/status/507681667147112450
3. http://www.express.co.uk/comment/expresscomment/683183/proud-making-June-23rd-INDEPENDENCE-DAY-Nigel-Farage-Brexit
4. http://www.independent.co.uk/news/uk/politics/brexit-recession-economy-what-happens-nigel-farage-speech-a7099301.html
5. https://twitter.com/ianbremmer/status/746309494267875328?ref_src=twsrc%5Etfw&ref_url=http%3A%2F%2Fdailycaller.com%2F2016%2F06%2F24%2Fhere-are-the-most-absurd-liberal-reactions-to-brexit%2F
6. http://www.cbsnews.com/news/donald-trump-us-politicians-react-to-brexit-vote/
7. https://www.washingtonpost.com/news/post-politics/wp/2016/06/24/in-scotland-trump-celebrates-brexit-vote/?utm_term=.ba6251efb025
8. http://www.cnn.com/2016/06/24/politics/us-election-brexit-donald-trump-hillary-clinton/
9. https://www.nytimes.com/2016/06/25/us/politics/is-brexit-the-precursor-to-a-donald-trump-presidency-not-so-fast.html?_r=0
10. http://www.lifezette.com/polizette/establishment-gets-their-comeuppance/
11. http://www.politico.com/story/2016/06/hardly-anybody-wants-to-speak-at-trumps-convention-224815
12. http://washingtonmonthly.com/2016/06/27/no-one-wants-to-speak-at-the-gop-convention/
13. https://www.fbi.gov/news/pressrel/press-releases/statement-by-fbi-director-james-b-comey-on-the-investigation-of-secretary-hillary-clinton2019s-use-of-a-personal-e-mail-system
14. http://www.nbcnews.com/storyline/data-points/hillary-clinton-s-lead-over-trump-shrinks-after-controversial-week-n607351
15. https://poll.qu.edu/pennsylvania/release-detail?ReleaseID=2365
16. http://www.washingtontimes.com/news/2006/nov/15/20061115-122626-4892r/
17. http://www.nielsen.com/us/en/insights/news/2016/third-night-of-2016-republican-national-convention-draws.html
18. http://www.cnn.com/2016/07/20/politics/laura-ingraham-donald-trump-media/

19. http://time.com/3923128/donald-trump-announcement-speech/
20. Donald J. Trump, *Time to Get Tough: Making America #1 Again* (Washington, DC: Regnery, 2011), p. 147.
21. http://thehill.com/blogs/pundits-blog/presidential-campaign/288611-transcript-ted-cruz-addresses-republican-convention
22. http://abcnews.go.com/Politics/full-text-donald-trumps-2016-republican-national-convention/story?id=40786529
23. http://www.dailywire.com/news/7714/top-left-wing-reactions-trumps-speech-robert-kraychik
24. http://www.newsbusters.org/blogs/nb/samantha-cohen/2016/07/22/msnbcs-willie-geist-donald-trump-painted-picture-dystopian-mad
25. http://www.rollingstone.com/politics/features/trumps-appetite-for-destruction-how-disastrous-convention-doomed-gop-w430546
26. http://www.nationalreview.com/corner/438612/donald-trumps-republican-convention-was-failure
27. https://www.nytimes.com/2016/07/22/opinion/campaign-stops/the-dark-knight.html
28. http://www.salon.com/2016/07/22/his_dark_materials_after_that_diabolical_masterful_performance_donald_trump_could_easily_end_up_president/
29. http://www.latimes.com/politics/la-na-pol-pence-reagan-library-20160908-snap-story.html
30. http://www.newyorker.com/news/amy-davidson/five-questions-about-the-clintons-and-a-uranium-company
31. http://www.politifact.com/punditfact/statements/2015/apr/26/peter-schweizer/fact-checking-clinton-cash-author-claim-about-bill/
32. https://www.nytimes.com/2015/03/09/us/politics/hillary-clinton-faces-test-of-record-aiding-women.html?_r=0
33. https://www.nytimes.com/2015/04/24/us/cash-flowed-to-clinton-foundation-as-russians-pressed-for-control-of-uranium-company.html?_r=1
34. http://www.bigstory.ap.org/article/82df550e1ec646098b434f7d5771f625/many-donors-clinton-foundation-met-her-state
35. http://www.breitbart.com/big-government/2016/05/28/trump-campaign-clinton-cash-formula-give-money-bill-get-favors-hill/
36. https://www.bloomberg.com/politics/graphics/2016-presidential-campaign-fundraising/
37. http://www.politifact.com/truth-o-meter/statements/2015/oct/13/hillary-clinton/what-hillary-clinton-really-said-about-tpp-and-gol/
38. https://www.nytimes.com/2016/10/08/us/politics/hillary-clinton-speeches-wikileaks.html?_r=0
39. https://www.washingtonpost.com/news/the-fix/wp/2016/07/24/here-are-the-latest-most-damaging-things-in-the-dncs-leaked-emails/?utm_term=.ef3ea2081dd7
40. http://www.cnn.com/2016/07/28/politics/hillary-clinton-speech-prepared-remarks-transcript/
41. http://abcnews.go.com/Politics/full-text-khizr-khans-speech-2016-democratic-national/story?id=41043609
42. http://abcnews.go.com/Politics/donald-trump-father-fallen-soldier-ive-made-lot/story?id=41015051
43. https://twitter.com/JonahNRO/status/758836064278548481?ref_src=twsrc%5Etfw&ref_url=http%3A%2F%2Ftalkingpointsmemo.com%2Flivewire%2Fconservatives-agree-dnc-was-disaster-for-gop
44. https://mediamatters.org/video/2016/07/29/cnn-highlights-conservatives-praising-hillary-clintons-acceptance-speeech-democratic-national/212019
45. http://www.nbcnews.com/politics/2016-election/poll-clinton-opens-double-digit-lead-over-trump-n625676 and http://www.foxnews.com/politics/interactive/2016/08/03/fox-news-poll-aug-3-2016.html
46. https://www.nytimes.com/2016/08/08/business/balance-fairness-and-a-proudly-provocative-presidential-candidate.html?_r=0
47. http://www.lifezette.com/polizette/obamas-new-gop-henchmen/s

8

1. https://www.wsj.com/articles/steve-bannon-and-the-making-of-an-economic
   -nationalist-1489516113
2. https://www.nytimes.com/2016/08/18/us/politics/donald-trump-stephen-bannon-paul
   -manafort.html
3. Ibid.
4. https://www.nytimes.com/2016/09/03/us/politics/donald-trump-black-voters.html
5. http://www.chicagotribune.com/news/nationworld/politics/ct-trump-minority-outreach
   -campaign-20160902-story.html
6. http://www.politico.com/story/2016/09/donald-trump-detroit-african-american-church
   -227712
7. http://www.latimes.com/nation/politics/trailguide/la-na-trailguide-updates-transcript
   -clinton-s-full-remarks-as-1473549076-htmlstory.html
8. https://www.hillaryclinton.com/briefing/statements/2016/09/10/statement-from-hillary
   -clinton/
9. http://www.nbcnews.com/meet-the-press/meet-press-sept-11-2016-n646441
10. https://www.washingtonpost.com/news/the-fix/wp/2016/09/26/voters-strongly-reject
    -hillary-clintons-basket-of-deplorables-approach/?utm_term=.85af7b5d58e3
11. https://www.bostonglobe.com/opinion/2016/11/21/understanding-undecided-voters
    /9EjNHVkt99b4re2VAB8ziI/story.html
12. http://abcnews.go.com/Health/hillary-clinton-blood-clot-life-threatening-medical
    -experts/story?id=18101213 and https://www.washingtonpost.com/national/health-science
    /hillary-clintons-blood-clot-most-likely-in-a-leg-experts-say/2012/12/31/d2c853ea-5376
    -11e2-bf3e-76c0a789346f_story.html?utm_term=.87ba794f365f
13. http://thehill.com/media/295605-cnn-host-says-sexism-a-factor-in-clinton-health-coverage
14. https://twitter.com/brianstelter/status/775138314525433856
15. http://www.lifezette.com/polizette/hillarys-allergy-to-transparency/
16. http://www.nielsen.com/us/en/insights/news/2016/first-presidential-debate-of-2016-draws
    -84-million-viewers.html
17. Jonathan Allen and Amie Parnes, *Shattered: Inside Hillary Clinton's Doomed Campaign*
    (New York: Crown, 2017), p. 325.
18. http://www.politico.com/story/2011/04/birtherism-where-it-all-began-053563
19. http://www.cnbc.com/2016/09/27/why-the-donald-trump-who-appeared-on-stage-monday
    -cant-win.html
20. http://www.therepublic.com/2017/01/10/photo-gallery-mike-pences-high-school-years
    -at-columbus-north/
21. http://www.politico.com/story/2016/10/mark-kirk-donald-trump-comments-women
    -229328
22. https://twitter.com/bensasse/status/784726683920297984?lang=en
23. https://www.washingtonpost.com/news/the-fix/wp/2016/10/07/the-gops-brutal-responses
    -to-the-new-trump-video-broken-down/?utm_term=.9ebaad197638
24. http://www.bakersfield.com/special/business-conference/laura-ingraham-obama-and
    -clinton-an-epic-fail/article_ae8f0d4c-8db6-11e6-b6c8-076d66560ce3.html
25. http://www.nielsen.com/us/en/insights/news/2016/second-presidential-debate-of-2016
    -draws-66-5-million-viewers.html
26. https://www.vox.com/2016/10/9/13222302/donald-trump-jail-hillary-clinton-second-debate
27. https://thinkprogress.org/after-trump-talks-about-jailing-clinton-media-draw
    -comparisons-to-dictators-4a770c4adc83
28. https://www.mediamatters.org/video/2016/10/09/cnns-van-jones-trump-threatened-jail
    -hillary-clinton-thats-new-low-american-democracy/213682
29. https://www.nytimes.com/2016/10/12/world/americas/united-states-democracy-clinton
    -trump.html
30. http://www.cnn.com/2016/10/10/politics/clinton-trump-new-national-poll/
31. http://www.realclearpolitics.com/epolls/2016/president/us/general_election_trump_vs
    _clinton-5491.html

32. http://www.latimes.com/nation/politics/trailguide/la-na-trailguide-updates-the-trump-vs
-mcmullin-battle-for-utah-1477800901-htmlstory.html
33. http://www.nielsen.com/us/en/insights/news/2016/third-presidential-debate-of-2016-draws
-71-6-million-viewers.html
34. https://www.youtube.com/watch?v=WGomGRZIDIE&feature=youtu.be&t=15s
35. http://www.centerforpolitics.org/crystalball/2016-president/
36. http://www.cnbc.com/2016/11/07/donald-trump-will-lose-after-failing-to-learn-from-mitt
-romney.html
37. http://election.princeton.edu/2016/11/06/is-99-a-reasonable-probability/
38. http://www.cnn.com/videos/tv/2016/11/05/poll-expert-i-will-eat-a-bug-if-trump-exceeds
-240.cnn
39. http://twitchy.com/dougp-3137/2016/11/09/full-stop-frank-luntz-reversed-sure-thing
-prediction-as-it-became-clear-trump-was-defeating-hillary/
40. http://www.realclearpolitics.com/video/2016/11/10/oreilly_on_trump_the_people_revolted
_and_they_won.html
41. https://twitter.com/IngrahamAngle/status/796222735252918273
42. Allen and Parnes, *Shattered*, p. 379.

9

1. https://www.whitehouse.gov/inaugural-address
2. http://thehill.com/homenews/media/315324-msnbcs-chris-matthews-trump-inauguration
-speech-hitlerian
3. https://twitter.com/billkristol/status/822496003391705089?lang=en
4. https://twitter.com/billkristol/status/822491947998838785?lang=pt
5. http://www.breitbart.com/big-government/2016/12/06/trump-announces-japanese
-telecom-co-will-invest-50-billion-create-50000-jobs-u-s/
6. https://www.whitehouse.gov/the-press-office/2017/03/06/president-trump-congratulates
-exxon-mobil-job-creating-investment
7. http://www.ajc.com/business/delta-hire-000-workers-ceo-meets-with-trump/YEONpBVD
CVTgm5eP3qQp9L/
8. http://www.jsonline.com/story/news/2017/07/26/scott-walker-heads-d-c-trump-prepares
-wisconsin-foxconn-announcement/512077001/
9. https://www.ft.com/content/aef9fdab-6568-3385-8218-a6df04cdc3f7
10. https://www.reuters.com/article/us-usa-economy-idUSKBN1AA267 and https://www.
cnbc.com/2017/08/01/apple-tech-stocks-soar-after-hours-set-to-lead-dow-to-22000-record-
wednesday.html
11. http://thehill.com/regulation/329720-study-trump-has-eliminated-86b-in-regs
12. https://www.nytimes.com/2017/08/01/us/politics/fact-check-trump-claims-low
-unemployment-booming-economy.html
13. https://twitter.com/davidfrum/status/834859197451821056?lang=en
14. http://www.politico.com/story/2016/11/hillary-clinton-rural-voters-trump-231266
15. https://www.nytimes.com/2017/01/23/us/politics/tpp-trump-trade-nafta.html
16. http://www.cnn.com/2017/05/11/politics/china-us-beef-imports-trade-deal/
17. https://www.nytimes.com/2017/05/13/business/china-railway-one-belt-one-road-1-trillion
-plan.html
18. http://www.businessinsider.com/trump-china-deal-one-belt-one-road-2017-5
19. http://www.nbcnews.com/news/world/japan-backs-trump-further-action-north-korea
-pressure-china-n788021
20. https://www.wsj.com/articles/u-s-plans-trade-measures-against-china-1501635127
21. http://www.lifezette.com/referral/ingraham-top-gop-lawmakers-laughing-idea-wall-get
-built/
22. http://www.rollcall.com/news/politics/omnibus-spending-bill-budget-trump-agenda
#sthash.AeGtcwPQ.dpuf
23. https://www.washingtonpost.com/news/fact-checker/wp/2016/02/11/trumps-dubious
-claim-that-his-border-wall-would-cost-8-billion/?utm_term=.3a95532a43da

24. http://www.breitbart.com/big-government/2017/01/27/ten-questionable-federal-govt
    -expenditures-greater-than-trumps-border-wall/
25. http://www.fairus.org/news/illegal-immigration-costs-california-taxpayers-more
    -than-25-billion-a-year-finds-fair
26. http://www.lifezette.com/polizette/cruz-lifts-idea-cartel-funded-border-wall-ingraham/
27. http://prospect.org/article/democrats'-'working-class-problem'
28. http://www.latimes.com/local/lanow/la-me-border-wall-delay-san-diego-20170727-story
    .html
29. http://www.speaker.gov/video/wall-lets-get-it-done
30. http://www.politifact.com/truth-o-meter/statements/2017/apr/25/donald-trump/illegal
    -immigration-lowest-17-years-trump-said/
31. http://www.foxnews.com/politics/2017/04/20/sessions-to-potential-illegal-immigrants
    -dont-come-wait-your-turn.html
32. http://www.foxnews.com/politics/2017/05/11/trumps-tough-immigration-rhetoric-slows
    -illegal-border-crossings-were-at-trickle.html
33. https://www.wsj.com/articles/senate-republicans-rebuff-donald-trumps-health-care-push
    -1501630741; http://www.gallup.com/poll/1600/congress-public.aspx
34. http://www.breitbart.com/big-government/2017/07/26/the-six-senate-republicans-who
    -flip-flopped-in-favor-of-obamacare/
35. http://www.wnd.com/2017/04/buchanan-trump-reacted-to-syria-emotionally/
36. http://www.reuters.com/article/us-usa-election-trump-exclusive-idUSKCN12P2PZ
37. https://www.washingtonpost.com/politics/horrible-pictures-of-suffering-moved-trump
    -to-action-on-syria/2017/04/07/9aa9fcc8-1bce-11e7-8003-f55b4c1cfae2_story.html?utm
    _term=.5964514ff35e
38. http://fortune.com/2017/03/21/neil-gorsuch-opening-statement/
39. http://hosted.ap.org/dynamic/stories/U/US_TRUMP_MOOD?SITE=AP&SECTION
    =HOME&TEMPLATE=DEFAULT&CTIME=2017-05-14-13-47-46
40. http://www.breitbart.com/big-government/2017/05/03/finally-know-steve-bannons-white
    board-donald-trump-promises-voters/
41. http://www.breitbart.com/big-government/2017/05/16/dennis-kucinich-calls-high-bs
    -quotient-on-wapo-story-asks-who-leaked/
42. http://www.breitbart.com/big-government/2017/05/17/trump-under-siege-more-than-60
    -percent-of-nsc-employees-placed-by-obama/
43. https://www.washingtonpost.com/graphics/politics/trump-administration-appointee
    -tracker/database/
44. http://www.lifezette.com/polizette/trump-moving-swiftly-to-appoint-conservative-judges/
45. http://www.foxnews.com/politics/2017/08/02/ben-rhodes-new-focus-unmasking
    -investigation.html
46. http://www.newyorker.com/news/ryan-lizza/anthony-scaramucci-called-me-to-unload
    -about-white-house-leakers-reince-priebus-and-steve-bannon
47. http://time.com/4681094/reince-priebus-steve-bannon-cpac-interview-transcript/
48. https://www.washingtonpost.com/news/fact-checker/wp/2017/06/26/president-trumps
    -claim-that-ms-13-gang-members-are-being-deported-by-the-thousands/?utm_term
    =.159646c07bac
49. https://www.bloomberg.com/news/articles/2017-07-03/manufacturing-pickup-in-u-s
    -signals-boost-to-economic-growth
50. http://money.cnn.com/2017/07/05/news/economy/trump-trade-protectionism-g20/index
    .html
51. https://www.reuters.com/article/us-g20-germany-idUSKBN19R345 and https://www
    .wsj.com/articles/g-20-leaders-set-to-reach-compromise-on-trade-at-summit-14995
    13260?mod=e2fb
52. http://www.washingtonpost.com/wp-dyn/content/article/2011/01/13/AR2011011301532_5
    .html

INDEX